BRUSSELS

THE MINI ROUGH GUIDE

There are more than one hundred Rough Guide travel, phrasebook, and music titles, covering destinations from Amsterdam to Zimbabwe, languages from Czech to Thai, and musics from World to Opera and Jazz

Forthcoming titles include

Indonesia • New England • St Lucia • Toronto

Rough Guides on the Internet

www.r

D0967272

Rough Guide Credits

Text editor: Kieran Falconer
Series editor: Mark Ellingham
Typesetting: James Morris
Cartography: Maxine Burke, Michael Larby

Publishing Information

This first edition published March 1999 by
Rough Guides Ltd, 62–70 Shorts Gardens, London, WC2H 9AB

Distributed by the Penguin Group:

Penguin Books Ltd, 27 Wrights Lane, London W8 5TZ
Penguin Books USA Inc., 375 Hudson Street, New York 10014, USA
Penguin Books Australia Ltd, 487 Maroondah Highway,
PO Box 257, Ringwood, Victoria 3134, Australia
Penguin Books Canada Ltd, 10 Alcorn Avenue,
Toronto, Ontario, Canada M4V 1E4
Penguin Books (NZ) Ltd, 182–190 Wairau Road,
Auckland 10, New Zealand

Typeset in Bembo and Helvetica to an original design by Henry Iles.
Printed in Spain by Graphy Cems.

© Martin Dunford and Phil Lee. 336pp, includes index
A catalogue record for this book is available from the British Library.
ISBN 1-85828-411-2

BRUSSELS

THE MINI ROUGH GUIDE

by Phil Lee
and Martin Battersby

THE ROUGH GUIDES

We set out to do something different when the first Rough Guide was published in 1982. Mark Ellingham, just out of university, was travelling in Greece. He brought along the popular guides of the day, but found they were all lacking in some way. They were either strong on ruins and museums but went on for pages without mentioning a beach or taverna. Or they were so conscious of the need to save money that they lost sight of Greece's cultural and historical significance. Also, none of the books told him anything about Greece's contemporary life – its politics, its culture, its people, and how they lived.

So with no job in prospect, Mark decided to write his own guidebook, one which aimed to provide practical information that was second to none, detailing the best beaches and the hottest clubs and restaurants, while also giving hard-hitting accounts of every sight, both famous and obscure, and providing up-to-the-minute information on contemporary culture. It was a guide that encouraged independent travellers to find the best of Greece, and was a great success, getting shortlisted for the Thomas Cook travel guide award, and encouraging Mark, along with three friends, to expand the series.

The Rough Guide list grew rapidly and the letters flooded in, indicating a much broader readership than had been anticipated, but one which uniformly appreciated the Rough Guide mix of practical detail and humour, irreverence and enthusiasm. Things haven't changed. The same four friends who began the series are still the caretakers of the Rough Guide mission today: to provide the most reliable, up-to-date and entertaining information to independent-minded travellers of all ages, on all budgets.

We now publish more than 100 titles and have offices in London and New York. The travel guides are written and researched by a dedicated team of more than 100 authors, based in Britain, Europe, the USA and Australia. We have also created a unique series of phrasebooks to accompany the travel series, along with an acclaimed series of music guides, and a best-selling pocket guide to the Internet and World Wide Web. We also publish comprehensive travel information on our Web site: **www.roughguides.com**

Help Us Update

We've gone to a lot of effort to ensure that this first edition of *The Rough Guide to Brussels* is as up to date and accurate as possible. However, if you find we've missed something good or covered something which has now gone, then please write: suggestions, comments or corrections are much appreciated.

We'll credit all contributions, and send a copy of the next edition (or any other Rough Guide if you prefer) for the best letters. Please mark letters: "Rough Guide Brussels Update" and send to:

Rough Guides, 62–70 Shorts Gardens, London, WC2H 9AB, or
Rough Guides, 375 Hudson St, New York NY 10014.
Or send email to: mail@roughguides.co.uk

Online updates about this book can be found on
Rough Guides' Web site (see opposite)

The Authors

Phil Lee has worked as a freelance for the Rough Guides for the last ten years. Previous books include the Rough Guides to Norway; Brussels; Mallorca and Menorca; and Canada. He has also written extensively for magazines and newspapers. He lives in Nottingham where he was born and raised.

Martin Battersby was born and raised in Leeds and supports Leeds United. He has lived and worked in Brussels for three years.

Acknowledgements

With special thanks to Pauline Owen and Kate Smith of Tourism Flanders-Brussels. Many thanks also to our diligent editor, Kieran Falconer; to Michael Larby of Cartographic Services, and Maxine Burke, for some beautiful maps; to Carole Mansur for eagle-eyed proofreading; and to James Morris for his excellent production skills. Lastly, but not least, we must say a big thanks to Peterjon Cresswell and Simon Evans of *The Rough Guide to European Football* – the lads did well.

CONTENTS

Introduction

Brussels is generally known to non-Belgians as the home of the EU. In fact, it forms but one layer of a city that has become, in postwar years at least, a thriving, cosmopolitan metropolis, a vibrant and fascinating place, with architecture and museums to rank among the best of Europe's capitals, not to mention a superb restaurant scene and an energetic nightlife. Moreover, most of the key attractions are crowded into a centre that is small enough to be absorbed over a few days, its boundaries largely defined by a ring of boulevards known as the "petit ring".

The layout of this city centre embodies historic class divisions. For centuries, the ruling class has lived in the Upper Town, an area of wide boulevards and grand mansions which looks down on the maze of tangled streets that characterize the Lower Town, traditionally home to shopkeepers and workers. This fundamental class divide has in recent decades been further complicated by discord between Belgium's two main linguistic groups, the Walloons (the French-speakers) and the Flemish (basically Dutch-speakers). As a cumbersome compromise, the city is Belgium's only officially bilingual region and by law all road signs, street names and virtually all published information must be in both languages, even though French-speakers make up nearly eighty percent of Brussels' population. As if this was not complex enough, since the 1960s the city has become much more ethnically diverse, with communities of immigrants from North Africa, Turkey, the Mediterranean and Belgium's former colonies as well as European administrators, diplomats and business people, comprising a quarter of the population.

Each of these communities leads a very separate, distinct existence and this is reflected in the number and variety of affordable ethnic restaurants. But, even without these, Brussels would still be a wonderful place to eat: its gastronomic reputation rivals that of Paris and London, and though restaurants are rarely inexpensive, there is great-value food to be had in many of the bars. The bars themselves can be sumptuous, basic, traditional or very fashionable – and one of the city's real pleasures. Another pleasure is shopping: Belgian chocolates and lace are de rigueur, but it's also hard to resist the charms of the city's art galleries, designer clothes shops and antique markets, not to mention the numerous specialist shops devoted to anything and everything from comic books to costume jewellery.

Many of the city's best bars and restaurants are dotted round the city centre, within the petit ring, and this is where you'll find the key sights. The Lower Town centres on the Grand-Place, one of Europe's most magnificent squares, boasting a superb ensemble of Baroque guild-houses and an imposing Gothic town hall, while the Upper Town weighs in with a splendid cathedral and a fine art museum of international standing, the Musées Royaux des Beaux Arts. Few visitors stray beyond the petit ring, but there are delights here too, principally in St Gilles and Ixelles, two communes (or boroughs) just to the south of the centre, whose streets are spotted with fanciful Art Nouveau residences including the old home and studio of Victor Horta, the architect of so many of the best houses in this period.

Belgium is such a small country, and the rail network so fast and efficient, that Brussels also makes a feasible base for many other day-trips. In Chapter Eight, we've selected six prime destinations, all within an hour's travelling time – the battlefield at Waterloo, the abbey ruins of Villers-la-Ville and a quartet of fascinating Flemish towns; Leuven, Antwerp, Ghent and Bruges.

Climate

Brussels – and Belgium – enjoys a fairly standard temperate climate, with warm, if mild, summers and cold winters, without much snow. The warmest months are usually June, July and August, the coldest December and January, when short daylight hours and weak sunlight can make the weather seem colder (and wetter) than it actually is. Rain is always a possibility, even in summer, which actually sees a greater degree of rainfall than autumn or winter. Warm days in April and May, when the light has the clarity of springtime, are especially appealing.

Average daily temperatures (°C)

Jan	Feb	Mar	Apr	May	June	July	Aug	Sept	Oct	Nov	Dec
1	4	7	11	13	18	19	18	17	12	7	3

Average monthly rainfall (mm)

Jan	Feb	Mar	Apr	May	June	July	Aug	Sept	Oct	Nov	Dec
66	61	53	60	55	76	95	80	63	83	75	88

THE GUIDE

Introducing the City

First-time visitors to **Brussels** are often surprised by the raw vitality of the **city centre**. It's not neat and tidy, and many of the old tenement houses are shabby and ill-used, but there's a buzz about the place that's hard to resist and it's here you'll find the majority of the city's sights and attractions, restaurants and bars. The centre is also surprisingly compact, sitting neatly within the rough pentagon of boulevards that enclose it (the petit ring) which follows the course of the fourteenth-century city walls, running from place Rogier in the north round to Porte de Hal in the south. The city centre is itself divided into two main areas. The larger, westerly portion comprises the Lower Town, built for the working and lower-middle classes and fanning out from the Grand-Place, while up above to the east lies the much smaller Upper Town, the traditional home of the Francophile upper classes. Broadly speaking, the boundary between the two zones follows the busy boulevard which swings through the centre under several names – Berlaimont, L'Impératrice and L'Empereur.

The Brussels area telephone code is ⓒ02.

The **Grand-Place** is the unquestionable centre of Brussels, a focus for tourists and locals alike, who come to admire its exquisite guildhouses and town hall. It's surrounded by the **Lower Town** whose cramped and populous quarters are bisected by one major north–south boulevard, variously named Adolphe Max, Anspach and Lemonnier. The Lower Town is at its most beguiling to the northwest of the Grand-Place, where the church of **Ste Catherine** stands amidst a cobweb of quaint, narrow lanes and tiny squares that also contains the beautiful church of **St Jean Baptiste au Béguinage**. By comparison the streets to the north of the Grand-Place are of less immediate appeal with dreary **rue Neuve**, a pedestrianized main street that's home to Brussels' mainstream shops and department stores, leading up to the clumping skyscrapers that surround the place Rogier and the **Gare du Nord**. This is an uninviting part of the city, but relief is at hand in the precise if bedraggled Habsburg symmetries of the **place des Martyrs** and – to the northeast of the Grand-Place – at the Belgian Comic Strip Centre, the Centre Belge de la Bande Dessinée. To the south of the Grand-Place lie the old working-class streets of the **Marolles** district and then the depressed and predominantly immigrant area in the vicinity of the **Gare du Midi**.

In Brussels, the languages of the French- and Flemish-speaking communities have parity. This means that every instance of the written word, from road signs to the yellow pages, has to appear in both languages. Visitors soon adjust, but on arrival this can be very confusing, especially in the names of the city's three main train stations: Bruxelles-Nord (in Flemish it's Brussel-Noord), Bruxelles-Centrale (Brussel-Centraal), and, most bewildering of the lot, Bruxelles-Midi

(Brussel-Zuid). Note that for simplicity we've used the French version of street names, sights, etc.

The **Upper Town** is quite different in feel from the rest of the city centre, a self-consciously planned, more monumental quarter, with statuesque buildings lining wide, classically imposed boulevards and squares. Appropriately, it's the home of the Belgian parliament and government departments, formal parks and the royal palace – the **Palais Royal**. More promisingly, it also accommodates the newly refurbished **Cathedral**, a fine Gothic edifice with wonderful stained-glass windows, the superb **Musées Royaux des Beaux Arts**, arguably Belgium's best collection of fine art, and some of the city's swishest shops clustered around the charming place du Grand Sablon. There's also the preposterous bulk of the Palais de Justice, which lords it over the rest of the city, commanding views that on clear days reach way across the suburbs.

Brussels by no means ends with the **petit ring**. Léopold II pushed the city limits out beyond the course of the old walls, grabbing land from the surrounding *communes* to create the irregular boundaries that survive today. To the **east**, he sequestered a rough rectangle of land where he laid out **Parc Léopold** and across which he ploughed two wide boulevards – Belliard and La Loi. These were designed to provide an imperial approach to the **Parc du Cinquantenaire**, whose self-glorifying and over-sized monuments were erected to celebrate Belgium's golden jubilee and now house three large if rather turgid museums – the pick is the **Musées Royaux d'Art et d'Histoire**. The boulevards were soon colonised by the city's bourgeoisie, but in the last few years they have been displaced by the brash concrete and glass tower blocks of the **EU Quarter**, amongst which is the flashy new **European Parliament**.

South of the city centre, **St Gilles** is an animated and cosmopolitan district, while neighbouring **Ixelles** has become the favoured hangout of the arty and the cool, its streets nurturing a handful of designer stores, and a growing number of chic bars and restaurants. These two *communes* also boast much of the best of the city's **Art Nouveau** architecture. Ixelles is bisected by **avenue Louise**, a prosperous corridor that's actually considered part of the city centre – and is home to the enjoyable **Musée Constantin Meunier**.

Further out, to the **southwest** of the city centre, lies the gritty suburb of **Anderlecht**, famous for its soccer team and also worth a visit for its Gueuze brewery and the fascinating Erasmus house, one-time residence of Desiderius Erasmus, who lodged here in 1521. Adjacent to this area is **Koekelberg**, the site of the Basilique du Sacré Coeur, another whopping pile built by Léopold II, and adjacent again is the *commune* of **Jette**, site of the Musée René Magritte. To the **north** of the city centre, beyond the tough districts of **St Josse** and **Schaerbeek**, is **Laeken**, city residence of the Belgian royal family, and **Heysel**, with its notorious soccer stadium and the **Atomium**, a clumsy leftover from the 1958 World's Fair.

Arrival

Brussels is the major gateway for Belgium. It's on the main routes heading inland from the Channel ports; trains arrive here direct from London via the Channel Tunnel; in addition, it is a convenient stop on the rail line between France and Holland. Brussels itself has a good public transport system which puts the main **points of arrival** – its airport, train and bus stations – within easy reach of the city centre.

By air

Arriving by air, you'll land at Brussels' **international airport** in Zaventem, 13km northeast of the city centre. There's a Destination Belgium tourist information desk in the arrivals hall (daily 6.30am–9.30pm) and they have a reasonable range of information on Brussels and its surroundings. They can also make hotel reservations, a service that is provided free – you just pay a percentage of the room rate as a deposit and this is then subtracted from your final hotel bill. There are several bureaux de change and ATMs in the arrivals hall too.

From the airport, **trains** run every twenty minutes to the city's main stations. The journey-time to Bruxelles-Centrale is about twenty minutes; the cost is F90 one-way, and tickets can be bought from the ticket office in the train station that is part of the airport complex. You can also pay the ticket inspector on the train, but there's a small surcharge. Trains run from around 5.30am until midnight; after that you'll need to take a **taxi** into the city centre – reckon on paying around F1400 for the trip. There's an hourly **bus** service from the airport complex through the city's northeastern suburbs to the Gare du Nord; the journey takes about 45 minutes – and much longer during rush hour.

By train

Brussels has three main **train stations** – Bruxelles-Centrale, Bruxelles-Nord and Bruxelles-Midi – each only a few minutes, by public transport, apart. Almost all **domestic** trains stop at all three but the majority of **international** services only stop at Bruxelles-Midi, including Eurostar trains from London and Thalys express trains from Amsterdam, Paris, Cologne and Aachen.

Bruxelles-Centrale is, as its name suggests, the most central of the stations, a five-minute walk from the Grand-Place; **Bruxelles-Nord** lies amongst the bristling tower blocks of the business area just north of the main ring road; and **Bruxelles-Midi** is located in a depressed area just to the south of the city centre. Note that on bus timetables and on maps of the city transit system, Bruxelles-Nord appears as "Gare du Nord", Bruxelles-Centrale as "Gare Centrale" and Bruxelles-Midi as "Gare du Midi". The former name stands for the mainline train station while the latter usually signifies the métro stop.

Bruxelles-Midi and Bruxelles-Nord are linked by **métro** with several services (principally #23 and #55) shuttling underneath the city centre between the two stations. To reach the Grand-Place from either Bruxelles-Nord or Bruxelles-Midi, simply take the prémétro (#23 or #55) to the **Métro Bourse** station, and it's a couple of minutes' walk from there. Bruxelles-Centrale is on the **métro** line #1. It's easily reached from the other two train stations by simply jumping on the next available mainline train. If you arrive late at night, it's best to take a taxi to your hotel or hostel – and you should certainly avoid the streets around Bruxelles-Midi.

By bus

Most **international bus** services to Brussels, including those from Britain, are operated by Eurolines, whose terminal is in the Bruxelles-Nord station complex. Belgium's comprehensive rail network means that it's unlikely that you'll arrive in the city by **long-distance domestic bus**, but if you do, Bruxelles-Nord is the main terminal for these services too.

Information

Aside from the office at the airport, there are two **tourist information offices** in Brussels, both located right in the centre of town. The main one is the **TIB** (Office de Tourisme et d'Information de Bruxelles), in the Hôtel de Ville on the Grand-Place (Mon–Sat 9am–6pm; closed Sun Jan & Feb, March–April & Oct–Dec 10am–2pm, May–Sept 9am–6pm; ℂ513 89 40, fax 514 45 38), which handles information on the city only. It has a wide range of handouts, including free public transport and city maps, and sells a variety of general- and specialist-interest guides, the most useful of which is the detailed *All Brussels Guide and Map* (F60). In addition, the TIB issues a list of all the city's hotels and makes hotel **reservations** for free – the deposit is subtracted from your final hotel bill. It can help with public transport too: the TIB sells the 24-hour *carte d'un jour* pass (see below) and the 24-hour Tourist Passport (F300), which entitles bearers to free use of the city's public transport network and provides substantial discounts at a variety of sights. The TIB also operates a theatre and concert booking service; you can make reservations in person or via a special hotline (ℂ0800/21 2 21).

If you need a large map buy the *Girault Gilbert* map (F200), which comes complete with an index. It's available at the TIB and most city centre newsagents and bookshops.

The Bulletin (F90), the city's main English-language weekly, contains an excellent entertainment listings section, detailing what's on and where. The magazine is on sale at most downtown newsagents. The TIB also provides *The Bulletin*'s listings section – "What's On" – for free. The Wednesday supplement in the newspaper *Le Soir* is useful as well.

The **tourism centre** (Maison du Tourisme), nearby at rue Marché aux Herbes 63 (daily: April, May & Oct 9am–6pm; June–Sept 9am–7pm; Nov–March Mon–Sat 9am–6pm, Sun 1–5pm; ℃504 03 90, fax 504 02 70), provides information on the whole of Belgium. They do stock a few brochures on Brussels, but this is not their main concern – they leave the city largely to the TIB. They also operate a hotel room reservation service, but again it's for the rest of Belgium not Brussels.

BRUSSELS ON THE INTERNET

Tintin
www.tintin.be/
Blistering barnacles! Anything you've ever wanted to know.

Anderlecht football team
www.rsca.be/
'Ere we go, the thrilling fields of Anderlecht.

Beer
www.belgianstyle.com
More encouragement, if you need it.

Lace
www.belgian-lace.com
Examples of lacy bits for all occasions.

Magritte
www.virtuo.be/
More than 300 pics in this library and not just bowler hats.

Tourist Information
www.interpac.be/G7/brussels/brussels.html
Straight from the tourist board's mouth.

City transport

The easiest way to get around the city centre, within the petit ring, is to **walk**. To get from one side of the centre to the other, or to reach some of the more widely dispersed attractions, you will, however, need to use **public transport**. Operated by STIB (information line ©515 20 00), the urban system runs on an integrated mixture of bus, tram, underground tram (prémétro) and métro lines that covers the city comprehensively. It's a user-friendly network, with every métro station carrying métro system diagrams and with timetables posted at most bus and tram stops.

Tickets

Tickets are fairly cheap. A single ticket costs F50, a strip of five F240, and a strip of ten F330, available either from tram or bus drivers, métro kiosks, or from newsagents displaying the STIB sign. These can be used on any part of the STIB system. Tickets can also be obtained from automatic machines at most métro stations. A go-as-you-please *carte d'un jour*, for F130, allows for 24 hours of city-wide travel on public transport.

Métro, trams and trains

The **métro** system consists of two underground train lines – lines #1 and #2. Line #1 runs west–east through the centre, and splits into two branches (#1A and #1B) at either end to serve the city's suburbs. Line #2 circles the centre, its route roughly following that of the petit ring up above. Brussels has a substantial **tram** system serving the city centre and the suburbs. These trams are at their speediest when they go underground to form what is sometimes called the **prémétro**, part of the system which runs underneath the heart of the city from Bruxelles-Nord, through de Brouckère and Bourse, to Bruxelles-Midi, Porte de Hal and on underneath St Gilles.

There is a métro plan on map 9 at the back of the book. The symbol Ⓜ will be used throughout the book to denote a métro station.

At the **beginning of each journey**, you're trusted to stamp tickets yourself in the machines provided on the concourse. After that, the ticket is valid for an hour, during which you can get on and off as many trams, métros and buses as you like. The system can seem open to abuse, as ticket controls at the métro stations are almost non-existent and you can get on at the back of any tram without ever showing a ticket. But bear in mind that there are roving inspectors who impose heavy on-the-spot fines for anyone caught without a valid ticket. Finally, remember that doors on métros, trams and buses mostly have to be opened manually.

STIB **route maps** are available free from the tourist office and from most major métro stations. The STIB has information kiosks at Porte de Namur, Rogier and Midi métro stations. Amongst the multitude of routes, times of operation and frequency vary considerably, but key parts of the system operate from 6am until midnight. Lone travellers should avoid the métro late at night.

In addition to the STIB network are **local trains**, run by Belgian Railways, which connect different parts of the inner city and the outskirts, though unless you're living and working in the city, you're unlikely to need to use them. These trains shuttle in and out of the city's four smaller train stations: Bruxelles Chapelle; Bruxelles Quartier Léopold; Bruxelles Schuman; and Bruxelles Congrès.

Buses

De Lijn (℃526 28 28) runs **buses** from the city to the Flemish-speaking communities that surround the capital; TEC (℃010/230 53 53) does the same to the French-speaking areas. Most of these buses run from the Gare du Nord complex and many from place Rouppe (just off boulevard Lemonnier). Both companies also run services to other Belgian cities, but they can take up to four times longer than the train. There is also a limited and sporadic **night bus** service – often just one bus operating on a route between midnight and around 3am.

Taxis

Taxis don't cruise the streets but can be picked up at stands spread around the city – notably on Bourse, de Brouckère and Porte de Namur, at train stations and outside the smarter hotels. The minimum fare is F95 during the day and F170 at night. If you can't find one, phone Taxis Verts (℃349 49 49), Taxis Orange (℃513 62 00), or Autolux (℃411 12 21).

Guided tours

Organized tours are big business in Brussels. The TIB offers no fewer than 33 different guided tours, with everything from a quick stroll round the city centre to themed visits – following, for example, in the footsteps of René Magritte or visiting the pick of the city's Art Nouveau buildings. As a general rule the more exotic and unusual tours need to be booked well ahead of time with the TIB normally requiring at least two weeks' advance notice. The TIB also arranges **walking tours** of the Grand-Place and its surroundings, which you can join without reserving (1 daily: March–Sept Mon–Sat; times vary; F350 per person).

In addition, Brussels has around a dozen companies offering guided tours, many of which are run in conjunction with the TIB. For a **bus tour**, book with De Boeck, rue de la Colline 8 (℃513 77 44), which operates a wide range of excursions including a three-hour, breathless zip round the city and its major sights for F780 (students F600). Alternatively, Chatterbus, rue des Thuyas 12 (℃673 18 35), runs well-regarded **walking and public transport tours** (mid-June to mid-Sept daily; times vary). These city tours last about three hours and cost F300. Chatterbus supplements them with once- or twice-weekly (French-only) excursions devoted to a particular theme, for example Léopold II's Brussels or Belgian beers. Another recommendation is ARAU (Atelier de Recherche et d'Action Urbaines), boulevard Adolphe Max 55 (℃219 33 45), a heritage action group which provides tours exploring the city's architectural heritage with particular emphasis on Art Nouveau. Their three-hour bus tours are run once weekly at the weekend (times vary), from March through to December, and cost F600 each – double-check the tour you want has an English commentary.

Cyclists are catered for by Pro Vélo, rue Ernest Solvay 32a (℃502 73 55); they operate several half-day cycle tours round the city and its environs and also offer an evening city-centre excursion. The charge is F300 per tour, with bike hire costing an extra F200.

The Grand-Place

The **Grand-Place**, one of Europe's most beautiful squares, is tucked away amid the tangle of ancient cobbled lanes that lie at the heart of Brussels. It's the Gothic magnificence of the **Hôtel de Ville** – the town hall – which first draws the eye, but in its shadow is an exquisite sequence of late seventeenth-century guildhouses, whose gilded facades with their columns, scrolled gables and dainty sculptures encapsulate the Baroque ideals of exuberance and complexity. There's no better place to get the flavour of Brussels' past, and, as you nurse a coffee at one of the pavement cafés, its Eurocapital present.

**The area covered by this chapter is shown in detail
on colour map 4.**

Originally marshland, the Grand-Place was drained in the twelfth century, and by 1350 a covered **market** for bread, meat and textiles had appeared, born of an economic boom underpinned by a flourishing cloth industry. The market was so successful that it soon expanded beyond the boundaries of the square – hence the names of the narrow streets that maze around it: rues au Beurre and des Bouchers, marchés aux Herbes, aux Poulets and aux Fromages. On the square itself, the city's merchants built themselves their headquarters, the guildhouses that cemented the Grand-Place's role as the commercial hub of the emergent city.

In the fifteenth century, with the building of the Hôtel de Ville, the square took on a civic and political function too, with the ruling dukes descending from their Upper Town residence to hold audiences and organize tournaments. Official decrees and pronouncements were read in the Grand-Place too, and justice was meted out with public executions. In 1482, however, Brussels, along with the rest of the Low Countries, became a fiefdom of the Habsburgs. The role of the Grand-Place was transformed by the fervently Roman Catholic **Philip II** of Spain (1555–98) who turned these executions into religious events as he strove to crush the city's Protestants – the opening shots of a bitter religious war that was to rack the Low Countries for the next hundred years. In 1568, after one failed attack, Philip dispatched a massive Spanish army to crush his heretical subjects. In anticipation of the arrival of the Spanish army, thousands fled the city and, as the local economy collapsed, thousands died of famine.

From Tuesday to Sunday, there's a modest flower and plant market on the Grand-Place (8am–6pm) and on Sundays (7am–2pm) there's a pet bird market here too. For more on markets, see p.242.

Religious conflict dogged the city for another twenty years, but when the Habsburgs finally captured the town in 1585 they were surprisingly generous, granting a general amnesty and promising to honour ancient municipal privileges. The city's economy revived and the Grand-Place resumed its role as a commercial centre. Of the square's medieval buildings, however, only parts of the Hôtel de Ville and one guildhouse survive today, the consequence of a 36-hour **French artillery bombardment** which pretty much razed Brussels to the ground in 1695.

THE GRAND-PLACE

Unperturbed, the city's **guilds** swiftly had their headquarters rebuilt, using their control of the municipal council both to impose regulations on the sort of construction that was permitted and to ward off the Habsburg governor's notions of a royal – as distinct from bourgeois – main square. The council was not to be trifled with. In an early example of urban planning, it decreed "(We) hereby forbid the owners to build houses on the lower market [ie the Grand-Place] without the model of the facade . . . first being presented to the Council . . . Any construction erected contrary to this provision shall be demolished at the expense of the offender." By these means, the guilds were able to create a homogeneous Grand-Place, choosing to rebuild in a distinctive and flamboyant Baroque which made the square more ornate and more imposing than before. This magisterial self-confidence was, in fact, misplaced, and the factories that were soon to render the guilds obsolete were already colonizing parts of the city. The industrialization of the city effectively becalmed the Grand-Place, and hence it has survived pretty much intact to this day.

THE HÔTEL DE VILLE

Map 4, C7. Forty-minute guided tours in English from April to September on Tues at 11.30am & 3.15pm, Wed 3.15pm & Sun 12.15pm; October to March on Tues at 11.30am & 3.15pm only; F75. Ⓜ Bourse.

From the south side of the Grand-Place, the newly scrubbed and polished **Hôtel de Ville** dominates the proceedings, its 96-metre spire soaring above two long series of robust windows whose straight lines are mitigated by fancy tracery, intricate corbels, striking gargoyles and an arcaded gallery. The edifice dates from the beginning of the fifteenth century when the town council decided to build itself a mansion that adequately reflected its wealth and power. The first part

THE HÔTEL DE VILLE

to be completed was the **east wing** and the original entrance is marked by the twin lions of the Lion Staircase, though the animals were only added in 1770. Work started on the **west wing** in 1444 and continued until 1480. Despite the gap, the wings are of very similar style, and you have to look hard to notice that the later wing is slightly shorter than its neighbour, allegedly at the insistence of Charles the Bold who – for some unknown reason – refused to have the adjacent rue de la Tête d'Or narrowed. The niches were left empty and the statues you see now, which represent leading figures from the city's past – are modern, part of a heavy-handed nineteenth-century refurbishment.

By any standard, the **tower** of the Hôtel de Ville is quite extraordinary, its remarkably slender appearance the work of Jan van Ruysbroeck, the leading spire specialist of the day who also played a leading role in the building of the cathedral (see p.46) and Sts Pierre et Guidon in Anderlecht (see p.98). Ruysbroeck had the lower section built square to support the weight above, choosing a design that blended seamlessly with the elaborately carved facade on either side – or almost: look carefully and you'll see that the main entrance is slightly out of kilter. Ruysbroeck used the old belfry porch as the base for the new tower, hence the misalignment, a deliberate decision rather than the miscalculation which, according to legend, prompted the architect's suicide. Above the cornice protrudes an octagonal extension where the basic design of narrow windows flanked by pencil-thin columns and pinnacles is repeated up as far as the pyramid-shaped spire, a delicate affair surmounted by a gilded figure of **St Michael**, protector of Christians in general and of soldiers in particular. The tower is off-limits and **guided tours** are confined to a string of lavish official rooms used for receptions and town council meetings. The most dazzling of these is the sixteenth-century **Council Chamber**, decorated with gilt moulding, faded tapestries and an oak floor inlaid with ebony. The entrance chamber at the top of the first flight of stairs is also of interest for its assortment of royal portraits. The Empress Maria Theresa of Austria is pictured side-saddle with her little feet (of which she was inordinately proud) poking out from her fancy lacy dress, while a gallant-looking Charles II sits astride his handsome steed, courtesy of Jan van Orley. This must have stretched Orley's imagination to the limit: Charles, the last of the Spanish Habsburgs, was – according to the historian J. H. Elliott – "a rachitic and feeble-minded weakling, the last stunted sprig of a degenerate line". Tours begin at the reception desk off the interior quadrangle; be prepared for the guides' overly reverential script.

THE GUILDHOUSES

Flanking and facing the Hôtel de Ville are the **guildhouses** which give the Grand-Place its character, their slender, gilded facades swirling with exuberant, self-publicizing carvings and sculptures. Decorated with semicircular arches and classical motifs, scroll work, supple bas-reliefs and statuettes, they represent the apotheosis of **Italian-Flemish architecture**, a melding of two stylistic traditions first introduced into the Low Countries by artists and architects returning from Italy in the early seventeenth century. Each guildhouse has a name, usually derived from one of the statues, symbols or architectural quirks decorating its facade – and the more interesting are described below.

On the west side of the square, at the end of the row, stands **no. 1: Roi d'Espagne**. This particularly fine building, which was once the headquarters of the guild of bakers, is named after the bust of Charles II (see above) on the upper storey. Charles is flanked by a Moorish and a Native American prisoner, symbolic trophies of war. Balanced on the balustrade are allegorical statues of Energy, Fire, Water, Wind,

Wheat and Prudence, presumably meant to represent the elements necessary for baking the ideal loaf. The guildhouse now holds the most famous of the square's bars, the *Roy d'Espagne* (see p.191), a surreal affair with animal bladders and marionettes hanging from the ceiling – and repro halberds in the toilets.

Nos. 2–3: Maison de la Brouette was the tallow makers' guildhouse, but it takes its name from the wheelbarrows etched into the cartouches. The figure at the top is St Gilles, the guild's patron saint.

Next door the three lower storeys of **Maison du Sac** at **no. 4** escaped the French bombardment of 1695. It was constructed for the carpenters and coopers, with the upper storeys being appropriately designed by a cabinet-maker, and featuring pilasters and caryatids which resemble the ornate legs of Baroque furniture.

The **Maison de la Louve**, at **no. 5**, also survived the French artillery, and was originally home to the influential archers' guild. The pilastered facade is studded with sanctimonious representations of concepts such as Peace and Discord, and the medallions just beneath the pediment carry the likenesses of four Roman emperors set above allegorical motifs indicating their particular attributes. Thus, Trajan is above the Sun, a symbol of Truth; Tiberius with a net and cage for Falsehood; Augustus and the globe of Peace; and Julius Caesar with a bleeding heart for Disunity. Above the door, there's a charming bas-relief of the Roman she-wolf suckling Romulus and Remus, while the pediment holds a relief of Apollo firing at a python; right on top the Phoenix rises from the ashes.

The **Maison du Cornet**, at **no. 6**, headquarters of the boatmen's guild, is a fanciful creation of 1697 sporting a top storey resembling the stern of a ship. Charles II makes another appearance here – it's his head in the medallion, flanked by representations of the four winds and of a pair of sailors.

The house of the haberdashers' guild, **Maison du Renard** at **no. 7**, displays animated cherubs in bas-relief play at haberdashery on the ground floor, while a scrawny, gilded fox – after which the house is named – squats above the door. Up on the third storey a statue of Justice, flanked by statues symbolizing the four continents, suggests the guild's designs on world markets – an aim to which St Nicolas, patron saint of merchants, glinting above, clearly gives his blessing.

On the south side of the square, this arcaded structure, **Maison de l'Étoile (no.8)**, is a nineteenth-century rebuilding of the medieval home of the city magistrate. In the passageway round the corner, on rue Charles Buls, the exploits of one Everard 't Serclaes are commemorated: in 1356 the Francophile Count of Flanders attempted to seize power from the Duke of Brabant, occupying the magistrate's house and flying his standard from the roof. 'T Serclaes scaled the building, replaced Flanders' standard with that of the Duke of Brabant, and went on to lead the recapturing of the city, events represented in bas-relief above a reclining statue of 't Serclaes. His effigy is polished smooth from the long-standing superstition that good luck will come to those who stroke it.

The mansion that takes its name from the ostentatious swan on the facade, **Maison du Cygne** at **no. 9**, once housed a bar where Karl Marx regularly met up with Engels during his exile in Belgium. It was in Brussels in February 1848 that they wrote the *Communist Manifesto*, only to be deported as political undesirables the following month. Appropriately enough, the Belgian Workers' Party was founded here in 1885, though nowadays the building shelters one of the city's more exclusive restaurants.

Maison de l'Arbre d'Or, at **no. 10**, is the only house on the Grand-Place still to be owned by a guild – the brewers' – not that the equestrian figure stuck on top gives any clues: the original effigy – of one of the city's Habsburg governors –

THE GUILDHOUSES

dropped off and the present statue, picturing the eighteenth-century aristocrat Charles of Lorraine, was moved here simply to fill the gap. Inside, the small and mundane **Musée de la Brasserie** (daily 10am–5pm; F100) has various bits of brewing paraphernalia; a beer is included in the price of admission.

The seven guildhouses (**nos. 13–19**) that fill out the east side of the Grand-Place have been subsumed within one grand facade whose slender symmetries are set off by a curved pediment and narrow pilasters, sporting nineteen busts of the dukes of Brabant. Perhaps more than any other building on the Grand-Place, the **Maison des Ducs de Brabant** has the flavour of the aristocracy – as distinct from the bourgeoisie – and, needless to say, it was much admired by the city's Habsburg governors.

The guildhouses and private mansions (**nos. 20–39**) running along the north side of the Grand-Place are not as distinguished as their neighbours, though the **Maison du Pigeon** (**nos. 26–27**), the painters' guildhouse, is of interest as the house where Victor Hugo spent some time during his exile from France – he was expelled after the French insurrection of 1848. The house also bears four unusual masks in the manner of the green man of Romano-Celtic folklore. The adjacent **Maison des Tailleurs** (**nos. 24–25**) is appealing too; the old headquarters of the tailors' guild is adorned by a pious bust of St Barbara, their patron saint.

MAISON DU ROI AND THE MUSÉE DE LA VILLE DE BRUXELLES

Map 4, D3. Mon–Fri 10am–12.30pm & 1.30–5pm, Sat & Sun 10am–1pm; F80. Ⓜ Bourse.

Much of the northern side of the Grand-Place is taken up by the late nineteenth-century **Maison du Roi**, a fairly faithful reconstruction of the palatial Gothic structure commissioned by Charles V in 1515. The emperor had a point to make: the Hôtel de Ville was an assertion of municipal independence and Charles wanted to emphasise imperial power by erecting his own building directly opposite. With its angular lines, spiky pinnacles and lacy stonework, the original Maison du Roi was an impressive building, but although its replacement, which was completed in the 1890s, is still quite grand, the arcaded galleries which were added interrupt the flow of the design. No expense was spared in its construction. When it turned out that the ground was too marshy to support the edifice Charles had approved, the architects began again, sinking piles deep into the ground and stretching cattle hides between them to keep the stagnant water at bay.

Despite its name, no sovereign ever lived here permanently, though this is where the Habsburgs sometimes stayed when they visited the city. It was also used as a sort of royal changing room: the future Philip II donned his armour here before joining a joust held in the Grand-Place, and the Archdukes Albert and Isabella dressed up inside before appearing on the balcony to shoot down a symbolic target that made them honorary members of the guild of crossbowmen. The Habsburgs also installed their tax men and law courts here, and used it to hold their more important prisoners – the counts of Egmont and Hoorn (see p.65) spent their last night in the Maison du Roi before being beheaded outside in the Grand-Place.

The building now holds the **Musée de la Ville de Bruxelles**, a wide-ranging but patchy collection whose best sections feature medieval fine and applied art – not that you'll glean much from the scanty (French and Flemish) labelling.

To the **left of the entrance**, there's a room full of Gothic sculpture retrieved from various city buildings. Pride of place goes to the eight prophets, complete with heavy

MUSÉE DE LA VILLE DE BRUXELLES

beards and eccentric headgear, who once decorated the porch of the Hôtel de Ville. A subsequent room contains a small but charming sample of eighteenth-century **glazed earthenware**, for which the city was once internationally famous. The finest work is by Philippe Mombaers (1724–54), whose workshop, on rue de Laeken, is credited with developing table decorations in the form of vegetables or animals – hence the splendid turkey, cod-fish, duck and cabbage soup tureens and casserole dishes.

The first of the rooms to the **right of the entrance** boasts superb **altarpieces** – or retables – the intricacy of which was a Brussels speciality, with the city producing hundreds of them from the end of the fourteenth century until the economic slump of the 1640s. Their manufacture was similar to a production line with panel- and cabinet-makers, wood carvers, painters and goldsmiths (for the gilding) working on several altarpieces at any one time. The standard format was to create a series of mini-tableaux illustrating Biblical scenes, with the characters wearing medieval gear in a medieval landscape. It's the extraordinary detail that impresses: look closely at the niche carvings on the whopping **Saluzzo altarpiece** and you'll spy the candlesticks, embroidered pillowcase and carefully draped coverlet of Mary's bedroom in the *Annunciation* scene, while the adjacent *Nativity* panel comes complete with a pair of cute little angels. Up above, in a swirling, phantasmagorical landscape (of what look like climbing toadstools), is the *Shepherds Hear the Good News*. Also in this room is Pieter Bruegel the Elder's *Wedding Procession*, a good-natured scene with country folk walking to church to the accompaniment of bagpipes.

The second room to the right is devoted to four large-scale **tapestries** and dated to 1516. The earliest of the four relates the legend of *Notre Dame du Sablon*, the tedious tale of the transfer of a statue of the Virgin from Antwerp to

Tapestry manufacture and design

Tapestry manufacture in Brussels began in the middle of the fifteenth century and soon came under the control of a small clique of manufacturers who imposed a rigorous system of quality control. From 1528 every tapestry made in Brussels had to bear the town's trademark – two "Bs" enclosed in a red shield. Brussels' tapestries were famous for their lavish raw materials – especially gold thread – and this also served to keep control of the industry in the hands of the few. Only rarely were weavers able to accumulate enough money to buy their materials, never mind their own looms.

The first great period of Brussels tapestry-making lasted until the middle of the sixteenth century, when religious conflict over-whelmed the city and many of its Protestant-inclined weavers migrated north to rival workshops. By the beginning of the seventeenth century, the industry had revived with about one hundred workshops. Later, however, French occupation and the shrinking of the Spanish market led to diminishing production, until the industry finally fizzled out in 1794.

Tapestry production was a cross between embroidery and ordinary weaving. It consisted of interlacing a wool weft above and below the strings of a vertical linen "chain", a process similar to weaving. However, the weaver had to stop to change colour, requiring as many shuttles for the weft as he had colours, as in embroidery. The design of a tapestry was taken from a painting to which the weaver made constant reference. Standard-size tapestries took six months to make and were produced exclusively for the very wealthy, the most important of whom would often insist on the use of gold and silver thread and the employment of the most famous artists of the day for the preparatory painting – Pieter Paul Rubens, Jacob Jordaens and David Teniers all had tapestry commissions.

Brussels (see p.65) – though fortunately the tapestry is much better than the story. A second tapestry, this one from 1580, tells the Arthurian legend of Tristan and Isolde, but easily the most striking is the *Solemn Funeral of the Roman Consul Decius Mus,* based on drawings by Rubens. This is an extraordinary work, crowded with classical figures of muscular men and fleshy women surrounding the consul, who won a decisive victory against the Samnites, securing Roman control of Italy in the third century BC. Decius is laid out on a chaise-longue and even inanimate objects join in the general mourning – with the lion heads, for instance, glancing sorrowfully at the onlooker.

The museum's upper floors are less diverting: the first floor has scale models of the city and various sections on aspects of its development, while the second holds the Manneken Pis' vast wardrobe, four hundred sickeningly saccharine costumes ranging from Mickey Mouse to a maharajah, all of them gifts from various visiting dignitaries.

AROUND THE GRAND-PLACE

In the 1890s, it was burgomaster **Charles Buls** who spearheaded the campaign to preserve the city's ancient buildings. One of his rewards was to have a street named after him, and this runs south from the Grand-Place in between the Maison de l'Étoile and the Hôtel de Ville to the corner of **rue des Brasseurs** (the first on the left), scene of a bizarre incident in 1873 when the French Symbolist poet Paul Verlaine shot his fellow poet and lover Arthur Rimbaud. This rash act earned him a two-year prison sentence – and all because Rimbaud had dashed from Paris to dissuade him from joining the Spanish army. Even today, there's still a slightly offbeat feel to the area, totally at odds with the respectable tourism of the Grand-Place, with gutsy bars and cheap Greek eateries running up the slope to rue des Éperonniers.

Moving on, rue de la Violette is the second turn on the left, and here at no. 6 the **Musée de Costume et de la Dentelle** (Map 4, C5; daily Mon–Fri 10am–12.30pm & 1.30–5pm, 4pm Oct–March, plus Sat & Sun 2–4.30pm; F80) has many examples of antique and modern lace mixed in with various temporary displays on costume. The museum rambles over three small floors and poor labelling doesn't elucidate, but the most interesting part of the permanent collection is on the top floor, where four wooden cupboards hold drawer after drawer of lace illustrating the work of all the principal centres of manufacture. Lace became an important Brussels product in the seventeenth century, and by the nineteenth century, when the industry reached its peak, the city had ten thousand lacemakers, all of them women. The lace made here was renowned for the intricacy of the designs and was in demand worldwide, bought by the rich to embellish their clothes. Nowadays lace is still made in Brussels, though on a much smaller scale, and it's still very expensive – especially from any of the shops around the Grand-Place.

....

F. Rubbrecht on the Grand-Place 23 will immediately satisfy your passion for lacy bits. See p.240 for a review.

....

From the foot of rue de la Violette, rue de l'Étuve runs south to the **Manneken Pis** (Map 4, B6), a diminutive statue of a pissing urchin stuck high up in a shrine-like affair protected from the hoards of tourists by an iron fence. The Manneken is supposed to embody the "irreverent spirit" of the city, or at least that is reputed to have been the intention of Jérôme Duquesnoy when he cast the original bronze statue in the 1600s to replace the medieval stone fountain that stood here before. It's likely that Duquesnoy invented the Manneken Pis and its popularity blossomed during the sombre, priest-dominated years following the Thirty Years' War, but it's possible his bronze replaced an earlier stone version of ancient provenance. There are all sorts of folkloric tales about its origins, from lost aristocratic children recovered when they were taking a pee, to peasant lads putting out dangerous fires and – least likely of the lot – boys slashing on the city's enemies from the trees and putting them to flight. As a talisman, it has certainly attracted the attention of thieves, notably in 1817 when a French ex-convict swiped it before breaking it into pieces. The thief and the smashed Manneken were apprehended, the former publicly branded on the Grand-Place and sentenced to a life of forced labour, while the fragments of the latter were used to create the mould in which the present-day Manneken was cast. It's long been the custom for visiting VIPs to donate a costume, and the little chap is regularly kitted out in different tackle – often military or folkloric gear, from C&W stetsons and chaps to golfers' plus fours and Donald Duck and Mickey Mouse outfits.

The Lower Town

The **Lower Town** is the commercial centre of Brussels, a bustling quarter that's home to most of the city's best restaurants, shops and hotels. It fans out from the Grand-Place, north, south and west to the boulevards of the petit ring, and east as far as the foot of the ridge which marks the start of the Upper Town (see Chapter 4), along the line of boulevards Berlaimont, L'Impératrice and L'Empereur. At its heart, the layout of the Lower Town remains essentially medieval, a labyrinth of narrow, cobbled lanes and alleys whose names mostly reveal their original purpose as markets – rue du Marché aux Fromages is an example. This medieval street pattern is interrupted by the boulevards that were inserted during the nineteenth century – part of a drive to modernize the city which saw the River Senne covered over and hundreds of culs-de-sac eliminated. But these boulevards have done little to disturb the jostle and jangle that give the Lower Town its character, with almost every street crimped by tall and angular town houses. There's nothing neat and tidy about all this, but that's what makes Brussels so intriguing –

The area covered by this chapter is shown in detail on colour map 3.

dilapidated terraces stand next to prestigious mansions and the whole place is dotted with superb buildings, everything from beautiful Baroque churches through to Art Nouveau department stores.

NORTHWEST OF THE GRAND-PLACE

Arguably the most diverting part of the Lower Town, the jumble of narrow streets and pocket-sized squares that spreads **northwest of the Grand-Place** to **place Ste Catherine** is crowded by the elegant, though often down-at-heel, town houses of the late nineteenth-century bourgeoisie. Pockets of stylish fashionability poke out here and there and the district has lots of great bars. There are also a couple of especially fine buildings, the Victorian **Bourse** and the Baroque church of **St Jean Baptiste au Béguinage**.

The Church of St Nicholas

Map 4, C2. Mon–Sat 8am–6.30pm, Sun 8am–12.30pm & 4–7.30pm; free. Ⓜ Bourse.

Walking northwest out of the Grand-Place along rue au Beurre, the pint-sized church of **St Nicholas**, on the right-hand side, dates from the twelfth century, though it's been heavily restored on several occasions, most recently in the 1950s when parts of the outer shell were reconstructed in a plain Gothic style. The church is dedicated to St Nicholas of Bari as the patron saint of sailors, or, as he's better known, Santa Claus. The church is unusual in so far as the three aisles of the nave were built at an angle to the chancel, in order to avoid a stream. It also carries a memento of the French bombardment of 1695 in the cannon ball embedded high up in the third pillar on the left the nave. Otherwise, the gloomy church hardly sets the pulse racing, although – among a scattering of *objets d'art* – there's a handsome, gilded copper reliquary shrine near the entrance. The shrine was made in Germany in the nineteenth century to honour a group of Catholics martyred by Protestants in Gorinchem in the Netherlands in 1572.

> **Maison Dandoy**, at rue au Beurre 31, is something of a city institution, a long-established confectioner's whose tasty specialities are macaroons and "spekuloos", a sugary brown, cinnamon-flavoured biscuit that's prepared in a variety of traditional and intricate moulds.

The Bourse and place St Géry

Beyond rue au Beurre rises the grandiose **Bourse** (Map 4, B2), formerly the home of the city's stock exchange, a Neoclassical structure of 1873 caked with fruit, fronds, languishing nudes and frolicking putti. This breezily self-confident structure sports a host of allegorical figures (Industry, Navigation, Asia, Africa, etc) which both reflect the preoccupations of the nineteenth-century Belgian bourgeoisie and, in their easy self-satisfaction, imply that wealth and pleasure are synonymous. The Bourse is in a bad state of repair, but the handsome town houses to either side are even worse – an unfortunate setting for two of the city's more famous cafés, the Art Nouveau *Falstaff*, on the south side at rue Henri Maus 17–23, and the fin-de-siècle *Le Cirio*, on the other side at rue de la Bourse 18. In front of *Le Cirio* are the glassed-in foundations of a medieval church and convent, unearthed by archeologists in the 1980s and now known rather grandly as **Bruxella 1238** (Map 4, B2). There are occasional guided tours of the site, although these are only of specialist interest – the tourist office on the Grand-Place can give you times.

The square in front of the Bourse – **place de la Bourse** – is little more than an unsightly, heavily trafficked pause along boulevard Anspach, but the streets on the other side of the boulevard have more appeal, with tiny **place St Géry** crowded by high-sided, somewhat run-down tenements, whose stone balconies and wrought-iron grilles speak of more prosperous days. The square is thought to occupy the site of the sixth-century chapel from which the medieval city grew, but this is a matter of conjecture – no archeological evidence has ever been unearthed and the only clue to the city's early history is in its name, literally "settlement in the marshes". Place St Géry has one specific attraction in the recently refurbished, late nineteenth-century covered market, the **Halles St Géry**, an airy, glass and iron edifice. The elegance of the structure is, however, obscured by a huge stone fountain plonked right in the middle – and moved here from the town of Grimbergen to the north of Brussels apparently for decorative reasons.

Rue Antoine Dansaert and place Ste Catherine

From place St Géry, it's a couple of minutes' stroll north to **rue Antoine Dansaert**, where the most innovative and stylish of the city's fashion designers have set up shop amongst the dilapidated old houses that stretch up to place du Nouveau Marché aux Grains. Amongst several outstanding boutiques, two of the best are Nicole Cadine, at no. 28, and the Art Halie shoe shop at no. 71. Stijl, at no. 74, showcases a bevy of big-name designers and there's strikingly original furniture at Max, at nos. 90 and 103.

Nearby, **place Ste Catherine** (Map 3, C4) is, despite its dishevelled appearance, at the heart of one of the city's most fashionable districts, not least because of its excellent seafood restaurants. Presiding over the square – and the proceedings of a daily market – is the **church of Ste Catherine** a battered nineteenth-century replacement for the Baroque original, of which the creamy, curvy belfry is the solitary survivor. Venture inside the church and you'll see a fourteenth-century Black Madonna and Child, a sensually carved stone statuette that was chucked into the Senne by Protestants, but fished out while floating on a fortuitous clod of peat.

Ste Catherine is open Mon–Sat 8.30am–5/6pm, Sun 9am–noon.

Quai aux Briques and the parallel quai aux Bois à Brûler extend northwest from place Ste Catherine on either side of a wide and open area that was once part of the city's main **dock**. Filled-in a few years ago, the route of the old waterway is easy to follow, a pleasant ten-minute jaunt to place de l'Yser and the Charleroi canal. On the way, you'll pass a motley assortment of nineteenth-century warehouses, shops and bars which maintain an appealing canalside feel – an impression heightened in the early morning when the streets are choked with lorries bearing trays of fish for local restaurants. From place de l'Yser, it's a brief walk east to place Rogier (see p.37).

St Jean Baptiste au Béguinage

Map 3, D4. July & Aug Tues–Sat 11am–5pm, Sun 10am–5pm; Sept–June Tues 10am–5pm, Wed, Thurs & Fri 10am–5pm plus occasional Sat and Sun morning; free. Ⓜ Ste Catherine.

Just north of place Ste Catherine lies **place du Samedi**, a pretty little square from where rue du Cyprès squeezes in between high old buildings to reach place du Béguinage, dominated by **St Jean Baptiste au Béguinage**, a supple, billowing structure dating from the second half of the seventeenth century. Recently restored, this beautiful church is the only building left from the Béguine convent founded here in the thirteenth century. The convent once crowded in on the church and only since its demolition – and the creation of the star-shaped place du Béguinage in 1855 – has it been possible to view the exterior with any degree of ease. There's a sense of movement in each and every feature, a dynamism of design culminating in three soaring gables where the upper portion of the central tower is decorated with pinnacles that echo those of the Hôtel de Ville. The church's light and spacious interior is lavishly decorated, the white stone columns and arches dripping with solemn-faced cherubs intent on reminding the congregation of their mortality. The nave and aisles are wide and open, offering unobstructed views of the high altar, but you can't fail to notice the enormous wooden pulpit featuring St Dominic preaching against heresy – and trampling a heretic under foot for good measure.

Around the back of the church, a short lane takes you through to a slender, tree-lined square framed by the austere Neoclassicism of the **Hospice Pacheco** (no access), built to house the destitute in the 1820s. It's a peaceful spot today, but the stern wall that surrounds the complex is a reminder of times when the hospice was more like a prison than a shelter, with draconian rules imposed with brutal severity.

The **Senne River** once flowed beside the hospice, but is no longer viewable here. By the nineteenth century it had become intolerably polluted – in the words of the Brussels writer, Camille Lemonnier, "the dumping ground, not only of industry, but also of the houses lining the river: it was not unusual to see the ballooned stomach of a dog mixed pell mell with its own litter..." After an outbreak of cholera in 1866, which killed over 3500 townsfolk, the river was piped underground and paved over.

NORTH OF THE GRAND-PLACE

The busy streets between the Grand-Place and the Gare du Nord hold many of the city's biggest shops and stores, especially along **rue Neuve**, as well as dozens of restaurants, notably on and around **rue des Bouchers**. The prime architectural attraction is the **place des Martyrs**, built by the Austrian Habsburgs.

Rue des Bouchers and the Galeries St Hubert

Just to the north of the Grand-Place, the quarter hinging on the pedestrianized **rue des Bouchers** is the city centre's restaurant ghetto, the narrow cobblestone lanes transformed at night into fairy-lit tunnels where restaurants vie for custom with elaborate displays of dull-eyed fish and glistening seafood. There's a feverish atmosphere here, of hard selling and high spending, and although there's no doubting the liveliness of the scene you may well prefer something less frenetic and more obviously Belgian. Tucked away down an alley off petite rue des Bouchers, at Impasse Schuddeveld 6, is the **Théâtre de Toone** (Map 4, D3), which puts on puppet plays in the *bruxellois* dialect – Brusselse Sproek or Marollien (see p.43). It's very much a city institution and there are performances Tuesday through Saturday – as well as an excellent bar. Nearby are the **Galeries St Hubert** (Map 4, F2), whose trio of glass-vaulted galleries – du Roi, de la Reine and the smaller des Princes – cut across the top of rue des

For further details or tickets for the
Théâtre de Toone, see p.259.

RUE DES BOUCHERS AND THE GALERIES ST HUBERT

35

Bouchers. Opened by Léopold I in 1847, these galleries were one of Europe's first shopping arcades, and the pastel-painted walls, classical columns and cameo sculptures still retain an aura of dignified sophistication.

Théâtre de la Monnaie and the Hôtel Métropole

Emerging at the north end of the Galerie du Roi, it's a brief walk down rue de l'Écuyer to **place de la Monnaie**, the drab and dreary modern square that's overshadowed by the huge **centre Monnaie** (Map 3, D5), housing offices, shops and the main city post office. The only building of interest here is the **Théâtre de la Monnaie** (Map 3, E5), Brussels' opera house, a Neoclassical structure built in 1819 and with an interior added in 1856 to a design by Poelaert, the architect of the Palais de Justice (see p.67). The theatre's real claim to fame, however, is as the starting-point of the revolution against the Dutch in 1830: a nationalistic libretto in Auber's *The Mute Girl of Portici* sent the audience wild, and they poured out into the streets to raise the flag of Brabant, signalling the start of the rebellion. The opera told the tale of an Italian uprising against the Spanish, and with such lines as "To my country I owe my life, To me it will owe its liberty" one of the censors should have seen what might happen given the revolutionary politics of that year.

For tickets and performance information about Théâtre de la Monnaie, see p.222.

On the far side of the centre Monnaie is traffic-choked boulevard Anspach which forks and widens at **place de Brouckère**, a busy junction that accommodates the **Hôtel Métropole**, whose splendidly ornate public areas date from 1895 and were once the haunt of the likes of Sarah Bernhardt and Isadora Duncan.

Rue Neuve and place des Martyrs

From place de la Monnaie, **rue Neuve** (Map 3, E4–F3) forges north, a workaday pedestrianized shopping street that's home to the big chain stores and the City 2 shopping mall. About halfway up, turn east along rue St Michel for the **place des Martyrs**, a cool, rational square imposed on the city by the Habsburgs in the 1770s. Long neglected, the square is very much the worse for wear – work has at last started on a thoroughgoing refurbishment – but there's still no mistaking the architectural elegance of the ensemble, completed in the last years of Austrian control. The only stylistic blip is the nineteenth-century centrepiece, a clumsy representation of the Fatherland Crowned rising from an arcaded gallery inscribed with the names of those 445 rebels who died in the Belgian revolution of 1830.

Rue Neuve meets the inner ring at **place Rogier**, beyond which glistening new office blocks march up rue du Progrès to the recently revamped **Gare du Nord** (Map 3, F1).

NORTHEAST OF THE GRAND-PLACE

The most obvious attraction to the northeast of the Grand-Place is the **Centre Belge de la Bande Dessinée**, the Belgian Comic Strip Centre, which details the leading role the country's artists and scriptwriters have taken in this sphere ever since *Tintin* first appeared in 1929. Spare time also for a visit to the Colonne du Congrès and the elegant squares and streets of the old middle-class residential district just behind.

Centre Belge de la Bande Dessinée

Map 3, F4. Tues–Sun 10am–6pm; F200.
Reference Library Tues–Thurs noon–5pm, Fri noon–6pm, Sat 10am–6pm; F50. Ⓜ Botanique.

Heading northeast from the Grand-Place, it takes about ten minutes to walk to the city's only surviving Horta-designed department store, the **Grand Magasin Waucquez**, situated amongst run-down offices and warehouses at rue des Sables 20. Recently restored after lying empty for many years, it's a wonderfully airy, summery construction, with light flooding through the stained glass that encloses the expansive entrance hall. It was completed in 1906, built for a textile tycoon, and exhibits all the classic features of Horta's work (see p.72) – from the soft lines of the ornamentation to the metal grilles, exposed girders and balustrades.

Around the entrance hall is a first-rate café, the *Brasserie Horta*, as well as the reference library, bookshop and ticket office of the **Centre Belge de la Bande Dessinée**. The displays are extensive and diverting and though the labelling is in French and Flemish only, an English guidebook is available free at reception. The exhibits begin at the top of the first flight of stairs with two modest sections outlining the processes involved in drawing comic strips and cartoon animation. There's also a small auditorium offering non-stop cartoons and documentaries. On the floor above, the grandly titled "Museum of the Imagination" begins by tracing the development of the Belgian comic strip up until 1960, with an especially interesting section on **Tintin**, the creation of Brussels-born Georges Remi, aka Hergé (1907–83). Remi's first efforts (non-*Tintin*) had been sponsored by a right-wing Catholic journal, *Le XXème Siècle*, and in 1929 when this same paper produced a kids' suplement – *Le Petit Vingtième* – Remi was given his first major break. Remi was responsible for a two- page comic strip and he created *Tintin in the Land of the Soviets*, a didactic tale about the evils of Bolshevism. Tintin's Soviet adventure lasted until May 1930 and the director of *Le XXème*

Siècle decided to stage a reception – as a PR stunt – to celebrate Tintin's return. Remi – along with a Tintin lookalike – hopped on a train just east of Brussels and when they pulled into the capital they were mobbed by scores of excited children. Remi and Tintin never looked back. Remi decided on the famous quiff straight away, but other features – the mouth and expressive eyebrows – only came later. His popularity was quite phenomenal – *Tintin* has been translated into fifty languages and over twenty million copies of the comic *Le Journal de Tintin*, Remi's own independent creation, have been sold. First published in 1946, this *Journal* also helped to popularise the work of some of the country's most creative cartoonists, including Willy Vandersteen and Edgar-Pierre Jacobs, whose theatrical compositions and fluent combination of genres – science fiction, fantasy and crime – are displayed in his *Blake and Mortimer*. Belgium's oldest comic-strip paper, the *Spiro Journal*, performed a similar service and was responsible for launching the career of André Franquin, the creator of the feckless anti-hero *Gaston Lagaffe*. Sadly, *Spiro* was also where *The Smurfs* first saw light of day, the creation of Peyo in 1958.

....

La Boutique Tintin, just off the Grand-Place at rue de la Colline 13, has all manner of Tintin paraphernalia.

....

On the top floor the "Museum of Modern Comic Strips" looks at new trends and themes. The comic strip has long ceased to be primarily aimed at children, but now focuses on the adult (sometimes very adult) market. A series of regularly rotated displays ably illustrates some of the best of this new work and there's also a programme of temporary exhibitions.

CENTRE BELGE DE LA BANDE DESSINÉE

Colonne du Congrès and place des Barricades

Moving east, it's another short walk up to the 47-metre-high **Colonne du Congrès** (Map 3, G5), on place du Congrès. Erected in 1850 to commemorate the country's first national parliament, the column sports a statue of Léopold I on top and four allegorical female figures down below, representing the freedoms enshrined in the Constitution – the freedoms of worship, association, education and of the press. The lions were added later, guarding the tomb of the unknown soldier in front of which burns the eternal flame honouring Belgium's dead of the two world wars. The column dominates a bleak belvedere, flanked by the blank glass and concrete administration buildings and offering a singularly unflattering view of the city.

Behind, beyond rue Royale and north of **rue du Congrès**, lies one of the most attractive parts of the city centre, a pocket-sized district where the grand mansions of the nineteenth-century bourgeoisie, built with dignified balconies and wrought-iron grilles, overlook wide, straight streets and fetching little squares. Some of the earliest houses, dating from the 1820s, overlook the **place des Barricades**, named to commemorate the fighting that took place against the Dutch in 1830. Victor Hugo was living in exile here at no. 4 when he was thrown out of Belgium for complaining to the government about *their* ban on refugees.

Le Botanique

Map 3, G3.

Running north from the Colonne du Congrès is **rue Royale**, a dead straight boulevard linking the place Royale with **Le Botanique**, an appealingly grandiose greenhouse dating from 1826. The building once housed the city's botanical gardens, but these were moved out long ago and the place has been turned into a Francophone cultural centre. The adjacent **park** slopes away to the west, its carefully manicured woods, lawns and borders decorated by statues and a tiny lake. Despite the proximity of the traffic-congested boulevards of the petit ring, it's a pleasant spot, though be warned that dodgy characters haunt its precincts in the evening.

St Josse

The district of **St Josse**, immediately north of Le Botanique, is somewhere you'll probably want to go only at night, the main attraction being its numerous (and inexpensive) Turkish restaurants. It's a compelling, uncompromisingly foreign neighbourhood, where men while away their days and nights over glasses of tea in cafés and head-scarved women emerge only during the day to shop. Dating from the 1840s, the vast, domed and severely dilapidated **Église de Ste Marie**, standing at the head of rue Royale, is the quarter's landmark, but life centres on **chaussée de Haecht**, joining rue Royale just beyond Le Botanique, packed with restaurants, snack bars and the odd shop selling fruit and veg, Turkish videos, and gimcrackery.

SOUTH OF THE GRAND-PLACE

Few tourists venture into the working-class districts to the **south of the Grand-Place**, either into the impoverished immigrant area around the **Gare du Midi** or the **Quartier Marolles,** on either side of rue Blaes. There is, however, a scattering of architectural sights, several atmospheric bars and restaurants and a pair of excellent **markets**.

ST JOSSE

Gare du Midi

The labyrinth of cobbled lanes immediately to the south-west of the Grand-Place makes for an enjoyable stroll, but inevitably you'll soon stumble on the two dead straight and uninteresting boulevards that run down from the Bourse to the **Gare du Midi** (Map 4, A10), which lies just beyond the petit ring. The area round the station is home to the city's many North African immigrants, a severely depressed and at times seedy quarter with an uneasy undertow by day and sometimes overtly threatening at night. There's a closed, ghettoized feel to the streets and in many of the cheap cafés and bars.

A good time to go to the Gare du Midi district is on a Sunday morning, when a vibrant souk-like market is held under the station's rail arches (see p.242). Don't miss out on the excellent choice of eating and drinking in the area as well.

Notre Dame de la Chapelle

Map 3, D8. June–Sept Mon–Fri 9am–5pm, Sat 1.30–5pm & Sun 1.30–3.30pm; Oct–May Mon–Fri 1–4pm; free. Ⓜ Gare Centrale.
If you'd rather avoid Midi, you could instead stroll south from the Grand-Place along rue de l'Étuve, passing the Manneken Pis (see p.27) before turning east down **rue des Alexiens**. This ends abruptly at boulevard de l'Empereur, a busy carriageway that disfigures this part of the centre. Across the boulevard, slightly to the north, you'll spy the crumbling brickwork of the **tour d'Angle**, a chunky remnant of the medieval city wall, while to the south gleams the recently restored **Notre Dame de la Chapelle**, a sprawling, broadly Gothic structure with an attractive if

somewhat incongruous Baroque bell tower. The city's oldest church, founded in 1134, has a well-proportioned nave, bathed in light from the huge clerestory windows and supported by heavyweight columns with curly-kale capitals. The pulpit is an extraordinary affair, a flashy, intricately carved hunk featuring Eli in the desert beneath the palm trees. The prophet looks mightily fed up, but then he hasn't realised that there's an angel behind him with a loaf of bread (manna). Also of note is the statue of Our Lady of Solitude, in the second chapel of the north aisle – to the left of the entrance. The Flemings were accustomed to religious statues whose clothing formed part of the original carving. It was the Spaniards who first dressed their statues in finery – and this is an example, gifted to the church by the Spanish Infanta in the 1570s. Yet the church's main claim to fame is the **memorial plaque** over the tomb of Pieter Bruegel the Elder. It was made by his son Jan and is located in the third chapel off the south aisle; Pieter is supposed to have lived and died just down the street at rue Haute 132.

The Quartier Marolles

Round the corner from the tour d'Angle, **rue de Rollebeek** (Map 3, D8) is a pleasant pedestrianized lane dotted with cafés and restaurants that will take you up into place du Grand Sablon (see p.66); or you can stroll down rue Blaes or the less appealing rue Haute, which together form the double spine of the **Quartier Marolles**, stacked on the slopes below the Palais de Justice. An earthy neighbourhood of run-down housing and cheap, basic restaurants, shops and bars, it's one of the few places in the city where you can still hear older people using the traditional dialect, **Brusselse Sproek** or Marollien. A brand of Flemish which has, over the centuries, been influenced by the languages of the city's overlords, it is now in danger of

dying out, and local people have set up an academy to preserve it. They propose – to add to the capital's linguistic
complexities – that all newcomers to Brussels should learn
one hundred words of the dialect. It's a colourful, ribald
language; you could make a start with *dikenek*, "big
mouth"; *schieve lavabo*, "idiot" (literally "a twisted toilet");
or *fieu* – "son of a bitch".

The Marolles neighbourhood grew up in the seventeenth
century as a centre for artisans working on the nearby mansions of Sablon. Industrialised in the eighteenth century, it
remained a thriving working-class district until the 1870s,
when the paving-over of the Senne led to the riverside factories closing down and moving out to the suburbs. The
workers and their families followed, abandoning Marolles to
the old and poor. Today, gentrification is creeping into the
district – along rue Blaes dilapidated houses are in the
process of restoration and the occasional restaurant or
antique shop has sprouted up among the bars and second-
hand clothes shops. **Place du Jeu de Balle** (Map 3, C10),
the heart of Marolles, is relatively unchanged, a shabby
square surrounded by rough-edged bars that is the scene of
the city's best flea market (see "Markets", p.242). The market is a daily event, but it's at its most hectic on Sunday
mornings, when the square and the surrounding streets are
completely taken over by pile after pile of rusty junk alongside muddles of eccentric bric-à-brac – everything from a
chipped buddha, a rococo angel or African idol, to horn-
rimmed glasses, a top hat or a stuffed bear.

The Upper Town

From the heights of the **Upper Town**, the Francophile ruling class long kept a beady eye on the proletarians down below, and it was here they built their palaces and mansions, churches and parks. Political power is no longer concentrated hereabouts, but the wide avenues and grand architecture of this aristocratic quarter – the bulk of which dates from the late eighteenth and nineteenth centuries – has survived pretty much intact, lending a dignified feel that's markedly different from the bustle of the Lower Town below.

The Lower Town ends and the Upper Town begins at the foot of the sharp slope which runs north to south from one end of the city centre to the other, its course marked – in general terms at least – by a traffic-choked boulevard that's variously named Berlaimont, L'Impératrice and L'Empereur. This slope is home to the city's **cathedral**, a splendid Gothic edifice that's recently been restored, but otherwise is little more than an obstacle to be climbed by a series of stairways. Among the latter, the most frequently used are the covered walkway running through the **Galerie Ravenstein** shopping arcade behind the **Gare Centrale**, and the open-air stairway that climbs up through the stodgy, modern

....

The area covered by this chapter is shown in detail on colour map 3.

....

buildings of the so-called **Mont des Arts**. Léopold II gave the area its name in anticipation of a fine art museum he intended to build, but the project was never completed, and the land was only properly built upon in the 1950s.

Above the rigorous layout of the Mont des Arts lie the exuberant **rue Royale** and **rue de la Régence**, which together make up the Upper Town's spine, a suitably smart location for the outstanding **Musées Royaux des Beaux Arts**, probably the best of Belgium's many fine art collections, and the surprisingly low-key **Palais Royal**. Further south, rue de la Régence soon leads to the well-heeled **Sablon** neighbourhood, whose antique shops and chic bars and cafés fan out from the medieval church of **Notre Dame du Sablon**. Beyond this is the monstrous **Palais de Justice**, traditionally one of the city's most disliked buildings.

THE CATHEDRAL

Map 4, I2. Daily 8am–6pm; crypt F40. Ⓜ Gare Centrale.

It takes only a couple of minutes to walk from the Grand-Place to the east end of rues de la Montagne and d'Arenberg, where a short, steep slope climbs up to the **Cathedral**, a fine Gothic building whose commanding position has been sorely compromised by a rash of modern office blocks. Begun in 1220, and three hundred years in the making, the cathedral is dedicated jointly to the patron and patroness of Brussels – St Michael the Archangel, and St Gudule, a vague, seventh-century figure whose reputation was based on gentleness.

The cathedral sports a striking twin-towered, whitestone **facade**, with the central doorway trimmed by fanciful tracery and statues of the Three Wise Men and the Apostles. The facade was erected in the fifteenth century in High Gothic style, but the intensity of the decoration fades away inside with the airy triple-aisled **nave**, completed a century before.

Other parts of the interior illustrate several phases of Gothic design – and a panel just inside the entrance explains what was built when; the chancel is the oldest part of the church, built in Early Gothic style around 1280.

The interior is short on furnishings and fittings, reflecting the combined efforts of the Protestants, who ransacked the church (and stole the shrine of St Gudule) in the seventeenth century, and the French Republican army, who wrecked the place a century later. One survivor is the massive oak **pulpit**, an extravagant chunk of frippery by the Antwerp sculptor Hendrik Verbruggen. Among several vignettes, the pulpit features Adam and Eve, dressed in rustic gear, being chased from the Garden of Eden, while up above the Virgin Mary stamps on the head of the serpent. The cathedral also boasts some superb sixteenth-century **stained-glass** windows, beginning above the main doors with the hurly-burly of the *Last Judgement*. Look closely and you'll spy the donor in the lower foreground with an angel on one side and a woman with long blonde hair (symbolising Faith) on the other. Each of the main colours has a symbolic meaning with green representing hope, yellow eternal glory and blue heaven.

There's more remarkable work in the **transepts**, where the stained glass is distinguished by the extraordinary clarity of the blue backgrounds. These windows are eulogies to the Habsburgs – in the north transept, Charles V kneels alongside his wife beneath a vast triumphal arch as their patron saints present them to God the Father, and in the south transept Charles V's sister, Marie, and her husband, King Louis of Hungary, play out a similar scenario. Both windows were designed by Bernard van Orley (1490-1541), long-time favourite of the royal family and the leading Brussels artist of his day. Finally, a stairway in the north side-aisle leads down to the Romanesque **crypt**, which gives an inkling as to the layout of the first church built on this site.

THE CATHEDRAL

GALERIE RAVENSTEIN AND THE MUSÉE DU CINÉMA

South of the cathedral, just up from the unenticing modernity of the carrefour de l'Europe roundabout, lies the **Gare Centrale**, a bleak Art Deco creation seemingly dug deep into the slope where Lower and Upper Town meet. From the station, a covered walkway leads up through the **Galerie Ravenstein** (Map 4, H6) shopping arcade to rue Ravenstein, home to the **Palais des Beaux Arts**, a drab, low-lying edifice designed by Victor Horta during the 1920s in complete contrast with his flamboyant earlier works. It holds a theatre and concert hall and hosts numerous temporary exhibitions, mostly of modern and contemporary art. Round the corner, up the stairway, the adjoining **Musée du Cinéma** (Map 4, I7; daily 5.30–10.30pm) has displays on the pioneering days of cinema and shows old movies every evening. One projection room presents two silent films with piano accompaniment every night, the other shows three early "talkies". From the museum, it's another short haul up the steps to rue Royale.

See Chapter 13 for further details on the city's classical music, cinema and performing arts. The Musée Victor Horta is described on p.72.

MONT DES ARTS

Map 4, F7.

The wide stone stairway that cuts up through the **Mont des Arts** also climbs the slope marking the start of the Upper Town. The stairs begin on **place de l'Albertine** where the figure of Queen Elizabeth, bouquet in hand, stands opposite a statue honouring her husband, Albert I, who is depicted in military gear on his favourite horse. Easily the most popular king Belgium has ever had, Albert became a national hero for his determined resistance to the Germans in World War I. He died in a climbing accident near Namur, in southern Belgium, in 1934.

The severe 1950s and 1960s buildings of the Mont des Arts house the main library and several government departments, and beyond – from the top – there are panoramic views of the city centre. Across the street, rue Montagne de la Cour, is the whimsical Art Nouveau of the **Old England** building, a glass and wrought-iron confection that started life as a store and has recently been refurbished with a view to housing the collection of the Musée Instrumental (see p.65). Incidentally, it takes its name from the eponymous British company who had the place built as their Brussels headquarters in 1899.

Close by – turn right at the top of the stairway – is the elegant **place du Musée**, the west side of which is occupied by the one remaining wing of the **Appartements de Charles de Lorraine**, a lavish abode built for the country's Austrian governor-general from 1749 to 1780. Recently restored, and scheduled to be open to the public in the next couple of years, the mansion has attractive marble floors and a plethora of Rococo decoration with Greek gods and cherubs scattered everywhere. Neither could Charles be accused of false modesty: stucco work proclaims the duke's military prowess and celebrates his skills as an alchemist. In case anyone missed the point, the statue of Hercules, just inside the main entrance bears the duke's face.

PLACE ROYALE

Map 3, F8.

Composed and self-assured, the **place Royale** forms a fitting climax to rue Royale, the dead straight backbone of

Belgium's Kings

Léopold I (1831–65). Foisted on Belgium by the great powers, Léopold, the first King of the Belgians, was imported from Germany, where he was the prince of Saxe-Coburg – and the uncle of Queen Victoria. Despite lacking a popular mandate, Léopold made a fairly good fist of things, keeping the country neutral as the great powers had ordained.

Léopold II (1865-1909). Energetic and forceful, Léopold II encouraged the urbanisation of his country and promoted its importance as a major industrial power. He was also the man responsible for landing Brussels with such pompous monuments as the Palais de Justice and for the imposition of a particularly barbaric colonial regime on the peoples of the Belgian Congo (now the Republic of Congo).

Albert I (1909–34). Easily the most popular of the dynasty, Albert's bravery in World War I, when the Germans occupied almost all of the country, made the king a national hero whose untimely death, in a climbing accident, traumatised the nation.

Léopold III (1934–51). In contrast to his predecessor, Léopold III had the dubious honour of becoming one of Europe's least popular monarchs. His first wife died in a suspicious car crash; he nearly lost his kingdom by remarrying (anathema in a Roman Catholic country); and he was badly compromised during the German occupation of World War II, when he remained in Belgium rather than face exile, fuelling rumours that he was a Nazi collaborator – though his supporters maintained that he prevented thousands of Belgians from being deported. After several years of heated postwar debate, the issue of Léopold's return from exile was put to a referendum in 1950. Just over half the population voted in Léopold's favour, but there was a clear French/Flemish divide, with opposition to the king concentrated in French-speaking Wallonia. Fortunately for Belgium, Léopold abdicated in 1951 in favour of his son,

Baudouin I (1951–93). A softly spoken family man, Baudouin did much to restore the popularity of the monarchy, not least because he was generally thought to be even-handed in his treatment of the French- and Flemish-speaking communities. He also hit the headlines in April 1990 by standing down for a day so that an abortion bill (which he as a Catholic had refused to sign) could be passed.

Albert II (1993–). The present king will have his work cut out if he wants to become the national figurehead that his father was. The Belgian royal family is one of the few unifying forces in a country divided by French-Flemish antagonisms; one slip off the linguistic tightrope could have untold consequences.

the Upper Town which runs the 2km north to the suburb of St Josse (see p.41). Precisely symmetrical, the square is framed by late eighteenth-century mansions, each an exercise in architectural restraint, though there's no mistaking their size nor the probable cost of their construction. Pushing into this understated opulence is the facade of the church of **St Jacques sur Coudenberg** (Tues–Sat 10am–6pm, Sun & Mon 3–6pm; free), a fanciful version of a Roman temple with a colourfully frescoed pediment representing Our Lady as Comforter of the Depressed – and a building so secular in appearance that the French Revolutionary army had no hesitation in renaming it a Temple of Reason. The French also destroyed the statue of a Habsburg governor that originally occupied the middle of the square, and its replacement – a dashing equestrian representation of Godfrey de Bouillon, one of the leaders of the first Crusade – dates from the 1840s.

PLACE ROYALE

THE PALAIS ROYAL

Map 3, G8. Late July–Sept Tues–Sun 10.30am–4.30pm; free.
Ⓜ Trone.

Around the corner from place Royale, the long and low
Palais Royal is something of an anticlimax, a sombre
nineteenth-century conversion of some late eighteenth-
century town houses, begun by King William I, the Dutch
royal who ruled both Belgium and the Netherlands from
1815 to 1830. The Belgian rebellion of 1830 polished off
the joint kingdom and since then the kings of independent
Belgium haven't spent much money on the palace. Indeed,
although it remains their official residence, the royals have
lived elsewhere (in Laeken, see p.105) for decades and it's
hardly surprising, therefore, that the **palace interior** is formal and unwelcoming. It consists of little more than a pre-
dictable sequence of opulent rooms – all gilt trimmings,
parquet floors, and endless royal portraits, though the tapestries designed by Goya and the magnificent chandeliers of
the Throne Room make a visit (just about) worthwhile.
The same cannot be said for the displays in the palace
annexe, the **Hôtel Bellevue**, on the corner of place des
Palais and rue Royale, where the **Musée de la Dynastie**
(Tues–Sun 10am–4pm; free) charts the brief history of the
Belgian royal family, and will thrill only ardent monarchists.

PARC DE BRUXELLES AND PLACE DU TRÔNE

Opposite the Palais Royal, the **Parc de Bruxelles** (Map 3,
G7) is the most central of the city's larger parks, along whose
tree-shaded footpaths civil servants and office workers stroll
at lunchtime, or race to catch the métro in the evenings.
They might well wish the greenery was a bit more interesting. Laid out in the formal French style in 1780, the park
undoubtedly suited the courtly – and courting – rituals of

the times, but today the straight footpaths and long lines of trees merely seem tedious. Furthermore, the classical statues that once cheered things up are in a dire state of repair.

Beside the park's southeast corner stands the **Palais des Académies**, a grand edifice that once served as a royal residence, but now accommodates the Francophone Academy of Language and Literature. Just beyond is the **place du Trône**, where the big and bold equestrian statue of Léopold II was the work of Thomas Vinçotte, whose skills were much used by the king – look out for Vinçotte's chariot on top of the Parc du Cinquantenaire's triumphal arch (see p.91).

From place du Trône, it's a few minutes' stroll east to the EU Parliament building or you can head north for the ten-minute walk along boulevard du Régent to the Musée Charlier.

The EU Quarter is covered in Chapter 6.

Musée Charlier

Map 3, H5. Mon 10am–5pm, Tues–Thurs 1.30–5pm, Fri 1.30–4.30pm; F100. Ⓜ Arts-Loi or Madou.

The enjoyable **Musée Charlier**, at avenue des Arts 16, just off the petit ring near place Madou, illustrates the artistic tastes of Belgium's upper middle class at the end of the nineteenth century. It holds the collection of Henri van Cutsem, a wealthy businessman who bought two adjacent properties here in 1890. Cutsem merged and modified the two buildings so that he could display his collection to best effect, even going to the trouble of having Victor Horta install glass roofs. He subsequently bequeathed the house and its contents to a sculptor he knew and admired, Guillaume Charlier (1854–1925). Charlier kept the collection pretty much intact and it includes a wide range of fine and applied arts, from Belgian tapestries and antique French furniture to Chinese porcelain and paintings by a number of lesser-known Belgian artists.

Each of the dozen or so rooms is crammed with artefacts, and it's this jumbled diversity which is the museum's principal charm. Nevertheless, in the Concert Room it's still worth tracking down James Ensor's *Flowers and Butterflies*, and Eugene Laermans' *The Promenade*, showing peasants out walking.

The Musée Constantin Meunier is described on p.77.
For more on James Ensor, see p.62.

THE MUSÉES ROYAUX DES BEAUX ARTS

Map 3, E8. Musée d'Art Ancien Tues–Sun 10am–noon & 1–5pm; Musée d'Art Moderne Tues–Sun 10am–1pm & 2–5pm; F150. Ⓜ Trone.

A few metres from place Royale, at the start of rue de la Régence, the **Musées Royaux des Beaux Arts** comprise two museums, one displaying modern art, the other older works. Together they make up Belgium's most satisfying, all-round collection of fine art, with marvellous collections of work by – amongst many – Pieter Bruegel the Elder, Rubens and the surrealists Paul Delvaux and René Magritte.

Both museums are large, and to do them justice you should see them in separate visits. Finding your way around is made easy by the detailed English-language **museum plan** on sale at the entrance (F20). The older paintings – up to the beginning of the nineteenth century – are exhibited in the **Musée d'Art Ancien**, where the blue area shows paintings of the fifteenth and sixteenth centuries, including the Bruegels, and the brown area concentrates on paintings of the seventeenth and eighteenth centuries, with the collection of Rubens (for which the museum is internationally famous) as the highlight. The orange area comprises the small and undistinguished Gallery of Sculptures. The **Musée d'Art Moderne** has a yellow area devoted to nineteeth-century works, notably the canvases of Ostend-born James Ensor, and a green area whose eight subterranean levels cover the twentieth century.

The Musée d'Art Ancien also hosts, in the red area, a prestigious programme of temporary exhibitions. A supplementary admission fee is usually payable and for the most popular you'll need to buy a ticket ahead of time; the ticket may specify the time of admission. The larger exhibitions may cause some disruption to the permanent collection, so treat the room numbers we've given with a little caution. Inevitably, the account below just scratches the surface; the museum's **bookshop** sells a wide range of detailed texts including a well-illustrated guide to the collections for F525.

Musée d'Art Ancien

Well presented, if not exactly well organized, the **Musée d'Art Ancien** is saved from confusion by its colour-coded zones – blue, brown, orange and red. It's a large collection and it's best to start a visit with the **Flemish primitives**.

Rogier van der Weyden and Dieric Bouts

Rooms 11 and 12 hold several paintings by Rogier van der Weyden, the official city painter to Brussels in the middle of the fifteenth century. When it came to portraiture his favourite technique was to highlight the features of his subject – and tokens of rank – against a black background. The *Portrait of the Grand Bâtard de Bourgogne* is a good example with Anthony, the illegitimate son of Philip the Good, casting a haughty, tight-lipped stare to his right while wearing the chain of the Order of the Golden Fleece and clasping an arrow, the emblem of the guild of archers.

In **Room 13**, the two panels of the *Justice of the Emperor Otto* are the work of Weyden's contemporary, the Leuven-based Dieric Bouts. The story was well known: in revenge for refusing her advances, the empress accuses a nobleman of attempting to seduce her. He is executed, but the man's wife remains convinced of his innocence and subsequently proves her point by means of an ordeal by fire where she holds a red hot iron bar.

Hans Memling and the Master of the Legends of St Lucy and St Barbara

Room 14 has some plain portraits by Hans Memling as well as his softly hued *Martyrdom of St Sebastian*. Legend has it that Sebastian was an officer in Diocletian's bodyguard until his Christian faith was discovered, at which point he was sentenced to be shot to death by the imperial archers. Left for dead by the bowmen, Sebastian recovered and Diocletian had to send a bunch of assassins to finish him off with cudgels. The tale made Sebastian popular with archers across Western Europe, and Memling's picture – showing the trussed up saint serenely indifferent to the arrows of the firing squad – was commissioned by the guild of archers in Bruges around 1470. In the same room, the Master of the Legend of St Lucy weighs in with a finely detailed and richly allegorical *Madonna with Saints*, where, with the city of Bruges in the background, the Madonna presents the infant Jesus for the adoration of eleven holy women. Decked out in elaborate medieval attire, the women have blank, almost expressionless, faces, but each bears a token of her sainthood which would have been easily recognised by a medieval congregation. St Lucy, whose assistance was sought by those with sight problems, holds two eyes in a dish.

In **Room 15**, there's more early Flemish art in the shape of the *Scenes from the Life of St Barbara*, one panel from an original pair by the Master of the Legend of St Barbara. One of the most popular of medieval saints, Barbara, so the story goes, was a woman of great beauty whose father locked her away in a tower to keep her away from her admirers. The imprisoned Barbara became a Christian whereupon her father, Dioscurus, tried to kill her, only to be thwarted by a miracle that placed her out of his reach – a part of the tale that's ingeniously depicted in this painting. Naturally, no self-respecting saint could escape so easily, so later parts of the story have Barbara handed over to the local prince, who tortures her for her faith. Barbara resists and the prince orders Dioscurus to kill her himself, which he does only to be immediately incinerated by a bolt of lightning.

School of Hieronymus Bosch

Moving on, **Room 17** boasts a copy of the Hieronymus Bosch *Temptations of St Anthony* that's in the Museu Nacional in Lisbon. No one is quite sure who painted this triptych – it may or may not have been one of Bosch's apprentices – but it was certainly produced in Holland in the late fifteenth or early sixteenth century. The painting refers to St Anthony, a third-century nobleman who withdrew into the desert, where he endured fifteen years of temptation before settling down into his long stint as a hermit. It was the temptations that interested Bosch – rather than the ascetic steeliness of Anthony – and the central panel has an inconspicuous saint sticking desperately to his prayers surrounded by all manner of fiendish phantoms. The side panels develop the theme – to the right Anthony is tempted by lust and greed, and on the left Anthony's companions help him back to his shelter after he's been transported through the skies by weird-looking demons.

Cranach, Gerard David and Matsys

Next door, **Room 18** holds works by Martin Luther's friend, the Bavarian artist Lucas Cranach, whose *Adam and*

Eve presents a stylized, Renaissance view of the Garden of Eden with an earnest-looking Adam on the other side of the Tree of Knowledge from a coquettish Eve, painted with legs entwined and her teeth marks visible on the apple. **Room 21** displays a couple of panels by Gerard David, a Bruges-based artist whose draughtsmanship may not be of the highest order, but whose paintings do display a tender serenity, as exhibited here in his *Adoration of the Magi* and *Virgin and Child*.

In **Room 22**, Quentin Matsys is well represented by the *Triptych of the Holy Kindred*. Matsys' work illustrates a turning point in the development of Flemish painting, and in this triptych, which was completed in 1509, Matsys abandons the realistic interiors and landscapes of his Flemish predecessors in favour of the grand columns and porticos of the Renaissance, with each scene rigorously structured, its characters – all relations of Jesus – assuming lofty, idealized poses.

Bruegel

The museum's collection of works by the Bruegel family, notably **Pieter the Elder** (1527–69), is concentrated in **Room 31**. Although he is often regarded as the finest Netherlandish painter of the sixteenth century, little is known of Pieter the Elder's life, but it's likely he was apprenticed in Antwerp and he certainly moved to Brussels in the early 1560s. He also made at least one long trip to Italy, but judging by his oeuvre, he was – unlike most of his "Belgian" contemporaries – decidedly unimpressed by Italian art. He preferred instead to paint in the Netherlandish tradition and his works often depict crowded Flemish scenes in which are embedded religious or mythical stories. This sympathetic portrayal of everyday life revelled in the seasons and was worked in muted browns, greys and bluey greens with red or yellow highlights. Typifying this approach, and on display here, are the *Adoration of the Magi* and the *Census at Bethlehem* – a scene that Pieter, his son, repeated on several occasions – two particularly absorbing works with the traditionally momentous events happening, almost incidentally, among the bustle of everyday life. The versatile Pieter also dabbled with the lurid imagery of Bosch, whose influence is seen most clearly in *The Fall of the Rebel Angels*, a frantic panel painting which had actually been attributed to Bosch until Bruegel's signature was discovered hidden under the frame. *The Fall of Icarus* is, however, his most haunting work, its mood perfectly captured by Auden in his poem "Musée des Beaux Arts":

> *In Bruegel's* Icarus, *for instance: how everything turns away*
> *Quite leisurely from the disaster; the ploughman may*
> *Have heard the splash, the forsaken cry,*
> *But for him it was not an important failure; the sun shone*
> *As it had to on the white legs disappearing into the green*
> *Water; and the expensive delicate ship that must have seen*
> *Something amazing, a boy falling out of the sky,*
> *Had somewhere to get to and sailed calmly on.*

Rubens and his contemporaries

Apprenticed in Antwerp, **Rubens** (1577–1640) spent eight years in Italy studying the Renaissance masters before returning home, where he quickly completed a stunning series of paintings for Antwerp Cathedral. His fame spread far and wide and for the rest of his days Rubens was inundated with work, receiving commissions from all over Europe. In **Room 52**, the popular misconception that Rubens painted nothing but chubby nude women and muscular men is dispelled with a sequence of portraits, each aristocratic head drawn with great care and attention to detail – in particular, note the exquisite, brilliant white ruffs adorning the Archduke Albert and Isabella. *Studies of a Negro's Head* is likewise wonderfully observed, a preparation

MUSÉE D'ART ANCIEN

for the black magus in the *Adoration of the Magi*, a luminous work that's one of several huge canvases next door in **Room 62**. Here you'll also find *The Ascent to Calvary*, an intensely physical painting, capturing the confusion, agony and strain as Christ struggles on hands and knees under the weight of the cross. There's also the bloodcurdling *Martyrdom of St Lieven*, whose cruel torture – his tongue has just been ripped out and fed to a dog – is watched from on high by cherubs and angels.

Two of Rubens' pupils, Anthony van Dyck (1599–1641) and Jacob Jordaens (1593–1678), also feature in this part of the museum with the studied portraits of the former clustered in **Room 53** and the big and brassy canvases of Jordaens dominating **Room 57**. Like Rubens, Jordaens had a bulging order-book and for years he and his apprentices churned out paintings by the cart load. His best work is generally agreed to have been completed early on – between about 1620 and 1640 – and there's evidence here in the two versions of the *Satyr and the Peasant,* the earlier work clever and inventive, the second a hastily cobbled together piece that verges on buffoonery.

Close by, in **Room 60**, is a modest sample of Dutch painting, including a couple of sombre and carefully composed Rembrandts (1606–69). One of them – the self-assured *Portrait of Nicolaas van Bambeeck* - was completed in 1641, when the artist was finishing off his famous *Night Watch*, now exhibited in Amsterdam's Rijksmuseum. Rembrandt's pupils are displayed in the same room, principally Nicolaes Maes (1634–93), who is well represented by the delicate *Dreaming Old Woman*.

Musée d'Art Moderne

To reach the **Musée d'Art Moderne** you'll need to use the underground passageway which leads from the main museum entrance to **Level –2** of the yellow area, whose nine-teeth-century, mostly Belgian paintings are spread over five small floors – two underground and three above. Another stairway on Level -2 leads down to the six subterranean half-floors that constitute the green area of twentieth-century works. The green area is comparatively small and has an international flavour, with the work of Belgian artists – including René Magritte and Paul Delvaux – supplemented by the likes of Dalí, Picasso, Chagall, Henry Moore, Miró, Matisse and Francis Bacon.

David and his contemporaries

The obvious highlight of **Level –2** is Jacques-Louis David's famous *Death of Marat*, a propagandist piece of 1793 showing Jean-Paul Marat, the French revolutionary hero, dying in his bath after being stabbed by Charlotte Corday. David (1748–1825) has given Marat a perfectly proportioned, classi-cal torso and a face which, with its large hooded eyes, looks almost Christ-like, the effect heightened by the flatness of the composition and the emptiness of the background. The dead man clasps a quill in one hand and the letter given him by Corday in the other, inscribed "my deepest grief is all it takes to be entitled to your benevolence". The other note, on the wooden chest, is written by Marat and begins "You will give this warrant to that mother with the five children, whose husband died for his country". This was David's paean to a fellow revolutionary for, like Marat, he had voted for the execution of Louis XVI, was a Jacobin – the deadly rivals of the Girondins, who were supported by Corday – and a member of the revolutionary Convention, which commis-sioned this picture. He was also a leading light of the Neoclassical movement and became the new regime's Superintendent of the Fine Arts. He did well under Napoleon, too, but after Waterloo David, along with all the other regicides, was exiled, ending his days in Brussels.

MUSÉE D'ART MODERNE

Realists and Symbolism

Two floors up, **Level +1** features the work of the Social Realists, whose paintings and sculptures championed the working class. One of the early figures in this movement was Charles de Groux (1825–70), whose *Poor People's Pew* is typical of his work, but it's Constantin Meunier who is really worth seeking out and he's well represented by two particularly forceful bronzes, *Firedamp* and *The Iron Worker*. Their friend Eugene Laermans (1864–1940) shifted from the Realist style into more Expressionistic works, as in the overtly political *Strike Night* and *The Corpse,* a sorrowful vision that is perhaps Laermans' most successful painting. The museum has little work by Vincent van Gogh, but it's here you'll find his fiery *Portrait of a Peasant*.

The Symbolists are clustered on **Level +2** and amongst them are the disconcerting paintings of Fernand Khnopff (1858–1921), a founding member of Les XX (see p.83) art movement. Khnopff painted his sister, Marguerite, again and again, using her refined, almost plastic, beauty to stir a vague sense of passion – for she's desirable and utterly unobtainable in equal measure. His haunting *Memories of Lawn Tennis* is typical of his oeuvre, a work without narrative, a dream-like scene with each of the seven women bearing the likeness of Marguerite. In *Caresses* Marguerite pops up once more, this time with the body of a cheetah pawing sensually at an androgynous youth.

James Ensor

Pressing on, **Level +3** has a sprinkling of French Impressionists and Post-Impressionists – Monet, Seurat, Gauguin – and a superb sample of the work of **James Ensor** (1860–1949). Ensor, the son of an English father and Flemish mother, spent nearly all of his long life working in Ostend, his home town. His first paintings were rather sombre portraits and landscapes, but in the early 1880s he switched to a more Impressionistic style, delicately picking out his colours as in *The Lady in Blue*. It is, however, Ensor's use of masks which sets his work apart – ambiguous carnival masks with the sniff of death or perversity. His *Scandalized Masks* of 1883 was his first mask painting, a typically unnerving canvas that works on several levels, whilst his *Skeletons quarrelling for a Kipper* (1891) is one of the most savage and macabre paintings you're ever likely to see.

Cubists, Expressionists and Fauvists

A stairway leads down from Level -2 to the six subterranean half-floors which hold an extremely varied collection of modern art and sculpture. It's a challenging collection of international dimensions that starts as it means to continue – at the entrance to **Level -3/4** – with a lumpy, uncompromising Henry Moore and an eerie Francis Bacon, *The Pope with Owls*. Beyond lies an assortment of works by Picasso, Braque and Matisse, a Dufy *Port of Marseille*, and two fanciful paintings by Chagall, one of which is the endearingly eccentric *The Frog that Wanted to Make Itself as Big as a Bull*. Another highlight is Léon Spillaert's evocations of intense loneliness, from monochromatic beaches to empty rooms and train cars. Spillaert lived in Ostend, the setting for much of his work, including the piercing *Woman on the Dyke*. Another noteworthy Belgian is Constant Permeke, whose grim and gritty Expressionism is best illustrated by *The Potato Eater* of 1935.

Delvaux, Magritte and current art

Level -5/6 is given over to the Surrealists. There's a fine Dalí, *The Temptation of St Anthony*, a hallucinatory work in which spindly legged elephants tempt the saint with fleshy women, and a couple of de Chirico's paintings of dressmakers' dummies. Of the Belgian Surrealists, **Paul Delvaux** is

MUSÉE D'ART MODERNE

represented by his trademark themes of ice-cool nudes set against a disintegrating backdrop as well as trains and stations: see the *Evening Train*. Even more elusive is the gallery's collection of paintings by **René Magritte** (1898–1967), perplexing works, whose weird, almost photographically realized images and bizarre juxtapositions aim to disconcert. Magritte was the prime mover in Belgian surrealism, developing – by the time he was thirty – an individualistic style that remained fairly constant throughout his entire career. It was not, however, a style that brought him much initial success and, surprising as it may seem today, he remained relatively unknown until the 1950s. The museum has a substantial sample of his work amongst which two of the more intriguing pieces are the baffling *Secret Player* and the subtly discordant *Empire of Lights*.

Most of the work down on **Level -7/8** is by living artists and although displays are regularly rotated you'll usually spot – amongst mostly modern incomprehensible stuff – the swirling abstracts of Brussels-born and Paris-based Pierre Alechinsky.

The Musée Magritte is covered on p.104.

THE SABLON NEIGHBOURHOOD

From place Royale it's a short walk along rue de la Régence to the **place du Petit Sablon**, (Map 3, E9), a small rectangular area which was laid out as a public garden in 1890 after previous use as a horse market. The garden is surrounded by a wrought-iron fence decorated with 48 statuettes representing the medieval guilds and inside, near the top of the slope, are ten more slightly larger statues honouring some of the country's leading sixteenth-century figures. The ten are hardly household names in Belgium never mind anywhere else, but one or two may ring a few bells – Mercator, the geographer and cartographer responsible for Mercator's projection of the earth's surface; William the Silent, the founder of the Netherlands; and the painter Bernard van Orley. Here also, on top of the fountain, are the figures of the counts Egmont and Hoorn, beheaded on the Grand-Place for their opposition to the Habsburgs in 1568 (see p.23).

Count Egmont is further remembered by the **Palais d'Egmont** (no entry) at the back of the square. This elegant structure was originally built in 1534 for Françoise of Luxembourg, mother of the executed count. It was remodelled on several subsequent occasions and in 1972 it was here that Britain signed the treaty admitting it to the EEC. Back at the foot of the park, on the corner of rue de la Régence, is the dusty and neglected **Musée Instrumental** (Map 3, E9; Tues–Fri 9.30am–4.45pm, Sat 10am–4.45pm; F80). The museum will soon be moving to the Old England building at the top of the Mont des Arts, but in the meantime you'll have to make do with a series of half-hearted displays showing only a fraction of a huge collection of over six thousand musical instruments. If you do pop in, one of the few highlights is the display devoted to Adolphe Sax, the Belgian-born inventor of the saxophone. Sax certainly had a vivid imagination – some of his wilder contraptions, like the oddly contorted saxhorn, are quite remarkable.

Notre Dame du Sablon and the place du Grand Sablon

Opposite the Musée Instrumental, the sooty fifteenth-century church of **Notre Dame du Sablon** (Map 3, E8; daily Mon–Fri 9am–6pm, Sat & Sun 10am–6pm; free) began life as a chapel for the guild of archers in 1304. Its fortunes were, however, transformed when a statue of

Mary, with healing powers, arrived from Antwerp in 1348. The chapel became a centre of pilgrimage and a proper church – in high Gothic style – was built to accommodate its visitors. The statue of Mary no longer exists, but a dinky little votive boat serves as a reminder of the story, and it sits above the inside of the entrance. The woman in the boat is one Béatrice Sodkens, the pious creature whose visions prompted her to procure the statue and bring it here. The occasion of its arrival in Brussels is still celebrated annually in July by the Ommegang procession (see p.271).

The church's **nave** is dark and gloomy, making it hard to pick out the Gothic detail, but there's no missing the lofty vaulted ceiling or the fancily carved stone tracery. Look out also for the grotesque tombstone of Claude and Jacqueline Bouton, members of Charles V's entourage, which, resting against the wall near the entrance, displays two graphically realistic skeletons. More conspicuous is the black and white marble **funerary chapel** in the north transept – a Baroque mausoleum for the earthly remains of the Tour and Taxis family, local worthies who founded the Belgian postal system.

Behind the church, the **place du Grand Sablon** (Map 3, E8) is one of Brussels' most charming squares, a sloping wedge of cobblestones flanked by tall and slender town houses plus the occasional Art Nouveau facade. The square serves as the centre of one of the city's wealthiest districts, and is busiest at weekends, when an antiques market clusters below the church. Many of the shops on Sablon and the surrounding streets are devoted to antiques and art, and you could easily spend an hour or so window-browsing from one to another – or you can soak up the atmosphere eating or drinking in one of Sablon's cafés. The **Musée Postal et Musée des Télécommunications** (Tues–Sat 10am–4.30pm; free), at no. 40, holds a complete collection of Belgian stamps and oodles of old telecommunications equipment.

PALAIS DE JUSTICE AND PLACE LOUISE

From place du Grand Sablon follow rue de la Régence up the hill to place Poelaert, named after the architect who designed the immense **Palais de Justice**, (Map 3, D10), a great Greco-Roman wedding cake of a building, dwarfing the square and everything around it. It's possible to wander into the main hall of the building, a sepulchral affair with tiny audience tables where lawyers huddle with their clients, but really it's the size alone that is impressive – not that it pleased the several thousand townsfolk who were forcibly evicted so that the place could be built. Poelaert became one of the most hated men in the capital, and, when he went insane and died in 1879, it was widely believed a *steekes* (witch) from the Marolles had been sticking pins into an effigy of him. The square is also the site of two war memorials: the one on the corner, dating to 1923, pays tribute to the Anglo-Belgian alliance, the other in the middle of the square commemorates Belgian dead with Art Deco soldiers following an angel.

A stone's throw from the Palais de Justice, **place Louise**, part square, part traffic junction (Map 3, E10), heralds the start of the city's most exclusive shopping district. It's here and in the immediate vicinity that you'll find designer boutiques, jewellers and glossy shopping malls as well as the discreet emporia of the likes of Hermès, Gucci and Chanel. The glitz spreads east along boulevard de Waterloo and south down avenue Louise, which is described on pp.77–79.

St Gilles, Avenue Louise and Ixelles

Full of tiny squares and twisting streets, home to a plethora of local bars and some of the capital's finest Art Nouveau houses, the neighbouring areas of **St Gilles** and **Ixelles**, just south of the petit ring, make a great escape from the hustle and bustle of the city centre. This is Brussels without the razzmatazz and tourists are few and far between, especially in **St Gilles**, the smaller of the two *communes*, which is often regarded as little more than an example of inner-city decay. Frankly, this is true enough of its most westerly section, comprising the depressing immigrant quarters of **Gare du Midi** and the downtrodden streets of **Porte de Hal**, but St Gilles gets more beautiful the further east it spreads, its run-down streets left behind for refined avenues interspersed with dignified squares.

Ixelles, for its part, is one of the capital's most attractive and exciting outer areas, with a couple of enjoyable museums, a diverse street-life and elegant squares – like the serene **place Châtelain**. Historically, Ixelles has long drawn artists, writers and intellectuals – Karl Marx,

Auguste Rodin and Alexandre Dumas all lived here – and even today it retains an arty, sometimes Bohemian feel. The *commune* has a good nightlife, too, and you're never far away from the action, whether it be the **Porte de Namur**, with its arcades and cinemas, or **Matongé** – the vibrant social centre of the district's Central African community, packed with late-night African bars, cafés and restaurants.

....

The area covered by this chapter is shown in detail on colour map 6.

....

Ixelles is divided in two by **avenue Louise**, whose character is entirely different, as befits an administrative anomaly: the boulevard is counted as part of the city centre, and has been home to the haute bourgeoisie ever since Léopold II had the avenue laid out in the 1840s. It's here you'll find some of the city's most expensive shops and hotels, pricey jewellers, slick office blocks and the interesting **Musée Constantin Meunier**, sited in the sculptor's old house.

More than anything else, however, it's the dazzling array of **Art Nouveau** buildings clustering the streets of St Gilles and Ixelles which really grab the attention, and there's a concentration of some of the finest on and around the boundary between the two *communes* – in between chaussée de Charleroi and avenue Louise. In particular, there's Horta's own house, now the glorious **Musée Horta**, as well as examples of the work of Paul Hankar and Armand van Waesberghe. Access to most of the city's Art Nouveau buildings is restricted, so you can either settle for the view from outside, or enrol on one of ARAU's specialist tours (see p.14).

ST GILLES

One of the smallest of the city's *communes*, **St Gilles** is also one of the most varied, stretching from the impoverished, sometimes threatening streets round the **Gare du Midi** and **Porte de Hal** to the affluent precincts of avenue Louise. In the poorer quarters, generations of political and economic refugees from the Mediterranean and North Africa have established themselves. The easterly sections of St Gilles are much more relaxed – and relaxing – and it's here you'll find the district's architectural highlight, the **Musée Horta**.

Porte de Hal and the Hôtel Winssinger

The imposing **Porte de Hal** (Map 6, C3), standing on the edge of St Gilles at the southern tip of the petit ring, is the only one of the city's seven medieval gates to have survived – the rest were knocked down by Napoleon, but this one was left untouched because it was a prison. The gate is a massive, heavily fortified affair, with towers and turrets, battlements and machicolations, and – although it was clumsily remodelled in the 1870s – it gives a good idea of the strength of the city's former defences. The interior has several appropriately dark and gloomy rooms and holds the **Musée du Folklore** – or will do when it reopens after a thoroughgoing revamp.

Heading south from the gateway, down the chaussée de Waterloo, you're soon in the impoverished heart of St Gilles, with the elaborate, rather dilapidated Art Nouveau houses of **rue Vanderschrick** running off to the right. On the first corner of this side street is the chic café *Porteuse d'Eau* (see "Drinking"), but this is the only sign of gentrification around here, and, as an outsider, it's hard not to feel intrusive as you push on towards the soulless **place de Bethléem**, with its cheap and seedy restaurants. In fact, it's better to press on down the chaussée de Waterloo to the morning **parvis de St**

Gilles market (Tues–Sun 6am–noon) selling fruit and veg, at rue du Fort. A detour east up rue de Rome brings you to rue de l'Hôtel des Monnaies where, at no. 66, you'll find Victor Horta's **Hôtel Winssinger** (Map 6, D4). Dating from the 1890s, Horta's most creative period, the building sports a wide facade, with large ground-floor windows and a cluster of smaller windows. The front is relatively unscathed, but the interior has been badly mauled by subsequent alterations.

The Barrière de St Gilles and the Maison and Atelier Dubois

From the Hôtel Winssinger continue south down rue de l'Hôtel des Monnaies until you reach **Barrière de St Gilles** – a seven-road junction that was, until the middle of the nineteenth century, the site of a toll gate. Close by, south again up avenue Paul Dejaer, is the *commune's* **Hôtel de Ville** (Map 6, C7), a heavy-duty, pseudo-Renaissance edifice, and behind that, at the top end of avenue Jef Lambeaux, rises the ersatz medieval castle which holds the prison.

Heading east from the prison, take the first right off avenue Ducpétiaux and turn left at the end – down avenue de la Jonction – to reach avenue Brugmann, where at no. 80 you'll find another Horta house, the **Maison and Atelier Dubois**. Completed in 1906, towards the end of Horta's Art Nouveau period, the building is much simpler than some of his earlier works, though it still bears some of his familiar trademarks – a well-lit interior, exquisite carpentry in mahogany and oak, a mosaic floor, and a marble staircase. The building is not open to the public, but the exterior – a modest but subtle facade with curvaceous windows set off by the careful use of wrought iron – is mightily impressive.

From here, a short stroll northeast up avenue Brugmann will bring you onto the chaussée de Charleroi, within easy striking distance of the **Musée Victor Horta**.

Musée Victor Horta

Map 6, F6. Tues–Sun 2–5.30pm; weekdays F150, weekends F200. Tram #91, #92.

The **Musée Victor Horta**, just off the chaussée de Charleroi at rue Américaine 23 & 25, occupies the two houses Horta designed as his home and studio at the end of the nineteenth century, and was where he lived until 1919. The only Horta house fully open to the public, the museum was opened in the late 1960s, part of a sustained cam-

Victor Horta

The son of a shoemaker, **Victor Horta** (1861–1947) was born in Ghent, where he failed in his first career, being unceremoniously expelled from the city's music conservatory for indiscipline. He promptly moved to Paris to study architecture, returning to Belgium in 1880 to complete his internship in Brussels with Alphonse Balat, the architect to King Léopold II. Balat was a traditionalist, responsible for the classical facades of the Palais Royal – amongst many other prestigious projects – and Horta looked elsewhere for inspiration. He found it in the work of William Morris, the leading figure of the English Arts and Crafts movement, whose designs were key to the development of **Art Nouveau**. Taking its name from the Maison de l'Art Nouveau, a Parisian shop which sold items of modern design, Art Nouveau rejected the imitative architectures which were popular at the time – Neoclassical and neo-Gothic – in favour of a innovatory style that was characterised by sinuous, flowing lines. In England, Morris and his colleagues had focused on book illustrations and furnishings, but in Belgium Horta extrapolated the new style into architecture, experimenting with new building materials – steel and concrete – as well as traditional stone, glass and wood.

In 1893, Horta completed the curvaceous **Hôtel Tassel** (see p.76), Brussels' first Art Nouveau building – "hôtel" meaning town house. Inevitably, there were howls of protest from the traditionalists, but no matter what his opponents said, Horta never lacked for work again. The following years – roughly 1893 to 1905 – were Horta's most inventive and prolific. He designed over forty buildings, including the **Hôtel Solvay** (see p.76) and the **Hôtel Winssinger** (see p.70) as well as his own beautifully decorated house and studio, now the **Musée Victor Horta** (see p.72). The delight Horta took in his work is obvious, especially when employed on private houses, and his enthusiasm was all-encompassing – he almost always designed everything from the blueprints to the wallpaper and carpets. He never kept a straight line or sharp angle where he could deploy a curve, and his use of light was revolutionary, often filtering through from above, atrium-like, with skylights and as many windows as possible. Curiously, Horta also believed that originality was born of frustration, and so he deliberately created architectural difficulties, pushing himself to find harmonious solutions. Horta felt that the architect was as much an artist as the painter or sculptor, and so he insisted on complete stylistic freedom. It was part of a well-thought out value system that allied him with both Les XX (see p.83) and the Left; as he wrote, "My friends and I were reds, without however having thought about Marx or his theories."

Completed in 1906, the **Maison and Atelier Dubois** (see p.71) and the **Grand Magasin Waucquez** department store (p.38) were transitional buildings signalling the end of Horta's Art Nouveau period. His later works were more Modernist constructions, whose understated lines were a far cry from the ornateness of his earlier work. In Brussels, the best example of his later work is the Palais des Beaux-Arts of 1928 (see p.48).

paign to stop the destruction of Brussels' architectural heritage and to publicise the charms of Art Nouveau. From the outside the building is quite modest, a dark, narrow terraced house with a fluid facade and almost casually knotted and twisted ironwork, but it is for his interiors that Horta is famous. Inside is a sunny, sensuous dwelling exhibiting all the architect's favourite flourishes – wide, bright rooms spiralling around a superbly worked staircase, wrought iron, stained glass, sculpture and ornate furniture and panelling made from several different types of wood.

The dining room is superb, an inventive blend of white enamelled brickwork and exposed structural metal arches on a parquet floor. Lining the walls are six bas-reliefs carved by Pierre Braecke, five of which portray the arts depicted by the muses above the dresser: painting, music, sculpture, literature, and architecture – with the sixth holding out a model of the Aubecq mansion, built by Horta in 1899 and demolished in 1950. The staircase is quite stunning, a dainty spiralling affair, which runs through the centre of the house up to the skylight, ensuring the house gets as much light as possible. Decorated with painted motifs and surrounded by mirrors, it remains one of Horta's most ingenious creations. Also of interest is the modest but enjoyable selection of paintings, many of which were given to Horta by friends and colleagues, including works by Félicien Rops and Joseph Heymans.

WESTERN IXELLES

Heading east from the Musée Victor Horta, take the first turning on the left – rue Africaine – for the parvis de la Trinité, the site of the church of **Ste Trinité** (Map 6, G7), a run-down but imposing Baroque structure whose dark columns dominate the skyline. The most interesting feature is the extravagant west front, which was originally part of the church of St Augustin (1620), demolished to make way for the place de Brouckère in 1896. The facade was moved here block by block and although pollution and years of neglect have left their mark, it's still – with its pointed pediments and columns – an impressive structure. Unfortunately, the church is rarely open – a real shame because when viewed from inside the stained-glass windows are almost luminescent.

Just beyond the church, detour south down rue de l'Amazone and you'll soon find yourself on **place Châtelain**, a quaint and endearing square lined by restaurants, bars, and cafés. Best known for its Wednesday food **market** (see p.242) – where you can buy home-made wines, fine cheeses, and a mouth-watering selection of cakes and pastries – it's also a relaxing place for a quiet drink or a spot of lunch; for breakfast, *Le Pain de Châtelain* serves what many locals regard as the best croissants in town (see p.166).

Rue Defacqz – the Art Nouveau of Paul Hankar

From place Châtelain, it's a short stroll north up rue Simonis to **rue Defacqz** (Map 6, G5–6), the site of several charming Art Nouveau houses. Three were designed by **Paul Hankar** (1859–1901), a classically trained architect and contemporary of Horta, who developed a real penchant for sgraffiti – akin to frescoes – and multicoloured brickwork. Hankar was regarded as one of the most distinguished exponents of Art Nouveau and, at **no. 48**, the house he built for the Italian painter Albert Ciamberlani in 1897 sports a fine, flowing facade, decorated with sgraffiti representing the Ages of Man. **Number 50** is a Hankar creation too, built for another painter, René Janssens, in 1898, whilst the architect's old home, at **no. 71**, features four sgraffiti beneath the cornice – one each for morning, afternoon, evening and night. Hankar designed his home in the early 1890s, making it one of the city's earliest Art Nouveau buildings.

Rue Faider and the Hôtel Tassel

There are more Art Nouveau treats in store on neighbouring **rue Faider** where **no. 83** boasts a splendidly flamboyant facade with ironwork foliage round the windows and faint frescoes of languishing pre-Raphaelite women, all to a design by Armand Van Waesberghe. Directly opposite is rue **Paul Émile Janson** at the bottom of which, at no. 6, is the celebrated **Hôtel Tassel** (Map 6, H5), the building that made Horta's reputation. The sinuous facade is appealing enough, with clawed columns, stained glass and spiralling ironwork, but it was with the interior that Horta really made his mark, an uncompromising fantasy featuring a fanciful wrought-iron staircase and walls covered with linear decoration. It's also a striking example of the way in which Horta tailor-made his houses to suit the particular needs of clients. In this case it was built for an amateur photographer and includes a studio and projection room.

Horta's Hôtel Solvay and Hôtel Max Hallet

At the end of rue Paul Émile Janson you hit avenue Louise, where a right turn will take you after a couple of hundred metres to the **Hôtel Solvay** (Map 6, I6), at no. 224 – another Horta masterpiece, and, like the Musée Horta, containing most of the original furnishings and fittings. The 33-year-old Horta was given complete freedom and unlimited funds by the Solvay family (they made a fortune in soft drinks) to design this opulent town house, whose facade is graced by bow windows, delicate metalwork and contrasting types of stone. Inside, Horta commissioned an artist to paint a scene from the Solvay's summer cottage on the first staircase landing, but typically chose the dominant colours himself. Also on avenue Louise, five minutes' further along at no. 346, is Horta's **Hôtel Max Hallet** (Map 6, J8), a comparatively restrained structure of 1904 where the straight and slender facade is decorated with elegant door and window iron grilles. Just beyond, the modern sculpture stranded in the middle of the traffic island looks like a pair of elephant tusks, but is in fact a representation of the "V" for Victory sign of World War II. Named *Phénix 44*, it's the work of Olivier Strebelle.

From the Max Hallet residence, it's a quick tram ride north to the smart commercialism of place Louise or a ten-minute stroll south to the Musée Constantin Meunier (see below).

AVENUE LOUISE

Named after the eldest daughter of its creator, Léopold II, **avenue Louise** (Map 6, F2–J9) slices southeast from the petit ring, its beginnings lined by some of the city's most expensive shops and boutiques. Further along, shops give way to plush apartment blocks, the most visible part of the wealthy residential area which occupies the side streets around the avenue. It's here you'll find the diverting **Musée Constantin Meunier** which displays a large sample of the work of the late nineteenth-century sculptor, and the **Abbaye de la Cambre**, whose pleasant gardens and old brick buildings are sited in the diplomatic zone at the end of the avenue.

The Musée Constantin Meunier

Map 6, I9. Tues–Fri & alternate weekends 10am–noon & 1–5pm; free. Tram #93, #94.

The **Musée Constantin Meunier**, just off avenue Louise, about 500m beyond Victor Horta's Hôtel Max Hallet (see p.76), is at rue de l'Abbaye 59. It's housed in the unassuming home and studio of Brussels-born Constantin Meunier, who lived here from 1899 until his death at the age of 74 six years later. Meunier began as a painter, but it's as a sculptor that he's best remembered, and the museum has an extensive collection of his dark and brooding bronzes.

The biggest and most important pieces are in the room at the back, where a series of muscular men with purposeful faces stand around looking heroic – *The Reaper* and *The Sower* are typical. There are oil paintings in this room, too: gritty industrial scenes like the coalfield of *Black Country Borinage* and the gloomy dockside of *The Port*, one of Meunier's most forceful works. In the other rooms, you'll find a few watercolours and drawings as well as more statues honouring the working class and its sufferings – there's *The Glass-blower*, *The Shrimp Fisherman* and the hunched figure of *Pain*. Meunier was angered by the harsh living conditions of Belgium's workers, particularly (like van Gogh before him) the harsh life of the coal miners of the Borinage. This anger fuelled his art, which asserted the dignity of the working class in a style that was to be copied by the Social Realists of his and later generations. According to Hobsbawm's *Age of Empire*, "Meunier invented the international stereotype of the sculptured proletarian."

The Abbaye de la Cambre

Map 6, K9. Mon–Fri 9am–noon & 3–6pm; free. Tram #93, #94.

In a lovely little wooded dell on the other side of avenue Louise from the museum, and approached via rue de l'Aurore, lies the **Abbaye de la Cambre**. Of medieval foundation, the abbey was suppressed by the French Revolutionary army and its attractive eighteenth-century brick buildings, which surround a pretty little courtyard, are now used by several government departments. On the courtyard is the main entrance to the lovely little abbey

church, whose nave, with its barrel vaulting, is an exercise in simplicity. The church is an amalgamation of styles incorporating both Gothic and Classical features and it holds one marvellous painting, Albert Bouts' *The Mocking of Christ*, an early sixteenth-century work showing a mournful, blood-spattered Jesus. Behind the abbey's buildings are the walled and terraced **gardens**, an oasis of peace away from the hubbub of avenue Louise.

Beyond the abbey, at the end of avenue Louise, the **Bois de la Cambre** is unpleasantly crisscrossed by the main commuter access roads in its upper reaches, but a good deal more agreeable around the lake that lies further to the south. It's Brussels' most popular park, bustling with joggers, dog-walkers, families and lovers at weekends, and is the northerly finger of the large **Forêt de Soignes** (see p.108), whose once mighty forests bear a clutch of dual carriageways, and, more promisingly, scores of quiet footpaths.

EASTERN IXELLES

Eastern Ixelles radiates out from the petit ring, its busy streets spined by the **chaussée d'Ixelles**, whose unpromising beginnings – beside the Porte de Namur – should not deter: things get interesting just five minutes' walk down the boulevard at the **Galerie d'Ixelles**, the shopping centre of Ixelles' Central and North African community. In sharp contrast to the designer boutiques of the **Galerie Toison d'Or** across the road, this is packed with tiny shops selling anything from batik cloths to bizarre wigs and cosmetics.

On the far side of the **Galerie d'Ixelles** is the **chaussée de Wavre**. Head south past the exotic fruit stores and take the second right and you'll find yourself in the heart of **Matongé**, the social centre of the African quarter. The area is thronged with small cheerful bars and cafés playing African music and serving cheap beer and traditional food.

The tiny pedestrianised **rue de Longue Vie** is the liveliest street, and consists of a dozen terraced bars and restaurants and even has a top-notch restaurant serving Portuguese specialities. When the bars close, which is usually well past 3am, you can always head to *Mambo*, a small club close by on chaussée de Wavre, where you can dance all night every night to the sounds of high-pitched guitars and African rhythms.

Musée Camille Lemonnier

Map 6, J2. Admission by prior arrangement only, Mon–Fri 9am–noon & 2–6pm; free.

The tiny **Musée Camille Lemonnier**, just along the street from *Mambo* at chaussée de Wavre 150, is dedicated to the eponymous Belgian intellectual, writer, dramatist and essayist, who was an influential member of the city's cultural elite for almost fifty years. A sharp-witted Francophone, **Lemonnier** (1844–1913) started out writing for a literary review, the *Journal des Artistiques*, and subsequently turned his hand to novels, books of art criticism – including the *Histoire de Beaux-Arts en Belgique* (1887) – and political texts. There were also monographs on the artists of the day – for instance Henri de Braekeleer, Alfred Stevens and Constantin Meunier – as well as oodles of stuff on the avant-garde Les XX (see p.83). Inevitably, Lemonnier's acid tongue created hostility and arguments concerning the merits of many painters ensued, most violently with Ensor.

Set up by Camille's daughter Louise in 1946, the **museum** is housed in an attractive late nineteenth-century building and holds an eclectic collection of *objets d'art*, everything from sculptures and paintings to gilded books. In the main room upstairs are paintings by Louise and these hang alongside portraits of her father by Emile Claus, Constantin Meunier and Isidore Verheyden. Other paintings of note include *The Fair* by Victor Gilsoul, and the bleak *Hunter in the Snow* by Emile Verheyden, Lemonnier's cousin. The finest of the sculptures are *The Foolish Song* by Jef Lambeaux and *Eternal Spring* by Auguste Rodin.

St Boniface and place Fernand Cocq

There's little else to detain you on the chaussée de Wavre, though you could drop by **Fil à Terre**, at no. 198, a comic-strip book shop and bar which has an extensive reading room holding more than 3000 comics. Otherwise, the best bet is to backtrack to rue de Longue Vie, and turn down rue de la Paix, which leads you to the imposing, Gothic pile of **St Boniface** (Map 6, I2). From the outside the church looks distressed and run down, but the cool interior boasts cathedral-like arches and immaculate stained-glass windows. Directly in front of the church lies the appealing **place St Boniface**, home to a number of laid-back café-bars including the immensely popular *L'Ultime Atome* (see "Drinking").

From St Boniface, it's a short stroll along the chaussée d'Ixelles to **place Fernand Cocq**, a small rectangular square named after a one-time Ixelles burgomaster, and lined by a good selection of bars, including Flemish-run *Volle Gas* and trendy *L'Amour Fou*. The square's centrepiece is the **Maison communale** (Map 6, J3), an imposing Neoclassical building built by the Flemish architect Vanderstraeten for the opera singer Maria Malibran, née Garcia (1808–36), and her lover, the Belgian violinist Charles de Bériot. Malibran was one of the great stars of her day and her contralto voice created a sensation when she first appeared on the stage in London in 1825. Her father, one Manuel Garcia, trained her and organised her tours, but pushed his daughter into a most unfortunate marriage in New York. Mr Malibran turned out to be a bankrupt and Maria pluckily left husband and father behind, returning to Europe to pick up her career. She was fantastically successful and had this Ixelles mansion built for herself and Bériot in 1833. After her death, the house lay uninhabited until it was bought by the Ixelles *commune* in 1849; the gardens in which Maria practised were reduced to the small park which now stands in the square's centre.

Musée d'Ixelles

Map 6, K4. Tues–Fri 1–7pm, Sat & Sun 10am–5pm; permanent collection free; admission charged for temporary exhibitions.

The excellent **Musée d'Ixelles**, rue Jean van Volsem 71, is located about ten minutes' walk southeast of place Fernand Cocq – just off the chaussée d'Ixelles. Established in an old slaughterhouse in 1892, the museum was enlarged and refurbished a few years back and since then it has built up an excellent reputation for the quality of its temporary exhibitions, ranging from Belgian surrealism through to Russian modernism. The permanent collection is mainly nineteenth- and early twentieth-century French and Belgian material, but there's a small sample of earlier paintings in the first wing, including *Tobie and the Angel* by Rembrandt and a sketch, *The Stork*, by Albrecht Dürer. In the same wing, Jacques-Louis David, one-time revolutionary and the leading light among France's Neoclassical painters, is well represented by *The Man at the Gallows.* There's also a wonderful collection of haunting works by Charles Herman, one of a group of Belgian realists who struggled to get their work exhibited in the capital's salons: until the late 1870s the salons would contemplate only Romantic and Neoclassical works. Also, look out for the large collection of posters featuring the work of Toulouse-Lautrec – thirty of his total output of thirty-two are displayed here.

The museum's two other wings hold an enjoyable sample

of the work of the country's leading modern artists, from well-known figures such as the surrealists Magritte, Paul Delvaux and Marcel Broodthaers (*Casserole of Mussels*) to less familiar artists such as Edgar Tytgat, Rik Wouters and

Les XX

Founded in 1883, Les XX was an influential group of twenty Belgian painters, designers and sculptors, who were keen to bring together all the different strands of their respective crafts. For ten years, they staged an annual exhibition showcasing both domestic and international talent and it was here that Cézanne, Manet, Seurat and Gauguin were all exhibited at the very beginning of their careers. With members as diverse as Ensor and the architect-designer Henri van de Velde, Les XX never professed to be united by the same artistic principles, but several of its members, including Rysselberghe, were inordinately impressed by the Post-Impressionism of Seurat, whose pointillist *The Big Bowl* created a sensation when it was exhibited by Les XX in 1887.

Les XX – and the other literary-artistic groupings which succeeded it – were part of a general avant-garde movement which flourished in Brussels at the end of the nineteenth century. This avant-garde was deeply disenchanted with Brussels' traditional salon culture, not only for artistic reasons but also because of its indifference to the plight of the Belgian working class. Such political views nourished close links with the fledgling Socialist movement, and Les XX even ran the slogan "art and the people have the same enemy – the reactionary Bourgoisie". Indeed, the Belgian avant-garde came to see art (in all its forms) as a vehicle for liberating the Belgian worker, a project regularly proclaimed in *L'Art Moderne,* their most authoritative mouthpiece.

LES XX

Constant Permeke. There's a smattering of sculptures, too, with the main event being Rodin's *La Lorraine* and *J.B. Willems*. Rodin used to have a studio nearby at rue Sans Souci 111, in the heart of Ixelles, and this was where he designed his first major work, *The Age of Bronze*. When it was exhibited in 1878, there was outrage: Rodin's naturalistic treatment of the naked body broke with convention and created something of a scandal – he was even accused of casting his sculptures round live models.

South to the étangs d'Ixelles

Beyond **place Fernand Cocq**, the chaussée d'Ixelles winds a tedious route south to place Flagey and then continues on to the first of two little lakes, the **étangs d'Ixelles** (Map 6, K6). Running alongside the first lake is well-heeled **avenue des Éperons d'Or**, where there are several good examples of Art Nouveau. Numbers 3 to 14, designed by the Delune brothers, are particularly striking, and so is "The Tower", on the corner of **avenue G. Macau**, built by Caluwaers for Baron Snoy. Across the lake stands another Delune creation at **rue du Lac 6**, a narrow house with exquisite stained-glass windows and decorated with aqua-floral designs inspired by Japanese woodcuts.

Another Art Nouveau architect, Ernest Blérot, specialised in wrought ironwork and demonstrated his virtuosity by building houses in pairs to heighten the effect. A good example of this can be found on the west side of the lake at **avenue Général de Gaulle 38** and **39**.

Southeast to Cimetière d'Ixelles

From the étangs d'Ixelles head east to place Flayet and take bus #11 south to Cimetière d'Ixelles, the last resting place of several well-known artistic figures including Victor Horta and Camille Lemmonier. It's also the burial place of General Georges Boulanger, who fled to Brussels with his mistress Marguerite Bonnemain, after a failed coup in Paris. Madame de Bonnemain died soon after arriving in Brussels, prompting the general to commit suicide on her grave two months later. Their joint tomb simply bears the names Marguerite and Georges, with the words "*A bien-tôt*" (See you soon) below hers, and "*Ai-je bien pu vivre deux mois sans toi*" (Did I really live for two months without you?).

The EU Quarter and Le Cinquantenaire

In the middle of the nineteenth century, Léopold II extended the boundaries of Brussels east of the petit ring to incorporate the grandiloquent monuments and grassy parks he had constructed. Smart residential areas followed along with a series of museums whose large collections reflected, so the king believed, Belgium's proper position amongst the leading industrial nations. Much of Léopold's grand design has survived – and provides the district's key attractions – but today it's overlaid with the uncompromising office blocks of the EU. These high-rises coalesce hereabouts to form the loosely defined EU Quarter – properly the **Quartier des Institutions Européennes**, home to the European Commission, whose civil servants support and advise the EU's ultimate decision-making body, the Brussels-based Council of Ministers, and various committees of the European Parliament (which sits in Strasbourg).

The area covered by this chapter is shown in detail on colour map 2.

To enjoy a visit to this part of the city, you'll need to follow a clear itinerary, one which avoids the worst of the EU area, where the streets groan with traffic and a vast building programme has turned whole blocks into dusty construction sites. Essentially, this means dodging – as far as possible – rues de la Loi and Belliard, the two wide boulevards that serve as the area's main thoroughfares. The best place to start is in the vicinity of **Parc Léopold**, where – just a few minutes' stroll from the petit ring – you'll find the intriguing **Musée Wiertz**, exhibiting the huge and eccentric paintings of the eponymous artist, and the brand-new **European Parliament building**. From here, it's a ten-minute walk to **Le Cinquantenaire**, one of Léopold's most excessive extravagances, a triumphal arch built to celebrate the golden jubilee of Belgian independence and containing three museums, the pick of which is the wide-ranging **Musées Royaux d'Art et d'Histoire**.

FROM PLACE DU TRÔNE TO THE EUROPEAN PARLIAMENT BUILDING

Part of the petit ring and on the métro line, **place du Trône** (Map 2, F7) is distinguished by its double lion gates and life-size statue of Léopold II, perched on his horse. From here, **rue du Luxembourg** heads east to bisect a small park whose northern half contains a modest memorial to Julien Dillens, a popular nineteenth-century sculptor responsible for the effigy of Everard 't Serclaes on the Grand-Place (see p.21). Just along the street, the **place du Luxembourg** has had varying fortunes, but now it's on the up, with fashionable cafés moving in as three-storey, stone-trimmed houses are refurbished. The reason for this gentrification is near at hand: follow the signs (to rue Wiertz)

The EU in Brussels

The **European Union** is operated by three main institutions, each of which does most of its work in Brussels:

The **European Parliament** sits in Strasbourg, but meets in Brussels for around six, two-day plenary sessions per year. It's the only EU institution to meet and debate in public. During sessions, MEPs sit in political blocks and not in national delegations; there are eight blocks at present. The Parliament has a President and 14 Vice-Presidents, each of whom is elected for two and a half years by Parliament itself. The President (or a Vice-President) meets with the leaders of the political groups to plan future parliamentary business. Supporting and advising this political edifice is a complex network of committees and these are mostly based in Brussels.

The **Council of Ministers** consists of the heads of government of each of the member states and the President of the European Commission (see below). They meet regularly in the much-publicized "European Summits". Most Council meetings are not, however, attended by the heads of government, but by a delegated minister. There are complex rules regarding decision-making: some subjects require only a simple majority, others need unanimous support. This political structure is underpinned by scores of committees and working parties made up of both civil servants and political appointees. These committees and working parties are based in Brussels.

The **European Commission** acts as the EU's executive arm and board of control, managing funds and monitoring all manner of agreements. The 20 Commissioners are political appointees, nominated by their home country, but once they're in office they are responsible to the European Parliament. The president of the Commission is elected for a three-year period of office. Over 10,000 civil servants work for the Commission, whose headquarters are in Brussels.

through the tatty railway station (Gare du Quartier Léopold) on the far side of the square and you'll behold a gigantic, new EU office block whose undulating lines sweep way down to rue Belliard. There's a breach in this edifice dead ahead, and just beyond it – through the passageway and down the steps – is the equally new **European Union Parliament building** (Map 2, H7), another glass and steel behemoth equipped with a curved glass roof that rises to a height of 70m. Completed in 1997, the building contains a large, semicircular assembly room as well as the offices of the President of the Parliament and their General Secretariat. The building has its admirers but is known locally as the "caprice des dieux".

MUSÉE WIERTZ

Map 2, H7. Tues–Fri 10am–noon & 1–5pm; alternate weekends 10am–noon & 1–5pm; free. ©508 33 50. Ⓜ Trône.

Behind the European Parliament building at rue Vautier 62, the **Musée Wiertz** is devoted to the works of one of the city's most distinctive, if disagreeable, nineteenth-century artists. Once immensely popular – so much so that Thomas Hardy in *Tess of the d'Urbervilles* could write of "the staring and ghastly attitudes of a Wiertz museum" – Antoine Wiertz painted vast religious and mythological canvases, featuring gory hells and strapping nudes, which were critically well-received at the time. The core of the museum is housed in his studio, a large, airy space that was built for him by the Belgian state on the understanding that he bequeathed his oeuvre to the nation. Delightful pictures include *The Burnt Child* and *The Thoughts and Visions of a Severed Head* – not for the squeamish. There are also a number of smaller, quite elegantly painted quasi-erotic pieces featuring coy nudes. A couple of adjoining rooms contain further macabre works, such as *Premature Burial* and *Hunger*,

Folly, Crime – in which a madwoman is pictured shortly after hacking off her child's ear and throwing it into the cooking pot – as well as more saucy girls in various states of undress. Wiertz eventually came to believe that he was a better painter than his artistic forebears, Rubens and Michelangelo. Judge for yourself.

MUSÉE DES SCIENCES NATURELLES

Map 2, I8. Tues–Sat 9.30am–4.45pm & Sun 9.30am–6pm; F150. Ⓜ Trône.

The **Musée des Sciences Naturelles**, just along the street from the Musée Wiertz, at rue Vautier 29, holds the city's natural history collection. It's a large, sprawling museum divided into fifteen clearly signed areas, each of which focuses on a particular aspect of the natural world, and several of which try to be child-friendly – robotic dinosaurs and suchlike. The dinosaur section is, indeed, the most impressive, featuring **iguanodons** whose skeletons parade across the ground floor. Iguanodons were two-legged herbivores who grazed in herds and a whole group of them was discovered in the coal mines of Hainaut in the late nineteenth century. Other museum highlights include a first-rate collection of tropical shells, an insect room, a section comparing the Arctic and Antarctic, and a whale gallery featuring eighteen skeletons, including the enormous remains of a blue whale.

PARC LÉOPOLD

Map 2, I7.

On rue Vautier, almost opposite the Musée Wiertz, a scruffy back entrance leads into the rear of **Parc Léopold**, a hilly, leafy enclave landscaped around a lake. The park is pleasant enough, but its open spaces were encroached upon years ago when the industrialist Ernest Solvay began constructing the educational and research facilities of a prototype science centre here. The end result is a string of big, old buildings that spreads along the park's northern periphery. The most interesting is the first you'll come to, the newly refurbished **Solvay Library** (no set opening times), a splendid barrel-vaulted structure with magnificent mahogany panelling. Down below the library and the other buildings, at the bottom of the slope, is the main entrance to Parc Léopold, where a set of stumpy stone gates bear the legend "Jardin royal de zoologie". Léopold wanted the park to be a zoo, but for once his plans went awry.

From the front entrance to the park, it takes a little less than ten minutes to walk east along traffic-choked rue Belliard to Parc du Cinquantenaire.

LE CINQUANTENAIRE

Map 2, K6.

The wide and largely featureless lawns of the **Parc du Cinquantenaire** slope up towards a gargantuan **triumphal arch** surmounted by a huge and bombastic bronze entitled *Brabant Raising the National Flag*. The arch, along with the two heavyweight stone buildings it connects, comprise **Le Cinquantenaire**, which was placed here by Léopold II for an exhibition to mark the golden jubilee of the Belgian state in 1880. By all accounts the exhibition of all things made in Belgium and its colonies was a great success, and the park continues to host shows and trade fairs of various kinds, while the buildings themselves – which are a brief walk from the Métro Merode – contain extensive collections of art and applied art, weapons and cars, displayed in three separate museums.

Musées Royaux d'Art et d'Histoire

Tues–Fri 9.30am–5pm, Sat & Sun 10am–5pm; F150.

The **Musées Royaux d'Art et d'Histoire**, on the south side of the south wing of the complex, is made up of a maddening (and badly labelled) maze of pottery, carvings, furniture, tapestries, glassware and lacework from all over the world. There is almost too much to absorb in even a couple of visits, and your best bet is to pick up the plan and index at reception (F20) and select the areas which interest you most. There are enormous galleries of mostly run-of-the-mill Greek, Egyptian and Roman artefacts complete with mummies of a jackal, crocodile and falcon. Elsewhere, another part of the collection has an assortment of Near and Far Eastern gods, porcelain, jewellery and textiles, and there are pre-Columbian Native American carvings and effigies too.

The **European decorative arts** sections have the most immediacy and these are located on Level 1 (Rooms 45–75) and Level 2 (Rooms 89–105). They are divided into over twenty distinct collections, featuring everything from Delft ceramics, altarpieces, porcelain and silverware through to tapestries, Art Deco and Art Nouveau furnishings. It's all a little bewildering, with little to link one set of artefacts to another, but the sub-section entitled **The Middle Ages to Baroque** (Level 1, Rooms 53–70) is outstanding and comparatively easy to absorb. This sub-section makes a cracking start in **Room 53** with *The Triumph of the Virtues*, a set of eight Brussels' tapestries dating from the middle of the sixteenth century, the heyday of the city's tapestry industry. **Room 56** also contains some fine tapestries, earlier works manufactured in Tournai, in southern Belgium, during the fifteenth century. These are much less languid, depicting scenes of tense and often violent drama as in the *Battle of Roncesvalles*, in which Christians and Moors slug it out in a fearsome, seething battle scene. The museum prides itself on its collection of medieval altarpieces and **Room 57** contains one of the best, the *Passion Altarpiece*, which is animated with a mass of finely detailed wooden reliefs. This altarpiece was carved in Brussels in the 1470s whereas the *Passion Altarpiece* in **Room 61** was made in Antwerp some fifty years later and is, in consequence, even more extravagant, sporting a veritable doll's house of figures.

Room 62 holds several more sixteenth-century Brussels' tapestries, including one depicting *The Legend of Notre Dame of Sablon* (see p.65); **Room 66** has some fine alabasters from Mechelen, just north of Brussels; and **Room 68** boasts a delightful double bed, a fancy, canopied affair produced for a Swiss burgher in the 1680s. Finally, don't leave without poking your nose round the **Art Nouveau** sections, especially **Room 50**, where the display cases were designed by Victor Horta for a firm of jewellers, and now accommodate the celebrated *Mysterious Sphinx*, a ceramic bust of archetypal Art Nouveau design, the work of Charles van der Stappen in 1897.

Autoworld

Daily: April–Sept 10am–6pm; Oct–March 10am–5pm; F200.

Housed in a vast hangar-like building in the south wing of Le Cinquantenaire, **Autoworld** is a chronological stroll through the short history of the automobile, with a huge display of vintage vehicles, beginning with early turn-of-the-century motorized cycles and Model Ts. Perhaps inevitably, European varieties predominate: there are lots of vehicles from Peugeot, Renault and Benz, and homegrown examples, too, including a Minerva from 1925 which once belonged to the Belgian monarch. American makes include early Cadillacs, a Lincoln from 1965 that was also owned by the Belgian royals, and some great gangster-style Oldsmobiles; among the British brands, there's a practically

AUTOWORLD

new Rolls-Royce Silver Ghost from 1921, one of the first Austins, and, from the modern era, the short-lived De Lorean sports car. Upstairs is a collection of assorted vehicles that don't fit into the main exhibition. It's a bit of a mish-mash, but worth a brief look for some early Porsches and Volvos, classic 1960s Jags and even a tuk-tuk from Thailand. The museum's major drawback is its lack of recent vehicles – few cars date from after the mid-1970s. That said, there's good English labelling, at least on the downstairs exhibits, and a decent museum shop, with lots of automobile-related matter, including a great selection of model cars.

Musée Royal de l'Armée et d'Histoire militaire

Tues–Sun 9am–noon & 1–4.30pm; free.

In the north wing of Le Cinquantenaire, on the other side of the triumphal arch from the other two museums, the **Musée Royal de l'Armée et d'Histoire militaire** displays collections tracing the history of the Belgian army from independence to the present day by means of weapons, uniforms and paintings. There are also modest sections dealing with "Belgian" regiments in the Austrian and Napoleonic armies, and, more interestingly, the volunteers who formed the nucleus of the 1830 revolution. Most spectacular are the galleries devoted to armoured cars, artillery and military aircraft, though it's far from required viewing. One surprise is that from the top floor you can get out onto the triumphal arch and enjoy extensive views over the city.

RUE DE LA LOI AND AROUND

The office blocks of the EU are concentrated along and between the two wide boulevards – **rues de la Loi and Belliard** (Map 2, G5–6 to I7–6) – which Léopold II built to connect his Parc du Cinquantenaire with the city centre. It's not an interesting area to visit as the EU remains committed to modernistic, state-of-the-art high-rises. This is surprising given the difficulties the EU has had with its best-known construction, the **Centre Berlaymont**, a huge office building on rue de la Loi beside Métro Schuman. When it was opened in 1967, the Berlaymont was widely praised for its ground-breaking design, but in 1991 it was abandoned for health and safety reasons – the building was riddled with asbestos and work still continues on its refurbishment.

Although EU buildings dominate this segment of the city, a small stretch of late nineteenth-century urban planning has survived, a ten-minute walk **north of the Centre Berlaymont** past the shops and cafés of rue Archimède. Here, two pleasant and leafy plazas, squares Ambiorix and Marie-Louise, were laid out in the 1870s on what had previously been marshland. By the end of the century, they had formed, along with the short avenue Palmerston which linked them, one of the city's most fashionable suburbs, where the residences of the bourgeoisie included several splendid examples of Art Nouveau. Nowadays, **square Ambiorix** (Map 2, I5) is largely overshadowed by modern apartments, but you shouldn't miss the superb wrought-iron and swirling stone facade of no. 11, one of the city's most ornate Art Nouveau buildings and the one-time home of a painter by the name of Georges de Saint-Cyr. Nearby, on **avenue Palmerston**, the Villa Germaine, at no. 24, exhibits striking patterned tiles and multicoloured bricks and down at the foot of the street are three wonderfully subtle buildings by Victor Horta: there's the austere facade of no. 3, whose white and blue stone trimmings lead round to an exuberant side-entrance; no. 2 is a charming corner house with a delicately carved, fluted stone facade; and no. 4 has a rigorous design softened by arched lintels and mosaics.

RUE DE LA LOI AND AROUND

For more on Victor Horta, see p.72.

The south side of **square Marie-Louise** is occupied by a series of big old houses whose stone trimmings, balconies, dormer windows and high gables jostle each other. Leading off from the square is **rue du Taciturne** whose most interesting building is no. 34, a lavish structure with an elegant facade of intricate window grilles and tiny black columns. It was designed by Paul Saintenoy, who was also responsible for the Old England building (see p.49).

Rue du Taciturne leads back to rue de la Loi, from where it's a couple of minutes' walk west to Métro Maalbeek.

The Outlying Districts

Brussels pushes out in all directions from the city centre and the inner suburbs, its present-day perimeter enclosing no fewer than nineteen *communes* and marked by the ring road, the RO. Within this circle, the city's **outlying districts** are little known by tourists but they do hold a handful of first-rate attractions as well as some lesser sights. All of the places mentioned are within easy reach of the centre by public transport.

The gritty *commune* of **Anderlecht**, to the immediate west of the petit ring, comes top in the order of places to visit, not only because it is home to one of Europe's most famous football teams – Anderlecht (see p.248) – but also as the location of the fascinating Maison d'Erasme, where Erasmus holed up for a few months in 1521, and the Musée Bruxellois de la Gueuze, devoted to the production of the eponymous brew. **Koekelberg**, just to the north, is less well-endowed – it has only the colossal Basilique du Sacré Coeur to offer – while the adjacent *commune* of **Jette** musters the soon-to-opened Musée René Magritte, sited in the artist's old home and studio.

Continuing in a clockwise direction, the next *commune* is **Heysel**, where you'll find the Atomium, a hugely enlarged model of a molecule, and the infamous Heysel stadium, scene of the 1985 football crowd disaster. Next door is leafy **Laeken**, whose sprawling parkland is dotted with the accoutrements of the Belgian royals – their greenhouse, statues and monuments, as well as the main palace and a couple of regal follies, a Japanese tower and a Chinese pavilion.

The *communes* lying east and south of the city centre are of only modest appeal. **Woluwe St Pierre** has the Palais Stoclet, with its Klimt interiors, and beyond – further east still, beyond the ring road – is the small town of **Tervuren**, site of the Musée Royal de l'Afrique Centrale, whose assorted African artefacts were first brought together by Léopold II. To the south of the city lies the **Forêt de Soignes**, a great chunk of forest crisscrossed by footpaths and scattered with picnic sites. To the west of the forest there's the greenery of prosperous **Uccle**, too, not to mention the fine art collection of the Musée van Buuren.

....

**The area covered by this chapter is shown
on colour maps 1, 2 and 5.**

....

ANDERLECHT

No one could say **Anderlecht** was beautiful, but it has its attractive nooks and crannies, particularly in the vicinity of **Métro St Guidon** on line #1B. Come out of the station, turn left and it's a few metres down the slope to place de la Vaillance, a pleasant triangular plaza flanked by little cafés and the whitestone tower and facade of the church of **Sts Pierre et Guidon** (Map 2, I3; Mon–Fri 9am–noon & 2.30–6pm; free). The facade, which mostly dates from the fifteenth century, is unusually long and slender, its stonework graced by delicate flourishes and a fine set of gargoyles. Inside, the church has a surprisingly low and poorly lit nave in a corner of which is a vaulted chapel dedicated to **St Guido**, otherwise known as St Guy, a local eleventh-century figure. Of peasant origins, Guido entered the priesthood but he invested all of his church's money in an enterprise that went bust. He was sacked and spent the next seven years as a pilgrim, a sackcloth-and-ashes extravaganza that ultimately earned him a sainthood – as the patron saint of peasants and horses. The chapel contains a breezy *Miracle of St Guido* by Gaspard de Crayer, a local seventeenth-century artist who made a tidy income from religious paintings in the style of Rubens.

Elsewhere in the church, several of the walls are decorated with late medieval **murals** and although these are incomplete and difficult to make out in the prevailing gloom one or two make interesting viewing. On the north wall of the nave, look out for the brutal martydom of St Erasmus – who is having his guts ripped out – and opposite, in the Chapelle de Notre Dame de Grâce, the recently restored scenes from the life of St Guido. The **chancel** is of interest too – it was designed by Jan van Ruysbroeck, who was also responsible for the tower of the Hôtel de Ville (see p.17), and it contains two contrasting tombs. The earlier effigy, a recumbent knight wearing his armour, is conservative and formal, whereas the kneeling figure opposite is dressed in lavish, early Renaissance attire, his helmet placed in front of him as decoration.

Maison d'Erasme

Map 2, J3. Mon, Wed & Thurs, Sat & Sun 10am–noon & 2–5pm; F50. Ⓜ St Guidon.

From Sts Pierre et Guidon, it's just a couple of minutes' walk to the **Maison d'Erasme**, at rue du Chapitre 31 – walk east along the front of the church onto rue d'Aumale and it's on the right behind the distinctive red brick wall. Dating from 1468, the house, with its pretty dormer windows and sturdy symmetrical lines, was built to accommodate important visitors to the church. Easily the most celebrated of these guests was **Desiderius Erasmus** (1466–1536), who lodged here in 1521. By any measure, Erasmus was a remarkable man. Born in Rotterdam, the illegitimate son of a priest, Erasmus was orphaned at the age of thirteen and was then defrauded of his inheritance by his guardians, who forced him to become a monk. He hated monastic life and seized the first opportunity to leave, becoming a student at the University of Paris in 1491. Throughout the rest of his life, Erasmus kept on the move – travelling between the Low Countries, England, Italy and Switzerland – and everywhere he went, his rigorous scholarship, sharp humour and strong moral sense made a tremendous impact. He attacked the abuses and corruptions of the Church, publishing scores of polemical and satirical essays which were read all over Western Europe. He argued that most monks had "no other calling than stupidity, ignorance . . . and the hope of being fed."

These attacks reflected Erasmus' determination to reform the Church from within, both by rationalising its doctrine and rooting out hypocrisy, ignorance and superstition. He employed other methods too, producing translations of the New Testament to make the Scriptures more widely accessible, and coordinating the efforts of like-minded Christian humanists. The Church authorities periodically harassed Erasmus, but generally he was tolerated not least for his insistence on the importance of Christian unity. **Luther** was less indulgent, bitterly denouncing Erasmus for "making fun of the faults and miseries of the Church of Christ instead of bewailing them before God." The quarrel between the two reflected a growing schism amongst the reformers that eventually led to the Reformation.

MAISON D'ERASME

The **house** contains none of Erasmus' actual belongings, but a host of contemporary artefacts, all squeezed into half a dozen, clearly signed rooms. To get the most from a visit you should borrow the (English-language) catalogue from reception. The Cabinet de travail (study) holds original portraits of Erasmus by Holbein, Dürer and others, as well as a mould of his skull, but the best paintings are concentrated in the Salle du Chapitre (chapterhouse), which boasts a charmingly inquisitive *Adoration of the Magi* by Hieronymus Bosch, a gentle *Nativity* from Gerard David, and an hallucinatory *Temptation of St Anthony* by Pieter Huys. Huys was one of many artists to copy Bosch's more frantic work, though it's hard not to feel that the freakish beasts populating his painting are as much to titillate as terrify – and certainly the woman, as a symbol of temptation, is a good deal more voluptuous than anything Bosch would have painted.

Moving on, the Salle Blanche (white room) contains a good sample of first editions of Erasmus' work alongside an intriguing cabinet of altered and amended texts: some show scrawled comments made by irate readers, others are the work of the Inquisition and assorted clerical censors.

Musée Bruxellois de la Gueuze

Mon–Fri 8.30am–5pm Sat & Sun 10am–5pm; F100.
Ⓜ Gare du Midi.

The **Musée Bruxellois de la Gueuze**, rue Gheude 56, is located ten minutes' walk north of the Métro Gare du Midi via avenue Paul Henri Spaak and rue Limnander; to get there direct from Maison d'Erasme, take tram #56 from Métro St Guidon to Gare du Midi. Well worth the effort, the museum is a mustily evocative working brewery, still brewing Gueuze according to the traditional methods – and there's an excellent English-language leaflet to help you decipher what you see. The beer, made only of wheat, malted barley, hops and water, is allowed to ferment naturally, reacting with natural yeasts peculiar to the Brussels air, and is bottled for two years before it is ready to drink. The result is unique, as you can find out at the tasting at the end of a visit.

KOEKELBERG – SACRÉ COEUR

Map 1, C2. Church daily: Easter to Oct 8am–6pm; Nov to Easter 8am–5pm; free. Dome daily: Easter to Oct 9am–5pm; Nov to Easter 10am–4pm; F100.

From Métro Simonis – two short subway rides from Métro Gare du Midi – take tram #19 which rattles west round the edge of the lawns leading up to the ugliest church in the capital, the **Basilique du Sacré Coeur**, a huge structure – 140m long with a 90-metre-tall dome – which dominates the *commune* of **Koekelberg**. Begun in 1905 on the orders of Léopold II and still unfinished, the basilica was conceived as a neo-Gothic extravagance in imitation of the basilica to the Sacré Coeur in Montmartre, Paris – a structure which had made the Belgian king green with envy. But the construction costs proved colossal and the plans had to be mod-

René Magritte

René Magritte (1898–1967) is easily the most famous of Belgium's modern artists, his disconcerting, strangely haunting images a familiar part of popular culture. He was born in a small town just outside Charleroi, in southern Belgium. In 1915 he entered the Royal Academy of Fine Arts in Brussels and was a student there until 1920. His appearances were few and far between at the Academy as he preferred the company of a group of artists and friends fascinated with the **Surrealist**

movement of the 1920s. Their antics were supposed to incorporate a serious intent – the undermining of bourgeois convention – but the surviving home movies of Magritte and his chums fooling around don't appear very revolutionary today.

Initially, Magritte worked in a broadly Cubist manner, but in 1925, influenced by Giorgio de Chirico, he switched over to Surrealism and almost immediately stumbled upon the themes and images that would preoccupy him for decades to come. The hallmarks of his work were striking, incorporating startling comparisons between the ordinary and the extraordinary, with the occasional erotic element. Favourite images included men in bowler hats, metamorphic figures, enormous rocks floating in the sky, tubas, fishes with human legs, *bilboquets* (the cup and ball game), and juxtapositions of night and day – one part of the canvas lit by artificial light, the other basking in full sunlight. He also dabbled in word paintings, mislabelling familiar forms to illustrate (or expose) the arbitrariness of linguistic signs. His canvases were devoid of emotion, deadpan images that were easy to recognise but perplexing because of their setting – perhaps most famously, the man in the suit with a bowler hat and an apple for a face.

He broke with this characteristic style on two occasions, once during the War – in despair over the Nazi occupation – and again in 1948, to revenge long years of neglect by the French artistic establishment. Hundreds had turned up to see Magritte's first Paris exhibition, but they were confronted with crass and crude paintings of childlike simplicity. These so-called **Vache paintings** created a furore, and Magritte beat a hasty artistic retreat behind a smokescreen of self-justification. These two experiments alienated Magritte from most of the other Surrealists but in the event this was of little consequence as Magritte was picked up and popularized by an American art dealer, Alexander Iolas, who made Magritte very rich and very famous.

RENÉ MAGRITTE

ified. The result is a vaguely ludicrous amalgamation of the original neo-Gothic design with Art Deco features added in the 1920s. While you're here, it's worth climbing up to the top of the **dome** for a panoramic view of the city.

JETTE – MUSÉE RENÉ MAGRITTE

Map 1, C1. Wed–Sun 11am–5pm (provisional); F200.
Ⓜ Pannenhuis.

To the north, Koekelberg fades into the prosperous suburb of **Jette**, home to the **Musée René Magritte**, rue Esseghem 135, a brand-new museum scheduled to open by spring 1999.

This museum, occupying Magritte's home from 1930 to the mid-1950s, contains a plethora of the surrealist's paraphernalia, as well as a modest collection of his early paintings and sketches.

Magritte's mature work can be seen at the Musées Royaux des Beaux Arts (see p.63).

The main attraction is the ground floor (the part he lived in), which has been faithfully restored – even the decor and furnishings – to recreate the artist's style of living. Elsewhere, documentation, photos, letters, and art work, take up the first floor, the second is used for temporary exhibitions, and a number of Magritte's personal objects are displayed in the attic, including the easel used at the end of his life.

HEYSEL

Lying northwest of the city, **Heysel**, a 500-acre estate bequeathed to the authorities by Léopold II in 1909, is best described as a theme park without a theme. Its most famous attraction is the **Atomium** (daily: April–Aug 9am–8pm;

Sept–March 10am–6pm; F200) (Map 5, C2), a curious model of a molecule expanded 165 billion times, which was built for the 1958 World Fair in Brussels. The structure has become something of a symbol of the city. Unfortunately what it contains is an unremarkable science museum and the main interest is the feeling of disorientation when travelling from sphere to sphere by the escalator. If you're hoping to get a good view of the city from the top sphere, around 102m above the ground, you may well be disappointed by grey weather obscuring the view, in which case forego the rather high entrance fee and settle for viewing it from the outside.

The Atomium borders a large trade fair area – the **Parc des Expositions** where they held the World Fairs of 1935 and 1958 – and the **Stade du Roi Baudouin** (Map 5, B2), formerly the infamous Heysel football stadium (see p.246) in which 39 (mainly Italian) supporters were crushed to death when a sector wall collapsed in 1985. International fixtures are held here, and it will be the main Belgian venue for Euro 2000, which Belgium is hosting jointly with Holland. The **Bruparck** (Map 5, C2) leisure complex is also close by, and although its commercial nature is not to everybody's taste, it's a handy place to take the kids. The child-oriented attractions include Océade, a water funpark, a gigantic cinema complex called Kinepolis, and Mini-Europe, where you can see scaled-down models of selected European buildings (see p.257).

LAEKEN

Bordering Heysel on the east, and around 3km north of the city, leafy **Laeken** is home to the royal family, who occupy a large out-of-bounds estate and have colonized the surrounding parkland with their monuments and memorials. From the south, Laeken is best approached on tram #52 or #92.

Get off at the Araucaria tram stop, which is just behind the **Pavillon Chinois** (Map 5, H3) and just off avenue des Croix. This elegant and attractive replica of a Chinese pavilion was built here by Léopold II after he had seen one at the World Fair in Paris in 1900. The king intended his creation to be a fancy restaurant, but this never materialized and the pavilion now houses a first-rate collection of Chinese and Japanese porcelain (Tues–Sun 10am–4.30pm; F120; joint ticket with Tour Japonaise, F150). Across the road, and reached by a tunnel from beside the pavilion, is the matching **Tour Japonaise** (same times as Pavillon Chinois; F100), another of Léopold's follies, this time a copy of a Buddhist pagoda with parts made in Paris, Brussels and Yokohama, and now in use as a venue for temporary exhibitions – usually items from the Far East in the Musées Royaux d'Art et d'Histoire (admission extra, see p.92).

Around the corner behind the railings, along the congested avenue du Parc Royal, is the sedate **Château Royal** (no entry) (Map 5, H6), the main royal palace. Built in 1790, its most famous occupant was Napoleon, who stayed here on a number of occasions and signed the declaration of war on Russia here in 1812. Before the château is the **Serres Royales**, enormous greenhouses, built for Léopold II, covering almost four acres and sheltering a mind-boggling variety of tropical and Mediterranean flora. The only problem is the restricted opening hours – the greenhouses are open to the public only during April and May (times from the tourist office) and the queues to see them can be daunting.

Opposite the front of the royal palace, a wide footpath leads up to the fanciful neo-Gothic monument erected in honour of Léopold I, the focal point of the pretty **Parc de Laeken** (Map 5, F4). The park is also home to the Stuyvenbergh Castle, once the residence of Emperor Charles V's architect, Louis Van Bodeghem, although now used to accommodate high-ranking foreign dignitaries.

LAEKEN

One kilometre further south along avenue du Parc Royal is **Laeken cemetery**, the last resting place of many influential Belgians including the architect Joseph Poelaert (who designed the Palais de Justice), and artist Jef Dillen, whose tomb is marked by a copy of Rodin's *The Thinker*. Also buried here is Maria Felicia Garcia, the famous Spanish soprano better known as Maria Malibran (see p.81).

At the cemetery's entrance stands the neo-Gothic style church of **Notre Dame de Laeken**, which was designed by Joseph Poelaert and built in memory of Belgium's first Queen – Louise-Marie. Many of the country's royals are buried here within the Royal Crypt.

WOLUWE ST PIERRE

Four kilometres southeast of the city and directly north of Tervuren, is **Woluwe St Pierre** (Map 1, F3), a popular residential town most easily reached by tram #44 from Métro Montgomery. Unlike its sister town, Woluwe St Lambert, it was less scarred by the brutal urban development policy of the 1960s and 1970s and has managed to keep its small-town-in-the-country appeal.

The main attraction is the **Palais Stoclet**, at avenue de Tervuren 279–281, which was designed by architect Josef Hoffman. Its interior, with designs by Gustav Klimt, resembles the concept behind the Horta residence in being a "total work of art" with every fixture and fitting having been designed especially for the house. Sadly the interior is not open to the public; its exterior, however, is magnificent, particularly the staircase tower with the four figures of naked green men, and bronze circle sculptures by Metzner.

Further down at no. 346b, the **Musée du Transport urbain bruxellois** (early April to early Oct, Sat & Sun 1.30–7.30pm; F150) retraces the history of trams and buses over the last hundred years, although perhaps more enticing

WOLUWE ST PIERRE

is the trip on a 1930s tram to Parc Cinquantenaire or through the Forêt de Soignes, which is included in the entrance price.

From the museum take the second right down avenue Jules César, continuing on to avenue de l'Atlantique which runs into rue du Bemel, where, at no. 21, you'll find **Bibliotheca Wittockiana** (check the tourist office for dates of exhibitions, otherwise by appointment only). A private museum, it contains a large collection of rare and priceless books belonging to industrialist Michael Wittock, including a work decorated with shells that belonged to Queen Margot, wife of Henry of Navarre, as well as a Moroccan leather-bound book belonging to Marie Antoinette. From here **Parc Woluwe**, lined by the lovely Mellaerts ponds, is only a short walk east.

FORÊT DE SOIGNES

Some 5km southeast of the city and 2km south of Woluwe St Pierre, the leafy suburbs are left behind for the dense beech woodland of the **Forêt de Soignes**, one of Belgium's most beautiful national parks. Originally a royal domain used for hunting, it once covered over 27,000 acres. Sadly, more than a century and a half of development has taken it's toll. In the 1820s the king of the Netherlands gave the forest to the "General Society for promoting National Industry" and large parts of the forest were subsequently sold off, before it was turned over to the government in 1843. Further depletion followed when sections of the forest were cleared to make way for country estates, agricultural complexes and country houses, and in 1861 a huge slice was carved off to create a large urban park, now known as Bois de la Cambe (see p.259). Today just over one-third of the original forest remains.

What is left stretches from Bois de la Cambe in its most northerly reaches, 10km southeast to La Hulpe, and from Uccle in the west, some 9km east to the Arboretum Géographique which lies less than a kilometre south of Parc de Tervuren. Despite the piecemeal development, it still remains one of the region's most attractive spaces, and is a popular escape for walkers and cyclists, as well as horse riders, golfers and anglers.

To get there, take tram #44 from Métro Montgomery, a lovely trip, which takes you down the chestnut tree-lined avenue de Tervuren, past Parc de Woluwe, and into the forest, before reaching the terminus at Tervuren town. The forest is also accessible from Bois de la Cambe, although you have to cross the unpleasant chaussée de la Hulpe before you reach the forest's peaceful, winding footpaths.

TERVUREN

Just over 2km southeast of Woluwe St Pierre, the small town of **Tervuren** (Map 1, G3) is one of the prettiest (and greenest) places in the Brussels region. Bordered in the south by the beautiful Forêt de Soignes, dotted with grand old houses, and surrounded by lush woodland, it is no surprise the area is a popular place to live, particularly with British and Irish Eurocrats, although strangely enough it remains firmly off the tourist track.

Connected to the city by the ten-kilometre-long avenue de Tervuren, a route most easily covered by tram #44 from Métro Montgomery, its centrepiece is the impressive **Musée Royal de l'Afrique Centrale** situated in the Parc de Tervuren – an attractive park which is also home to a vast array of ancient trees, manicured lawns, lakes and flower-beds. Once here, a few other sights also merit a visit, particularly the church of St Jean l'Évangéliste, on Tervuren's main square, and the Arboretum, which lies half a kilometre to the south.

Musée Royal de l'Afrique Centrale

Tues–Fri 10am–5pm, Sat & Sun 10am-6pm; F80. Tram #44.

Without a doubt Tervuren's main attraction is the **Musée Royal de l'Afrique Centrale**. Only a short walk along Leuvensesteeweg from the Tervuren tram terminal, it is housed in a pompous, custom-built pile constructed on the orders of King Léopold II around 1900. Personally presented with the vast Congo River basin by a conference of the European powers in 1885, Léopold became one of the country's richest men as a result. His initial attempts to secure control of the area were abetted by the explorer – and ex-Confederate soldier – Henry Stanley, who went to the Congo on a five-year fact-finding mission in 1879, just a few years after he had famously found the missionary David Livingstone. Even by the standards of the colonial powers, Léopold's regime was too chaotic and too extraordinarily cruel to stomach, and in 1908, one year before the museum opened, the Belgian government took over the territory, installing a marginally more liberal state bureaucracy. The country gained independence as Zaire in 1960, and its subsequent history has been one of the most bloodstained in Africa.

The museum was Léopold's own idea, a blatantly colonialist and racist enterprise which treats the Africans as a naive and primitive people, and the Belgians as their paternalistic benefactors. Nevertheless, the collection is undeniably rich if a little old-fashioned, and sometimes positively eccentric: one room is entirely devoted to examples of different sorts of timber. Unsurprisingly there is little about Léopold's administration or its savagery. The most interesting displays cover many aspects of Congolese life, from masks, idols and musical instruments to weapons and an impressive array of dope pipes, and there's a superb 22-metre-long dugout canoe. The museum's grounds are also worth a stroll, with the formal gardens set around a series of geometric lakes, flanked by wanderable woods.

The Town

From the museum, backtrack for a few minutes along Leuvensestweg until you reach Kerkstraat, where you'll find the prettily cobbled town square and a few gems worth investigating. The square itself is dominated by the imposing church of **St Jean l'Évangéliste**, a thirteenth-century Gothic church which contains the tomb of the Duke of Brabant, Antoine of Burgundy, who was killed at Agincourt in 1415. Close by, at Kerkstraat 33, the **Schaakboard** art gallery (Sat & Sun 2pm–5pm; free) exhibits a modest but palatable collection of paintings (mainly landscapes) from the nineteenth-century Tervuren school. The square is also home to *Glacerie Mont Blanc*, where you can pause for one of the delicious home-made ice creams.

From here, continue on Kerkstraat which turns into Pardenmaktstraat, after which take the first left down Pauwstraat, which runs into Arboretumlaan; this will bring you to Tervuren's **Arboretum Géographique**. Originally part of the Forêt de Soignes, it was converted into an arboretum in 1905 on the instructions of Léopold II, and was used to train European officers for the African and Asian colonies. Today it's home to hundreds of different species of trees – redwoods, maples, Scots pines and larches, to name but a few – and is a great place for an afternoon stroll.

UCCLE

South of the city, **Uccle** (Map 1, A3), is connected to Ixelles by avenue Brugmann and is best reached by tram #92, which can be taken at either place Stéphanie, which is a few hundred metres from Métro Louise, or, if you're coming from the centre, rue de la Régence. Originally a string of hamlets, Uccle only became a suburb in the mid-nineteenth century when the aristocracy – attracted by the lush greenery – took up residence here.

Chapelle Notre Dame des Afflingés at rue de Stalle 50, just off avenue Brugmann, is a lovely little church which dates back to the fifteenth century. Its centrepiece is the beautiful stucco ceiling which was added in the seventeenth century. There's also an awe-inspiring statue of St Catherine.

From here, a ten-minute walk along avenue Vanderaey will bring you to the tranquil **Cimetière Dieweg**, unused for burials since 1958, though a waiver was granted allowing Hergé, the creator of Tintin, to be interred here in 1983.

From the cemetery continue east up Diewag, crossing avenue de Wolvendael, and on the left you'll find the entrance to **Parc de Wolvendael**, a historic 45-acre estate, which is mentioned in documents dating back to 1209. It makes a lovely place for a picnic and afterwards you can view (from outside only) the small white stone castle built in 1753. Close by is the beautiful Louis XV summerhouse, a lovely building which, sadly, has been converted into an unimpressive restaurant.

From the park, head north to avenue de Fré, where on the corner of chemin du Crabbegat you'll find **Le Cornet**, a one-time tavern much-frequented by artists and writers throughout the nineteenth and early twentieth centuries. In fact it is here that famous Belgian writer Charles de Coster sets a delightful scene in his epic novel *Till Ulenspiegel* (1867), where the hero, Till, meets women archers from Uccle.

Continue heading east along avenue de Fré, taking the first left after square de Fré up rue Roberts Jones until you reach avenue Léo Errera. Here, at no. 41, is the **Musée David et Alice van Buuren** (Mon 2–4pm, Sun 1–6pm; F300) a superb little gallery housed in a glorious Art Deco building which dates back to 1928. Established in 1973, it contains an amazing collection of paintings including a version of *The Fall of Icarus* by Bruegel the Elder, several pictures by van de Woestyne and James Ensor, some still lifes by Fantin-Latour, several landscapes by the sixteenth-century painter Joachim Patenier, and sketches by van Gogh. The picturesque, maze-like garden outside (daily 2–6pm), designed by Belgian landscape architect René Pechère, contains many rare species of rose, as well as 300 yew trees.

Day-trips from Brussels

Almost all of Belgium is within easy striking distance of Brussels, making the list of possible excursions nearly endless. In this chapter we've picked out six of the most appealing destinations, all within an hour's travelling time by bus or train from the capital. To the south of Brussels lies **Waterloo**, site of Napoleon's final defeat at the hands of the Duke of Wellington in 1815. The battlefield has long been a popular tourist attraction and was once part of the "grand tour". Also to the south of Brussels, deep in the wilds of French-speaking Brabant, lies the Cistercian abbey of **Villers-la-Ville**, perhaps the most beautiful medieval ruins in the country and a favourite, "romantic" spot for newlyweds to have their photo snapped. Different again is the Flemish city of **Leuven**, a vibrant university town to the east of Brussels that boasts lively bars and restaurants and a couple of especially fine Gothic buildings. The big city and port of **Antwerp**, to the north of the capital, is alluring too: it possesses a flourishing nightlife, medieval churches and first-rate museums as well as an unrivalled collection of the work of its favourite son, Peter Paul Rubens.

Accommodation price codes

All the **hotels** detailed in this chapter have been graded according to the following price categories. All the codes are based on the rate for the least expensive double room during high season.

① F1500–2000. ③ F2500–3000. ⑤ F4000–5000. ⑦ F6000 and
② F2000–2500. ④ F3000–4000. ⑥ F5000–6000.   over.

Flanders stretches west of Brussels as far as the North Sea. In medieval times, this was the most prosperous and urbanized part of Europe and its merchants grew rich from the profits of the cloth industry. Those heady days are recalled by **Bruges**, one of the most perfectly preserved medieval cities in Europe. It's easily the most popular tourist destination in Belgium and in summertime the crowds can be oppressive, which makes neighbouring **Ghent**, another fine old Flemish cloth town with superb architecture and excellent art museums, doubly appealing.

WATERLOO

Map 1, E9.

Waterloo, now a run-of-the-mill suburb about 18km south of the centre of Brussels, has a resonance far beyond its size. It was here on June 18, 1815, at this small crossroads town on what was once the main route into Brussels from France, that Wellington masterminded the battle which put an end to the imperial ambitions of Napoleon. Indeed, the battle actually had far more significance than even its generals realised, for not only was this the last throw of the dice for the formidable army born of the French Revolution, but it also marked the final end of France's prolonged attempts to dominate Europe militarily.

WATERLOO

The historic importance of Waterloo has not, however, saved the **battlefield** from interference – a motorway cuts right across it – and if you do visit you'll need a lively imagination to picture what happened and where, unless, that is, you're around to see the large-scale re-enactment which takes place every five years in June; the next one is scheduled for 2000. Scattered round the battlefield are several monuments and memorials, the most satisfying of which is the **Butte de Lion**, a huge earth mound that's part viewpoint and part commemoration. The battlefield is 3km north of the centre of Waterloo, where the **Musée Wellington** is the pick of the district's museums.

Arrival and information

To get to Waterloo from Brussels, catch the train from any of Brussels' three main stations (Mon–Fri 2 hourly, Sat & Sun 1 hourly; 20min), or take orange bus #W from place Rouppe (every 30min). The disadvantage with the train is that the railway station is a dreary 1km walk west from the centre of Waterloo along rue de la Station, whereas bus #W goes through Waterloo and then continues onto the battlefield. In the centre of Waterloo, bus #W stops outside the **Syndicat d'Initiative et de Tourisme**, at chaussée de Bruxelles 149 (daily: April–Oct 9.30am–6.30pm; Nov–March 10.30am–5pm; ℗02/354 99 10). They provide free town maps and have several booklets recounting the story of the battle. The most competent of them is titled *The Battlefield of Waterloo Step by Step*. The tourist office also sells (at F385) a combined ticket for all the battle-related attractions, though if you're at all selective (and you should be) this won't work out as a saving at all.

The Musée Wellington

Daily: April–Sept 9.30am–6.30pm; Oct–March 10.30am–5pm; F100.
The best starting point for a visit to Waterloo is next door to
the tourist office in the old inn where Wellington slept the
night before the battle. The inn has been turned into the
Musée Wellington detailing the events of the battle with
plans and models, and displaying the assorted personal effects
of Wellington, Alexander Gordon (his aide-de-camp) and
Napoleon. There are also copies of the messages Wellington
sent to his commanders during the course of the battle,
curiously formal epistles laced with phrases like "Could you
be so kind as..." and "We ought to...", as well as the artificial
leg of Lord Uxbridge: "I say, I've lost my leg," Uxbridge is
reported to have said during the battle, to which Wellington
replied, "By God, sir, so you have!" After the battle,
Uxbridge's leg was buried here in Waterloo, but it was
returned to London when he died to join the rest of his
body; as a consolation his artificial leg was donated to the
museum. Neither were the bits and pieces of dead soldiers
considered sacrosanct: tooth dealers roamed the battlefields
of the Napoleonic Wars pulling out teeth which were then
stuck on two pieces of board with a spring at the back –
primitive dentures known in England as "Waterloos".

The church of **Saint Joseph**, across the street, shelters
dozens of memorial plaques to the British soldiers who
died at Waterloo.

The battlefield – the Butte de Lion

From outside the tourist office, pick up orange bus #W
again and head on down to the **battlefield** – an undulating landscape of fields punctuated by the odd clump of
trees and the whitewashed walls of the occasional farm-
stead. Avoid the **Centre du Visiteur**, on route du Lion

WATERLOO

(daily: April–Sept 9.30am–6.30pm; Oct–March 10.30am–4pm; F200), and instead walk up the adjacent hundred-metre-high **Butte de Lion** (daily: same hours; F50), built by local women with soil from the battlefield to mark the spot where Holland's Prince William of Orange – later King William II of the Netherlands – was wounded. It's a commanding monument, topped by a regal 28-ton lion atop a stout column, and one that provides a panoramic view over the battlefield.

The Battle of Waterloo

Napoleon escaped from imprisonment on the island of Elba on February 26, 1815. He landed in Cannes three days later and moved swiftly north, entering Paris on March 20 just as his unpopular replacement – the slothful King Louis XVIII – high-tailed it to Ghent. Thousands of Frenchmen rushed to Napoleon's colours and, as soon as possible, Napoleon marched northeast to crush the two armies that threatened his future. Both were in Belgium. One, an assortment of British, Dutch and German soldiers, was commanded by the **Duke of Wellington**, the other was a Prussian army led by **Marshal Blücher**. At the start of the campaign, Napoleon's army was about 130,000 strong, larger than each of the opposing armies but not big enough to fight them both at the same time. Napoleon's strategy was, therefore, quite straightforward – he had to stop Wellington and Blücher from joining together – and to this end he crossed the Belgian frontier near Charleroi to launch a quick attack. On June 16, the French hit the Prussians hard, forcing them to retreat and giving Napoleon the opportunity he was looking for. Napoleon detached a force of 30,000 soldiers to harry the retreating Prussians, while he concentrated his main army against Wellington, hoping to deliver a knock-out blow. Meanwhile, Wellington had assembled his troops at **Waterloo**, on the main road to Brussels.

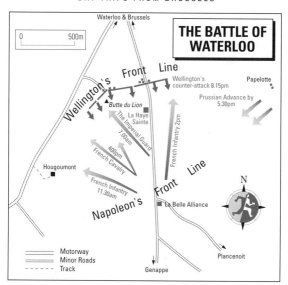

At dawn on **Sunday June 18**, the two armies faced each other. Wellington had some 68,000 men, about one third of whom were British, and Napoleon around 5,000 more. The armies were deployed just 1500 metres apart with Wellington on the ridge north of – and uphill from – the enemy. It had rained heavily during the night, so Napoleon delayed his first attack to give the ground a chance to dry. At **11.30am**, the battle began when the French assaulted the fortified farm of Hougoumont, which was crucial for the defence of Wellington's right. The assault failed and at approximately **1pm** there was more bad news for Napoleon when he heard that the Prussians had eluded their pursuers and were closing fast. To gain time he sent 14,000 troops off to impede their progress and at **2pm** he tried to regain the initiative by launching a large-scale infantry attack against Wellington's left. This second French attack also proved inconclusive and so at **4pm** Napoleon's cavalry charged Wellington's centre, where the British infantry formed into squares and just managed to keep the French at bay – a desperate engagement that cost hundreds of lives. By **5.30pm**, the Prussians had begun to reach the battlefield in numbers to the right of the French lines and, at **7.30pm**, with the odds getting longer and longer, Napoleon made a a final bid to break Wellington's centre, sending in his Imperial Guard. These were the best soldiers Napoleon had but, slowed down by the mud churned up by their own cavalry, the veterans proved easy targets for the British infantry, and they were beaten back with great loss. At **8.15pm**, Wellington, who knew victory was within his grasp, rode down the ranks to encourage his soldiers before ordering the large-scale counterattack that proved decisive. The French were vanquished and Napoleon subsequently abdicated, ending his days in exile on St Helena. He died there in 1821.

Waterloo's other museums

There are two more modest attractions at the base of the Butte – a dire wax museum, the **Musée de Cires** (April–Oct daily 9.30am–6.30pm; Nov–March Sat & Sun 10am–5pm; F60), and the **Panorama de la Bataille** (daily: April–Oct 9.30am–6.30pm; Nov–March 10.30am–4pm; F110 or F200 with Centre du Visiteur), where a circular naturalistic **painting** (1912–13) of the battle, a canvas no less than 110m in circumference, is displayed in a purpose-built, rotunda-like gallery.

WATERLOO'S OTHER MUSEUMS

Le Caillou

April–Oct 10am–6.30pm; Nov–March Tues–Sun 1–5pm; F60.

Napoleon spent the eve of the battle at **Le Caillou**, a two-storey brick farmhouse about 4km south from the Butte de Lion on the chaussée de Bruxelles, and you can visit this, too, though there are no public transport connections. The mementoes here, including Napoleon's army cot and death mask, are a memorial to the emperor and his army, but it's hardly riveting stuff.

VILLERS-LA-VILLE

Map 1, F9. April–Oct Mon & Tues noon–6pm, Wed–Sun 10am–6pm; Nov–March Wed, Thurs & Fri 1–5pm, Sat & Sun 10am–5pm; F150.

The ruined Cistercian abbey of **Villers-la-Ville** nestles in a lovely wooded dell about 35km south of Brussels, and is altogether one of the most haunting and evocative sights in the whole of Belgium. The first monastic community settled here in 1146, consisting of just one abbot and twelve monks. Subsequently the abbey became a wealthy local landowner, managing a domain of several thousand acres, with numbers that rose to about a hundred monks and three hundred lay brothers. A healthy annual income funded the construction of an extensive monastic complex, most of which was erected in the thirteenth century, though the less austere structures, such as the Abbot's Palace, went up in a second spurt of activity some four hundred years later. In 1794 the monastery was ransacked by French revolutionaries, and later on a railway was ploughed through the grounds. Today the site is wild and overgrown and the buildings are all in varying states of decay, but enough survives to pick out Romanesque, Gothic and Renaissance features and to make some kind of mental reconstruction possible.

Arrival and information

To get to Villers-la-Ville from Brussels, catch a Namur **train** and change at Ottignies; the journey takes about an hour. The abbey is 1.6km from the train station from beside the platform for trains to Ottignies; follow the sign pointing to Monticelli up the cobbled street and, after 100m, you'll reach a T-junction; turn right and follow the road round.

Villers-la-Ville **tourist office** (Tues–Fri 1–5pm, Sat 2–6pm, Sun 10am–6pm; ©071/87 98 98) is situated in a little building that was once the main gateway into the abbey – it's to the right of the present entrance. They sell an in-depth English guide to the abbey.

The ruins

From the entrance a path crosses the courtyard in front of the Abbot's Palace to reach the **warming room**, the only place in the monastery where a fire was kept going all winter, and which still has its original chimney. The fire provided a little heat to the adjacent rooms: on one side the monks' work-room, used for reading and studying; on the other the large Romanesque-Gothic **refectory**, lit by ribbed twin windows topped with a rose window. Next door is the **kitchen**, which contained the main drainage system to the river and a chimney for airing the room, and behind this lies the **pantry**, where a slice of the original vaulting has survived on top of a single column. Across the court, on the northwestern edge of the complex, is the **brewery**, one of the biggest and oldest buildings in the abbey.

The most spectacular building, however, is the **church**, which fills out the northeastern corner of the complex. It has the dimensions of a cathedral, with pure lines and elegant proportions, and displays the change from Romanesque to Gothic – the transept and choir are the first known examples

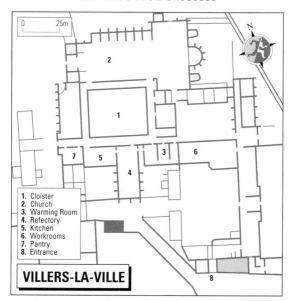

1. Cloister
2. Church
3. Warming Room
4. Refectory
5. Kitchen
6. Workrooms
7. Pantry
8. Entrance

VILLERS-LA-VILLE

of Gothic in the Brabantine area. It's 90m long and 40m wide with a majestic nave whose roof was supported on strong cylindrical columns. An unusual feature is the series of bull's-eye windows which light the transepts. Of the original twelfth-century **cloister** adjoining the church, only a pair of twin windows remain. Around the edge are tombstones and the solitary sarcophagus of the Crusader Gobert d'Aspremont.

LEUVEN

Map 1, F8.

About half an hour by train from Brussels, **Leuven** is home to Belgium's oldest university, whose students give the town a

LEUVEN

lively, informal air – and sustain lots of inexpensive bars and cafés. The key historical sights are the splendid Gothic Stadhuis and St Pieterskerk, a heavy-duty medieval church that towers over the main square, the Grote Markt. Otherwise, the centre is an undistinguished tangle of streets with a lot of the new and few remnants of the old, but then again it's something of a miracle that any of Leuven's ancient buildings have survived, since the town was badly shelled in both World Wars.

Arrival and information

It's an easy ten- to fifteen-minute walk west along Bondgenotenlaan from the train and adjacent bus station to the Grote Markt. Leuven's **tourist office** is a couple of minutes' walk southeast of the Grote Markt at Léopold Vanderkelenstraat 30 (Mon–Fri 9am–5pm & Sat 10am–1pm & 1.30–5pm; March–Oct also Sun 10am–1pm & 1.30–5pm; ©016/21 15 39). They sell a useful city brochure full of practical details including maps locating all the hotels, sights and museums. The tourist office will help to arrange accommodation for free, but frankly none of the town's hotels is very enticing and, with Brussels so near, there's not much reason to stay.

The Town

The centre of Leuven is marked by two adjacent squares, the more easterly of which is the **Fochplein**, basically just a road junction whose one noteworthy feature is the modern **Font Sapienza**, a wittily cynical fountain of a student literally being brainwashed by the book he is reading. Next door, the wedge-shaped **Grote Markt** is Leuven's architectural high spot, dominated by two late Gothic buildings – St Pieterskerk and the Stadhuis. The **Stadhuis** is the more flamboyant of the two, an extraordinarily light and lacy structure, studded with statues and tracery and crowned by soaring pinnacles. The interior is something of an anticlimax, with guided tours (Mon–Fri 11am & 3pm; Sat, Sun & holidays 3pm; F20) taking you through just four rooms, including an overblown salon in Louis XVI style and the neo-Gothic council chamber.

Across the square, **St Pieterskerk** (Tues–Sat 10am–noon & 2–5pm, Sun 2–5pm, plus mid-March to mid-Oct Mon 10am–noon & 2–5pm; free) is a rambling, heavily buttressed late-Gothic pile whose inelegant western facade defeated its architects. Work began on the present church in the 1420s and continued until the start of the sixteenth century when the Romanesque towers of the west facade, the last remaining part of the earlier church, were pulled down to make way for a grand design by Joos Matsys, the brother of Quentin (see p.58). It didn't work out – the foundations proved too weak – and finally, another hundred years on, the unfinished second-attempt towers were capped, creating the truncated versions that rise above the entrance today. Inside, the church is distinguished by its soaring nave whose enormous pillars frame a splendid **rood screen**. The nave's Baroque **pulpit** is also striking – a weighty wooden confection which shows St Norbert being thrown off his horse by lightning.

The **ambulatory** houses the **Museum voor Religieuze Kunst** (Museum of Religious Art; same times as church; F50), whose three key paintings comprise a copy of Rogier van der Weyden's triptych, *Descent from the Cross*, and two of the few surviving paintings by Weyden's apprentice, Dieric Bouts (c.1415–75), who worked for most of his life in Leuven.

South of the Grote Markt is the boisterous core of Leuven's student scene, the **Oude Markt**, a large cobblestone rectangle surrounded by cafés and bars in good-looking gabled houses; it's also the site of a bustling Friday

LEUVEN

market. To the immediate east of Oude Markt, Naamsestraat leads south past the imperious Baroque facade of the Jesuit **St Michielskerk**, restored after wartime damage, towards the **Groot Begijnhof**, a sixteenth-century enclave of mellow red brick houses tucked away beside the River Dijle. Once home to around three hundred *begijns* – women living as nuns but without taking vows – the Begijnhof was bought by the university in 1962 since when it has been painstakingly restored as student residences.

Eating and drinking

Ascoli, Muntstraat 17.
Tasty French-Italian food at reasonable prices – everything from pasta through to regional delicacies. Just south of the Grote Markt. Closed Wed.

De Oesterbar, Muntstraat 23.
Easily the best seafood restaurant in town with oysters the house speciality. Closed Sun & Mon.

Heaven's Door, Oude Markt 16.
Fashionable students' bar – one of several on this attractive square. Other trendy, popular places include *Eclips*, at no. 50, and *Gecko's*, at no. 2.

Lukemieke, Vlamingenstraat 55.
Inexpensive, home-made, vegetarian cooking. Excellent daily specials. A few minutes' stroll south of the centre, off Naamsestraat. Mon–Fri noon–2pm & 6–8.30pm.

Universum, Herbert Hooverplein.
A big and busy barn-like place stuffed with students and townies who shovel down platefuls of spaghetti and omelettes. A short walk southeast of the Grote Markt on the corner of Tiensestraat. Mon–Fri 11am–11pm.

LEUVEN

ANTWERP

Map 1, F7.

Belgium's second city, **Antwerp**, fans out from the east bank of the Scheldt about 50km north of Brussels. It's not an especially handsome city – the terrain is too flat and industry too prevalent for that – but it does possess a vibrant and intriguing centre sprinkled with some lovely old churches and distinguished museums, reminders of its auspicious past as centre of a wide trading empire. In particular, there is the enormous legacy of **Rubens**, whose works adorn Antwerp's galleries and churches. The French laid the foundations of the city's present economic success during the Napoleonic occupation and Antwerp is now one of Europe's premier ports. It has also become the focus of the international diamond industry and, in the last few years, of the more nationalistic amongst the Flemish, who regard the city as their capital in preference to Brussels. It also lays claim to the title of fashion capital of Belgium with many a young talent designing here.

Arrival and information

Most trains stop at **Centraal Station**, on the edge of the city centre about 2km east of the main square – the Grote Markt – and connected with the centre by **tram** (#2 or #15 to Groenplaats) from the adjacent Diamant underground station. The city transport information office in the Diamant underground station (Mon–Fri 8am–12.30pm & 1.30–4pm) sells tickets and maps (F60) of the transport system. A standard single fare costs F40, a ten-strip *Rittenkaart* F290, a 24-hour unlimited travel tourist card F110. Tickets (but not the *Rittenkaart*) are also available from bus and tram drivers.

Antwerp's **tourist office** is at Grote Markt 15 (Mon–Sat 9am–6pm, Sun 9am–5pm; ©03/232 01 03); they have a comprehensive range of information on the city and its sights, including maps and a number of specialist leaflets – principally a walking tour detailing where to see the works of Rubens and his contemporary, Jacob Jordaens. They will also make **hotel reservations** on your behalf at no charge: the modest deposit you pay is subtracted from your final hotel bill.

The City

The centre of Antwerp is **Grote Markt**, at the heart of which stands the **Brabo Fountain**, a haphazard pile of rocks surmounted by a bronze of Silvius Brabo, depicted flinging the hand of the giant Antigonus – who terrorized passing ships – into the Scheldt. The north side of Grote Markt is lined with daintily restored sixteenth-century **guildhouses**, though they are overshadowed by the **Stadhuis** (tours Mon, Tues, Thurs & Fri 11am, 2pm & 3pm, Sat 2pm & 3pm; F30), completed in 1566, and one of the most important buildings of the Northern Renaissance. Among rooms you can visit are the Leys Room, named after Baron Hendrik Leys, who painted the frescoes in the 1860s, and the Wedding Room, which has a chimneypiece decorated with two caryatids carved by Cornelius Floris, architect of the building.

Southeast of Grote Markt, the **Onze Lieve Vrouwe Cathedral** (Mon–Fri 10am–5pm, Sat 10am–3pm, Sun 1–4pm; F70) is one of the finest Gothic churches in Belgium, mostly the work of Jan and Pieter Appelmans in the middle of the fifteenth century. Inside, the seven-aisled nave is breathtaking, if only because of its sense of space, an impression that's reinforced by the bright, light stonework revealed by a recent refurbishment. Four early paintings by **Rubens** are displayed here, the most beautiful of which is the *Descent from the Cross*, a triptych painted after the artist's return from Italy that displays an uncharacteristically restrained realism, derived from Caravaggio.

It takes about five minutes to walk southwest from the cathedral to the **Plantin-Moretus Museum**, on Vrijdagmarkt (Tues–Sun 10am–4.45pm; F100), which occupies the grand old mansion of Rubens' father-in-law, the printer Christopher Plantin. One of Antwerp's most interesting museums, it provides a marvellous insight into how Plantin and his family conducted their business.

From here it's a brief stroll to another, the riverfront **National Maritime Museum** (Tues–Sun 10am–4.45pm; F100), which is located at the end of Suikerrui and inhabits the **Steen**, the remaining gatehouse of what was once an impressive medieval fortress. Inside, the cramped rooms feature exhibits on inland navigation, shipbuilding and waterfront life, while the open-air section has a long line of tugs and barges under a rickety corrugated roof. Crossing Jordaenskaai, it's a short walk east to the impressively gabled **Vleeshuis** (Tues–Sun 10am–4.45pm; F100), built for the guild of butchers in 1503 and now used to display a substantial but incoherent collection of applied arts – everything from antique musical instruments to medieval woodcarvings.

Just north of here, along Vleeshouwersstraat, **St Pauluskerk** (May–Sept daily 2–5pm; free) is a dignified late Gothic church built for the Dominicans in the early sixteenth century. Inside, the airy and elegant nave is decorated by a series of paintings depicting the "Fifteen Mysteries of the Rosary", including Rubens' exquisite *Scourging at the Pillar* of 1617.

East of the centre

It's a ten-minute walk east from the cathedral to the **Rubenshuis** at Wapper 9 (Tues–Sun 10am–4.45pm; F100),

ANTWERP

the former home and studio of the artist, now restored as a museum. Unfortunately, there are only one or two of his less distinguished paintings here, but the restoration of the rooms is convincing. Rubens died in 1640 and was buried in **St Jacobskerk**, north of here at Lange Nieuwstraat 73 (April–Oct Mon–Sat 2–5pm; Nov–March Mon–Sat 9am–noon; F50). Rubens and his immediate family are buried in the chapel behind the high altar, where in one of his last works, *Our Lady Surrounded by Saints*, he painted himself as St George, his two wives as Martha and Mary, and his father as St Jerome.

Further east still, the discreetly shabby streets just to the southwest of Centraal Station are home to the biggest **diamond** market in the world. The trade is largely controlled by Orthodox Jews, whose presence is often the only outward indication that the business exists at all, though there are a handful of gold and diamond shops at the top of Pelikaanstraat and the **Provinciaal Diamantmuseum**, at Lange Herentalsestraat 31 (daily 10am–5pm; free) has diamond cutting demonstrations every Saturday afternoon (1.30–4.30pm).

South of the centre

About ten minutes' walk southeast of Groenplaats, the **Mayer van den Bergh Museum**, at Lange Gasthuisstraat 19 (Tues–Sun 10am–4.45pm; F100), contains delightful examples of the applied arts, from tapestries to ceramics, silverware, illuminated manuscripts and furniture, in a crowded reconstruction of a sixteenth-century town house. There are also some excellent paintings, including works by Quentin Matsys and Jan Mostaert, but the museum's most celebrated work is Bruegel's *Dulle Griet* or "Mad Meg", a misogynistic allegory in which a woman, loaded down with possessions, stalks the gates of Hell.

Further south still (tram #8 from Groenplaats), the **Museum voor Schone Kunsten** (Fine Art Museum; Tues–Sun 10am–5pm; F150) has one of the country's finest art collections. Its early Flemish section features paintings by Jan van Eyck, Memling, Rogier van der Weyden and Quentin Matsys. Rubens has two large rooms to himself, in which one very large canvas stands out: the *Adoration of the Magi*, a beautifully human work apparently completed in a fortnight. The museum also displays a comprehensive collection of modern Belgian art with Paul Delvaux and James Ensor being particularly well represented.

Accommodation

Prinse, Keizerstraat 63 (©03/226 40 50, fax 225 11 48).
Smart if slightly characterless hotel in a rambling old house with its own courtyard. Good, quiet central location – only 5min walk north of the Rubenshuis. ⑦.

Rubens, Oude Beurs 29 (©03/222 48 48, fax 225 19 40).
Probably the best hotel in town, the *Rubens* is a lovely little hotel with tastefully furnished, modern rooms just a couple of minutes' walk north of the Grote Markt. ⑦.

Scoutel Jeugdverblifcentrum, Stoomstraat 3 (©03/226 46 06, fax 232 63 92).
Spick and span hostel-cum-hotel offering frugal but perfectly adequate doubles and triples with breakfast. It's situated about 5min walk from Centraal Station. There's no curfew (guests have their own keys), but be sure to check in before 6pm when reception closes. Reservations are advised. F2000 for under-25s, F2500 for over-25s.

Tourist Hotel, Pelikaanstraat 20 (©03/232 58 70, fax 231 67 07).
An inexpensive, if rather uninspiring, modern option near Centraal Station – OK for a night or two, though Pelikaanstraat can be noisy. ④.

ANTWERP

Eating

Hippodroom, Léopold de Waelplaats 10 (☏03/238 89 36).
Smooth and polished restaurant offering a wide range of Flemish
   dishes from around F700 per main course. Closed Sun.

Metalurgie, Grote Pieter Potstraat 1 (☏03/232 54 10).
Popular café-restaurant with good Flemish food, great mussels and
   a lively crowd. The decor has post-modernist touches in line with
   the menus, which are served on pieces of steel.

Pizzeria Da Toni, Grote Markt 6.
Tasty and swiftly served pasta and pizza.

De Stoemppot, Vlasmarkt 12 (☏03/231 36 86).
Stoemp is a traditional Flemish dish consisting of puréed meat and
   vegetables – and this is the best place to eat it. Closed Wed.

Drinking

Babblebox, Grote Pieter Potstraat 18.
Handily situated off Suikerrui, this small and darkly lit bar is an
   enjoyable place for a drink. One of several fashionable bars on
   this street.

Café de Muze, Melkmarkt 15.
With its bare brick walls and retro film posters, this laid-back and
   central little place is a popular spot. Occasional live music –
   mainly jazz and blues.

Het Elfde Gebod, Torfbrug 10.
On one of the tiny squares fronting the north side of the cathedral,
   this bar is something of a tourist trap, but it's still worth visiting for
   the kitsch religious statues which cram the interior; avoid the food.

De Vagant, Reyndersstraat 21.
Specialist gin bar serving an extravagant range of Belgian and
   Dutch jenevers in spruce, modern surroundings.

De Volle Maan, Oude Koornmarkt 7.
Lively, likeable and offbeat bar close to the Grote Markt. Very busy.

GHENT

Just 56km from Brussels, the Flemish city of **Ghent** has a long and illustrious history. It was the seat of the counts of Flanders and the largest town in western Europe during the thirteenth and fourteenth centuries, its prosperity built upon the cloth trade. It's now Belgium's third largest city, a thriving, busy sort of place with an amiable atmosphere and an outstanding assortment of medieval buildings, the pick of which is St Baafskathedraal, home to a remarkable painting, *Adoration of the Mystic Lamb* by Jan van Eyck. Ghent is less immediately picturesque than Bruges, but this is much to its advantage in so far as it's never overrun by tourists.

Ghent is shown in detail on colour map 8.

Arrival and information

Trains from Brussels pull in at **Ghent St Pieters station**, some 2km south of the city centre; **trams** #1, #10, #11 and #12 run to the central square, Korenmarkt. A couple of minutes' walk east of the Korenmarkt, the **tourist office** (Map 8, E4) is located in the old Cloth Hall, the Lakenhalle, on the Botermarkt (daily: April–Oct 9.30am–6.30pm; Nov–March 9.30am–12.30pm & 1.15–4.30pm; ℗09/226 52 32). They provide a comprehensive range of information, including a full list of **accommodation**, which they will book on your behalf for a refundable deposit. The best way to see the sights is on foot, but Ghent is a large city and you may find you have to use a **tram** or **bus** at some point. Standard single fares cost F40 and tickets can be bought direct from the driver.

GHENT

The City

The best place to start an exploration of Ghent's city centre is the mainly Gothic **St Baafskathedraal**, squeezed into the eastern corner of St Baafsplein (Map 8, F5; Mon–Sat 8.30am–6pm, Sun 1–6pm; free). St Baaf's mighty nave, begun in the fifteenth century, is supported by tall, slender columns that give the whole interior a cheerful sense of lightness, though the seventeenth-century marble screens spoil the effect by darkening the choir. In a small side **chapel** (April–Oct Mon–Sat 9.30am–noon & 2–6pm, Sun 1–6pm; Nov–March Mon–Sat 10.30am–noon & 2.30–4pm, Sun 2–5pm; F60) to the left of the entrance is Ghent's greatest treasure, Jan van Eyck's *Adoration of the Mystic Lamb*. The altarpiece's cover screens display a beautiful Annunciation scene with the archangel Gabriel's wings reaching up to the timbered ceiling of a Flemish house, while below the donor and his wife kneel piously alongside statues of the saints. Yet the restrained exterior painting is merely a foretaste of what's within – a striking, visionary work of art that was revealed only when the shutters were opened on Sundays and feast days. On the upper level sit God the Father, the Virgin and John the Baptist in gleaming clarity; to the right are musician-angels and a nude, pregnant Eve; and on the left is Adam plus a group of singing angels who strain to read their music. In the lower panel the Lamb, the symbol of Christ's sacrifice, is approached by bishops, saintly virgins and Old and New Testament figures in a heavenly paradise seen as a sort of idealized Low Countries. It's a fabulous painting, after which the rest of the cathedral is a something of an anticlimax, though you could drop by the **crypt** (same hours and ticket), which preserves features of the earlier Romanesque church. Full of religious bric-à-brac, the crypt displays several fine reliquaries and a superb medieval triptych, Justus van Gent's *Crucifixion of Christ*.

Just west of St Baaf's, the fifteenth-century **Lakenhalle** (Cloth Hall) is little more than an empty shell, whose first-floor entrance leads to the adjoining **Belfry** (tours daily; F100), a much-amended edifice from the fourteenth century. A glass-sided lift climbs up to the roof for excellent views over the centre. The facade niches of the **Stadhuis** across the street (Map 8, F4; tours May–Oct Mon–Thurs 2–4pm; F100) were intended to hold a statue, but the money didn't last; the present carvings, representing the powerful and famous in characteristic poses – including the architect Rombout Keldermans rubbing his chin and studying his plans for the building – were inserted only at the end of the last century. The interior is hardly riveting, but the tour does include a visit to the handsome Pacificatiezaal hall. The last of this central cluster of buildings is **St Niklaaskerk** (Map 8, E4; daily 10am–5pm; free), an architectural hybrid dating from the thirteenth century; inside, the giant-sized Baroque high altar is no mean piece, with its mammoth representation of *God the Father* glowering down its back surrounded by a flock of cherubic angels.

Dodging the trams of the Korenmarkt and heading west, you pass the main post office building, close to which the **St Michielsbrug** bridge (Map 8, D4) offers fine views of the towers and turrets that pierce the skyline. The bridge also overlooks the city's oldest harbour, the **Tussen Bruggen** (Between the Bridges), from whose quays **boats** leave for trips around the neighbouring canals from April to early November (every 15 minutes; daily; 10am–7pm; F160). The **Korenlei**, the western side of the harbour, is home to a series of solid, high-gabled merchants' houses dating from the eighteenth century, while the **Graslei**, opposite, accommodates the charming, late medieval guild-houses of the town's boatmen and grainweighers.

A couple of minutes' walk north of Graslei, **Het Gravensteen** (Map 8, D2; daily: April–Sept 9am–6pm;

GHENT

Oct–March 9am–5pm; F200), the Castle of the Counts of Flanders, looks sinister enough to have been lifted from a Bosch painting. Cold and cruel, its dark walls and unyielding turrets were first raised in 1180 as much to intimidate the town's unruly citizens as to protect them. Beside the main courtyard stand the castle's two main buildings, the **keep** on the right and to the left the **count's residence**, riddled with narrow, interconnected staircases set within the thickness of the walls. A self-guided tour takes you through the labyrinth.

East of the castle are the part-gentrified, medieval cobbled lanes and alleys of the **Patershol** (Map 8, E2), home to the most fashionable of the city's restaurants and the **Museum voor Volkskunde**, Kraanlei 65 (Tues–Sun: April–Oct 9am–12.30pm & 1.30–5.30pm; Nov–March 10am–noon & 1.30–5pm; F80), a series of restored almshouses where a chain of period rooms depicts local life and work in the eighteenth and nineteenth centuries.

South of the city centre, Ghent's main shopping street, **Veldstraat**, heads off towards the **Museum voor Schone Kunsten**, Nicolaas de Liemaeckereplein 3 (Tues–Sun 9.30am–5pm; F100), which holds the city's most extensive fine art collection. On display is a first-rate sample of Flemish painting including works by Bosch, Pieter Bruegel the Younger, Jordaens, van Dyck and Frans Hals.

Accommodation

Erasmus, Poel 25 (Map 8, C4; ℡09/224 21 95, fax 233 42 41). Ghent's most distinctive hotel, located in an old and commodious town house a few yards away from the Korenlei. A small, family-run hotel, where the breakfast is excellent. ④.

Gravensteen, Jan Breydelstraat 35 (Map 8, D3; ℡09/225 11 50, fax 225 18 50).
A small hotel in an attractively restored nineteenth-century mansion.

Some of the rooms are small, but they're snug enough and several overlook the castle. ④.

Youth Hostel, *Jeugdherberg De Draecke,* St Widostraat 11 (Map 8, D2; ✆09/233 70 50, fax 233 80 01).
Excellent, well-equipped and smart youth hostel in the city centre, 5min north of the Korenmarkt. Breakfast is included. F400 per person.

Eating

Patisserie Bloch, Veldstraat 60, on the corner with Volderstraat (Map 8, E5).
One of the best and busiest tearooms in town. Cakes, coffee and snacks 10am–5pm. Closed Sun.

Malatesta, Hooiaard 2 (Map 8, D3).
Fashionable and inexpensive café-restaurant offering tasty pizza and pasta dishes. Mon–Fri 11am–11pm.

't Marmietje, Drabstraat 30 (Map 8, D3).
Intimate restaurant on a side street off the Korenmarkt. Excellent traditional Flemish cuisine at reasonable prices. Closed Sun & Mon.

Pascalino, Botermarkt 11 (Map 8, F4).
Straightforward, inexpensive café offering snacks and filling meals of sound quality until 9.30pm every night. Handy location, opposite the Stadhuis.

Drinking

't Dreupelkot, Groentenmarkt 10 (Map 8, E3).
Cosy bar specializing in jenever, of which it stocks over 100 brands, all kept at icy temperatures.

De Tap en de Tepel, Gewad 7 (Map 8, D2).
Dark bar with an open fire and a clutter of antique furnishings. Wine is the main deal, served with a wide selection of cheeses. Closed Sun–Tues & most of Aug.

GHENT

Het Waterhuis aan de Bierkant, Groentenmarkt 9 (Map 8, E3).
Over 100 types of beer in a pleasant bar near the castle. An
informative beer menu makes choosing easy.

BRUGES

Bruges is one of the most beautifully preserved medieval
cities in western Europe and it draws visitors in their thousands. Inevitably, the crowds tend to overwhelm the town's
charms, but as a day-trip destination from Brussels – it's just
an hour away by train – Bruges is hard to resist: its museums hold some of the country's finest collections of Flemish
art and its intimate streets, woven around a pattern of narrow canals, live up to even the most inflated tourist hype.

Bruges is shown in detail on map 7.

Bruges came to prominence in the thirteenth century
when it shared effective control of the **cloth trade** with its
great rival, Ghent, turning high-quality English wool into
clothing that was exported all over the known world. It was
an immensely profitable business, and it made the city a
centre of international trade. By the end of the fifteenth
century, however, Bruges was in decline, principally
because the Zwin River – the city's vital link to the North
Sea – was silting up. By the 1530s, the town's sea trade had
collapsed completely, and Bruges simply withered away.
Frozen in time, Bruges escaped damage in both World Wars
to emerge the perfect tourist attraction.

Arrival and information

Bruges **train station** adjoins the **bus station** about 2km
southwest of the town centre. Beside the station, there's an
information and hotel booking office (Mon–Sat

10.30am–6pm; no phone), which will make reservations for a deposit which is deducted from your final hotel bill.

If the twenty-minute walk into town doesn't appeal, most of the **local buses** that leave from outside the train station head off either to the Biekorf or the neighbouring Markt, bang in the centre; the single fare costs F40. Just footsteps away from the Markt, at Burg 11 (Map 7, E5), the **tourist office** (April–Sept Mon–Fri 9.30am–6.30pm, Sat & Sun 10am–noon & 2–6.30pm; Oct–March Mon–Fri 9.30am–5pm, Sat & Sun 9.30am–1pm & 2–5.30pm; ©050/44 86 86, fax 44 86 00), provides an accommodation booking service and free maps and bus timetables.

Half-hour boat trips around the central canals leave every few minutes from a number of jetties south of the Burg; March–Nov daily 10am–6pm; F170. For the rest of the year there's a sporadic service on the weekend only.

The City

The older sections of Bruges fan out from two central squares, Markt and Burg. **Markt** (Map 7, D5), edged on three sides by nineteenth-century gabled buildings, is the larger of the two, an impressive open space, on the south side of which rises the octagonal **Belfry** (Map 7, C5; daily: April–Sept 9.30am–5pm; Oct–March 9.30am–12.30pm & 1.30–5pm; F100) was built in the thirteenth century when the town was at its richest. Inside, the staircase passes the room where the town charters were locked for safekeeping, and an eighteenth-century carillon, before emerging onto the roof. At the foot of the belfry, the quadrangular **Hallen** is a much-restored edifice dating from the thirteenth century, its arcaded galleries built to facilitate the cloth trade.

BRUGES

The Burg

Map 7, E5.

From the Markt, Breidelstraat leads through to the **Burg**, whose southern half is fringed by the city's finest group of buildings. One of the best of these is the **Heilig Bloed Basiliek** (Basilica of the Holy Blood; daily: April–Sept 9.30am–noon & 2–6pm; Oct–March Mon–Tues & Thurs–Sun 10am–noon & 2–4pm, Wed 10am–noon; free) on the right, named after the holy relic that found its way here in 1150. The basilica divides into two parts. Tucked away in the corner, the **lower chapel** is a shadowy, crypt-like affair, originally built at the beginning of the twelfth century to shelter another relic, that of St Basil, one of the great figures of the early Greek Church. Next door, approached up a wide staircase, the **upper chapel** was built at the same time but it's impossible to make out the original structure behind the excessive nineteenth-century decoration. The building may be disappointing, but the rock crystal phial that contains the Holy Blood is stored within a magnificent silver **tabernacle**, the gift of Albert and Isabella of Spain in 1611. One of the holiest relics in medieval Europe, the phial purports to contain a few drops of blood and water washed from the body of Christ by Joseph of Arimathea. The Holy Blood is still venerated in the upper chapel on Fridays at 6pm, and reverence for it remains strong, not least on Ascension Day when it is carried through the town in a colourful but solemn procession.

To the left of the basilica, the **Stadhuis** has a beautiful, turreted sandstone facade from 1376, though its statues of the counts and countesses of Flanders are much more recent. Inside, the magnificent Gothic Hall (daily: April–Sept 9.30am–5pm; Oct–March 9.30am–12.30pm & 2–5pm; F100) boasts fancy vault-keys depicting New Testament scenes and romantic paintings commissioned in 1895 to illustrate the history of the town.

<hr>

A combination ticket for Bruges' central museums,
the Groeninge, Arentshuis, Gruuthuse and Memling, is
available from any of the four and costs F400.

<hr>

The Groeninge Museum

Map 7, E7.

Heading south from the Burg, through the archway next to
the Stadhuis, Blinde Ezelstraat ("Blind Donkey Street")
leads south across the canal to the huddle of picturesque
houses crimping the **Huidenvettersplein**, the old tanners'
quarter that now holds some of the busiest drinking and
eating places in town. Nearby, the Dijver follows the canal
to the **Groeninge Museum**, Dijver 12 (April–Sept daily
9.30am–5pm, Oct–March Wed–Mon 9.30am–12.30pm &
2–5pm; F200), which boasts an outstanding collection of
early Flemish paintings. Among them are several works by
Jan van Eyck, who lived and worked in Bruges from 1430
until his death eleven years later. Featured also are works by
Rogier van der Weyden, Hans Memling, Gerard David and
Hieronymus Bosch, whose paintings are crammed with
mysterious beasts, microscopic mutants and scenes of awful
cruelty. The museum's selection of late sixteenth- and seventeenth-century paintings is far more modest, though
highlights here include canvases by Pieter Brueghel the
Younger and Pieter Pourbus. The modern paintings are distinguished by the spooky surrealism of Paul Delvaux and by
Constant Permeke, noted for his dark and earthy representations of Belgian peasant life.

The rest of the city centre

Also on the Dijver, in a big old mansion just west of the
Groeninge Museum, is the **Arentshuis Museum** (Map 7,
D7; same hours as the Groeninge), which contains two sep-

BRUGES

arate collections. The ground-floor **Kant Museum** displays an excellent sample of Belgian lace and upstairs is the **Brangwyn Museum**, which exhibits the moody naturalistic paintings of the artist Sir Frank Brangwyn, who was born in Bruges of Welsh parents in 1867.

The **Gruuthuse Museum** (Map 7, D7; same hours as the Groeninge) at Dijver 17, is sited in a rambling fifteenth-century mansion and holds a varied collection of fine and applied art, including intricately carved altarpieces, musical instruments, magnificent tapestries and many different types of furniture. Beyond the Gruuthuse rises the **Onze Lieve Vrouwekerk** (Map 7, C8; April–Sept Mon–Fri 10–11.30am & 2.30–5pm, Sat 10–11.30am & 2.30–4pm, Sun 2.30–5pm; Oct–March Mon–Sat 10–11.30am & 2.30–4.30pm, Sun 2.30–4.30pm; free), a massive shambles of a church among whose treasures are a delicate marble *Madonna and Child* by Michelangelo and the striking Renaissance mausoleums (F60) of Charles the Bold and his daughter Mary of Burgundy.

Opposite the church, the **St Jans Hospitaal** complex contains a well-preserved fifteenth-century dispensary and the small **Memling Museum** (Map 7, C8; April–Sept daily 9.30am–5pm; Oct–March Thurs–Tues 9.30am–12.30pm & 2–5pm; F100), which contains six exquisite works by Hans Memling, a German-born, fifteenth-century artist who spent most of his working life in Bruges. From here, it's a short walk northwest to the **Sint Salvators-kathedraal** (Map 7, B7; daily Mon 2–5.45pm, Tues–Fri 8.30–11.45am & 2–5.45pm, Sat 8.30–11.45am & 2–5pm & Sun 9am–noon & 3–5pm; free), a replacement for the cathedral destroyed by the French in the eighteenth century. Emerging from a long-term restoration, the soaring columns and arches are quite splendid, but it's the wonderful, flowing tapestries hanging in the choir which really catch the eye.

Accommodation

Adornes, St Annarei 26 (Map 7, G3; ☏050/34 13 36, fax 34 20 85).
Tastefully converted old Flemish town house with antique charm.
Great location, too, at the junction of two canals near the east
end of Spiegelrei. ④.

Egmond, Minnewater 15 (☏050/34 14 45, fax 34 29 40).
Rambling old house on the southern edge of the city centre. Attractive
rooms in a quiet location at surprisingly affordable prices. ④.

Passage Budget Hotel, Dweerstraat 28 (Map 7, A7; ☏050/34 02
32, fax 34 01 40).
Simple but well-maintained rooms a ten-minute stroll west of the Markt.
Next door to and run by the same owner as the *Passage Hostel*. ①.

Passage Hostel Dweerstraat 26 (Map 7, A3; same phone & fax as
Passage Budget Hotel).
The most agreeable hostel in Bruges, which accommodates 50 people
in 10 comparatively comfortable dormitories at F480 per person.

Walburg, Boomgaardstraat 13 (Map 7, F4; ☏050/34 94 14, fax 33
68 84).
Charming, family-run, four-star hotel with thirteen spacious if slightly
spartan rooms. In a quiet location two minutes' east of the Burg. ⑥.

Eating

Den Dyver, Dijver 5 (Map 7, E7; ☏050/33 60 69).
First-rate restaurant specializing in traditional Flemish dishes
cooked in beer – the quail and rabbit are magnificent. Expensive;
reservations advised. Closed Wed, also Tues in winter.

Erasmus, Wollestraat 35 (Map 7, D6).
Straightforward, brightly lit café with reasonably priced, mostly Flemish
dishes plus a wide range of Belgian brews. A couple of hundred
metres south of the Markt. Closed Mon except July & Aug.

BRUGES

CHAPTER ONE

Het Dagelijks Brood, Philipstockstraat 21 (Map 7, E5).

Excellent bread shop which doubles as a wholefood café with one,
long wooden table. Mouth-watering home-made soup and bread
makes a meal in itself. Central location, just footsteps away from
the Burg. Open 7am to 6pm; closed Tues.

Taverne Curiosa, Vlamingstraat 22 (Map 7, D5).

Lively bar-restaurant in an old vaulted cellar a couple of minutes'
walk north of the Markt. Specialities are grilled meats, smoked
fish and regional dishes, with a wide-ranging beer menu to wash
it down. Closed Mon and one week in July.

Drinking

't Brugs Beertje, Kemelstraat 5 (Map 7, B6).

Small and friendly speciality beer bar that claims a stock of two
hundred ales. Five minutes' walk southwest of the Markt, off
Steenstraat. Closed Wed.

't Dreupelhuisje, Kemelstraat 9 (Map 7, B6).

Tiny bar specializing in jenevers and advocaats, of which it has an
excellent range. Closed Tues.

De Garre, De Garre 1 (Map 7, D5).

Down an alley off Breidelstraat between the Markt and the Burg, this
cramped but cosy café-bar has a good range of Belgian beers
and tasty snacks. Closed Wed.

Oude Vlissinghe, Blekerstraat 2 (Map 7, F2).

With its wood panelling, old paintings and long wooden tables, this
is one of the oldest and most distinctive bars in Bruges. A couple
of minutes' walk from Jan van Eyckplein: follow Spinolarei and it's
a turning on the right.

LISTINGS

Accommodation

As a general rule most tourists head for the hotels in the narrow lanes around the **Grand-Place**, an attractive, though at times expensive, option which puts you at the centre of the action. If you want something a little quieter and cheaper, **Ste Catherine**, a ten-minute walk west of the Grand-Place in the Lower Town, is the place to make for. Here you'll find a good selection of low- to mid-range hotels and you're not too far away from trendy place St Géry, recently developed into one of the capital's hippest night-spots.

Another cluster of hotels can be found just beyond the southern edge of the centre in one of the older and more

Accommodation price codes

All the **hotels** detailed in this chapter have been graded according to the following price categories. All the codes are based on the rate for the least expensive double room during high season.

① F1500–2000   ③ F2500–3000   ⑤ F4000–5000
② F2000–2500   ④ F3000–4000   ⑥ F5000–6000
⑦ F6000 and over

prosperous residential areas around **avenue Louise**. Although on the outskirts of the city, access to the centre is fairly easy by métro, and in any case you can walk from here to the Grand-Place in less than twenty minutes. A number of budget hotels can also be found near **Métro Madou** and in the Middle Eastern-cum-African quarter around the nearby **place St Josse**. Despite being branded something of a "no-go" area at night-time, it's not as bad as people make out, and some of the hotels, though a bit frayed at the edges, are housed in elegant and old buildings.

Although Brussels has no shortage of places to stay, finding **accommodation** can still prove difficult, particularly in the spring and autumn when the capital enjoys its high seasons. However, as many of the capital's hotels cater for a European business clientele, **the low season** is generally considered to be July and August. This is mainly because the institutions of the European Union close down for the summer – and when the EU goes on holiday, so do the Eurocrats. The upshot is, in stark contrast to many other European cities, prices in some of the capital's larger hotels actually go down during the summer. Another bonus is that substantial **discounts** are offered **on weekends**, again when the suits have gone home (see *Hôtel Métropole* and the *Conrad International*).

Unless you fancy trudging halfway across the city only to find there's no room at the inn, book in advance, at least for the first night – but preferably for the first couple. **Hotel reservations** can be made from outside Belgium through the **tourist office** (℃02/513 89 40). If you do find yourself in the unfortunate position of being bedless, go to the tourist office on the Grand-Place; they can give you a list of hotels and make bookings on the spot. Alternatively, contact one of the **Bed and Breakfast agencies** (see p.159), or go to the Acotra Office, rue du Marché-aux-Herbes 110 (Mon–Fri 8.30am–6pm; ℃512 86 07), where you can book rooms in **youth hostels** for free.

ACCOMMODATION

Our listings are divided into the following areas:
the Grand-Place and around (p.149); the Lower Town
(see p.152); the Upper Town (see p.155); Ixelles and
Avenue Louise (see p.157); St Gilles (see p.158).

HOTELS

Prices in the capital's hotels vary hugely, although the golden rule is they are always negotiable, so don't be afraid to have a good haggle, and remember that many hotels offer group reductions. In most places **breakfast** is included in the price of the room, but this is not always the case so it's a good idea to check. Generally speaking, standards in Belgian hotels are fairly high and you can usually be sure that a wide range of facilities and services – bar, restaurant, TV, air conditioning – is available. Sadly **wheelchair** and **disabled access** is not always guaranteed so check beforehand. The imaginatively titled brochure *Hôtels*, available free from the Belgian tourist office, usually up-to-date, tells you exactly what's on offer, and ranks the capital's hotels according to a five-star system devised by the tourist office.

THE GRAND-PLACE AND AROUND

Amigo
Map 4, C4. Rue de l'Amigo 1–3 ©547 47 47; fax 513 52 77. Ⓜ Bourse. Just around the corner from the Grand-Place and in the middle of the old centre, this delightful hotel occupies an attractive 1950s building designed in the style of an eighteenth-century mansion and is decked out with assorted antiques, tapestries, and Flemish paintings. A charming and convivial place but, with the cheapest double costing F7750 per night, so it should be. ⑦

Aris

Map 4, D3. Rue du Marché-aux-Herbes 78–80 ©514 43 00; fax 514 01 19. Ⓜ Bourse.

Aesthetically not the most pleasing of buildings, despite the nineteenth-century stone facade – but the 55 modern rooms are clean and functional and you're only 50m from the Grand-Place. Though fairly expensive midweek, the prices come down as far as F3500 per double on a weekend. Facilities include TV, air conditioning and wheelchair access. ⑤

Auberge Saint-Michel

Map 4, D4. Grand-Place 15 ©511 09 56; fax 511 46 00. Ⓜ Gare Centrale.

The only place to look out over the Grand-Place, this impressive hotel occupies the duke of Brabant's old mansion and is the ideal location for exploring the centre. The rooms range from the small and basic at the back of the building (F3850) to the more elegant period rooms at the front (F5100), though for these it's probably wise to make an advanced booking. Think twice if you're a light sleeper – poor noise insulation and Grand-Place revellers may make you a grouch in the morning. ④

Le Dix-Septième

Map 4, F6. Rue de la Madeleine 25 ©502 57 44; fax 502 64 24. Ⓜ Gare Centrale.

Arguably the most charming hotel in Brussels, located in a tastefully renovated seventeenth-century mansion a 2min walk from the Grand-Place. Parquet flooring, crystal chandeliers, and pastel-painted woodwork add to the flavour. Doubles cost F6600, but the price drops to F5600 at weekends. ⑦

La Légende

Map 4, B5. Rue du Lombard 35 ©512 82 90; fax 512 34 93. Ⓜ Bourse.

Simple, no-frills accommodation in an old building set around a courtyard in the heart of the city. Standard double rooms just have sinks; however, for an extra F1200 you'll get your own shower and a TV. Although there are forty rooms available, book in advance – the cheap prices and a central location make it popular with tourists on a low budget. ①

La Madeleine

Map 4, F3. Rue de la Montagne 22–24 ©512 29 71; fax 502 13 50.
Ⓜ Gare Centrale.

An unattractive, two-storey hotel with around fifty clean and modern rooms. It won't feature in your photo album, but it's very handily placed just down the hill from Gare Centrale and close to some good restaurants on rue des Bouchers. ④

Matignon

Map 3, D6. Rue de la Bourse 10–12 ©511 08 88; fax 513 69 27.
Ⓜ Bourse.

Reasonably priced and modern, this three-star hotel is in an old renovated building. Although a bit on the cramped side, it has 37 small but perfectly functional rooms, a bar and a fairly good restaurant. Only 100m from the Grand-Place. Wheelchair access. ④

Meridien

Map 4, F5. Carrefour de l'Europe 3 ©548 42 11; fax 548 40 80.
Ⓜ Gare Centrale.

This modern 224-room hotel attracts the suit-and-briefcase brigade who are no doubt impressed by the five-star status and convenient location next to Gare Centrale. Although it doesn't have as much character as some of the hotels in the capital, it's worth noting that on weekends, right throughout the year, there's a fifty percent reduction on all rooms, which means you can pick up a standard double for F6000. Still not cheap, but just about worth it. ⑦

Mozart

Map 4, D5. Rue du Marché-aux-Fromages 15a ℭ502 66 61;
fax 502 77 58. Ⓜ Gare Centrale.

Relatively cheap rooms and a friendly atmosphere make it
worthy of consideration, but if you want to get any sleep make
sure you avoid the rooms overlooking "Pitta street", where
hordes of restless locals noisily consume falafel until the early
hours. ⑤

Vieille Lanterne

Map 4, A6. Rue des Grands Carmes 29 ℭ512 74 94; fax 512 13 97.
Ⓜ Gare Centrale.

A small but friendly, family-oriented pension close to the
Manneken Pis and only a short stroll from the Grand-Place.
Each room has a shower and, at F2100 for a double, it's good
value for money. There are only six rooms, so make sure you
reserve well in advance. Breakfast not included. ②

THE LOWER TOWN

Arlequin

Map 4, A6. Rue de la Fourche 17–19 ℭ514 16 15; fax 514 16 15.
Ⓜ de Brouckère.

A straightforward and slightly unkempt, three-star hotel with
modest rooms. It's not the *Dorchester*, but it's at the centre of
the downtown action. The staff are friendly and reservations
are not always necessary. ④

Astrid

Map 3, D4. Pl du Samedi 11 ℭ219 31 19; fax 219 31 70.
Ⓜ Ste Catherine.

Built in 1994, the *Astrid* isn't as old and atmospheric as some of
the other hotels in Ste Catherine – but if you're looking for a nice,
clean, modern hotel, look no further. Each one of the 100 rooms
comes equipped with a bathroom, TV, and strangely enough an

individual safe. If that doesn't impress you, the prices might – at weekends and during the low season a standard double costs as little as F3000. Group reductions offered and wheelchair access. ⑤

Atlas

Map 3, C5. Rue du Vieux Marché-aux-Grains 30–34 ℂ502 60 06; fax 502 69 35. Ⓜ Bourse.

Comfortable, four-star hotel situated only a 10min walk from the Grand-Place in the gentrifying Ste Catherine district. The rooms are fully equipped – bathroom, TV, mini-bar – and there's a F600 discount at weekends. Full wheelchair access. ⑤

La Bourse

Map 3, C5. Rue Antoine Dansaert 11 ℂ512 60 10; fax 512 61 39. Ⓜ Bourse.

Though a tad frayed around the edges, this hotel is popular with young budget tourists and it's easy to see why – it's within spitting distance of the fashionable place St Géry and only a stroll from the Grand-Place. A standard double with shower, toilet, and TV costs F2200, breakfast included. There are only around thirty rooms. ②

Hôtel Éperonniers

Map 3, E7. Rue des Éperonniers 1 ℂ513 53 66; fax 511 32 30. Ⓜ Gare Centrale.

A basic, and at times chaotic, hotel a couple of minutes' walk east of the Grand-Place. Just over half the rooms are equipped with a shower and cost about F400 more than the others, but the communal washing facilities are hardly enticing. Handy enough, but probably best reserved for emergencies. ②

George V

Map 4, B5. Rue 't Kint 23 ℂ513 50 93; fax 513 44 93. Ⓜ Bourse.

This ramshackle period hotel is attractively situated only a 5min walk from the Bourse and is pretty cheap by Brussels'

HOTELS: LOWER TOWN

standards, especially on weekends when the price drops by ten percent. Breakfast is thrown in, but it's not much to write home about. ②

Métropole

Map 3, D4. Pl de Brouckère 31 ℂ217 23 00; fax 218 02 20. Ⓜ de Brouckère.

Arguably Brussels' finest hotel, the Métropole dates back to 1895 and boasts some of the most exquisite Empire and Art Nouveau decor to be found in the capital. Although some rooms are routinely if spaciously modern, it's worth staying here simply for the restaurant (excellent but pricey) and the bar which is breathtaking in its beauty. A double room usually costs F14,000, but in July and August the price is slashed to a bargain F7000. ⑦

New Hotel Siru

Map 3, F3. Pl Rogier 1 ℂ203 35 80. Ⓜ Rogier.

Housed in a nineteenth-century building, this 101-room hotel was given a facelift in the late 1980s, when a team of 130 Belgian artists – painter Roger Somerville and sculptors César Bailleux and Hanneke Beaumont included – were given carte blanche to decorate the corridors, paint the walls, and put works of art in every bedroom. It's worth staying here at least one night for the novelty value, although the compact rooms aren't cheap (F3200 for the cheapest double in the high season and F2900 in July & August), and the area, though safe, is hardly attractive or at the centre of the action. ④

Opéra

Map 3, D5. Rue Grétry 57 ℂ219 43 43; fax 219 17 20. Ⓜ de Brouckère.

This two-star hotel, close to place de Brouckère, is "downtown" in every respect – small, basic rooms, few facilities and drab decor. In terms of location the price takes some beating. Group reductions available. ②

Orion

Map 3, C4. Quai au Bois à Brûler 51 ©221 14 11; fax 221 15 99.
Ⓜ Ste Catherine.

A modern hotel slap-bang in the middle of Ste Catherine.
Although it's not a first choice, you can usually get one of the
170 rooms without a reservation. Good-value breakfasts are an
extra F260. Wheelchair access. ④

Vendôme

Map 3, E3. Bd Adolphe Max 98 ©227 03 00.
Ⓜ Rogier or de Brouckère.

This modern, 106-room hotel is aimed at a business clientele,
although it attracts a few tourists in the low season when the
prices drop. A standard, medium-sized double room, fully
equipped with TV, en-suite bathroom, and a mini-bar, usually
costs F4850; however, in July and August you'll pick one up
for F3000. Breakfast is not included and the breakfast buffet is
not worth the additional F650. Eat out. ③

THE UPPER TOWN

Alfa Sablon

Map 3, E8. Rue de la Paille 2–4 ©513 60 40; fax 511 81 41. Tram
#91, #92, #93, #94.

Pleasant enough modern hotel situated right next to the
atmospheric place du Grand Sablon, known principally for its
antiques and collector's market. Unlike other hotels in the
vicinity, this one is slightly cheaper with a standard double
costing F3600 in July and August. Wheelchair access and
rooms for the disabled. ⑥

Astoria

Map 3, F7. Rue Royale 103 ©217 62 90; fax 217 11 50.
Ⓜ Gare Centrale.

Winston Churchill once stayed at this grand 120-room hotel,

HOTELS: UPPER TOWN

which is handily placed near the Parc de Bruxelles and the Palais Royal. Beautifully decorated with original turn-of-the-century fixtures and fittings and home to an Orient Express-style "Pullman Bar", the *Astoria* has a real time-warp feel to it. However, time travel doesn't come cheap these days, so expect to pay an arm, leg and torso for the experience. ⑦

Du Congrès

Map 3, H5. Rue du Congrès 40 ©217 18 90; fax 217 18 97.
Ⓜ Madou.

Another turn-of-the-century hotel fallen on hard times but still popular with budget tourists.Close to the cathedral, it's in slightly better condition than its main rival the *Madou* (see below). The clean and fairly comfortable rooms with shower and toilet, and the substantial breakfast, make it good value for money, and although on the outskirts, you're still only a 15min walk from the town centre. ③

Jolly Hotel du Grand Sablon

Map 3, E8. Pl du Grand Sablon 2-4 ©512 88 00; fax 512 67 66.
Tram #91, #92, #93, #94.

Pretty expensive for what you get, but this plush, 200-room hotel does look over the lovely place du Grand Sablon with its terraced cafés and designer shops. The excellent restaurant and convivial bar rate as the other main attractions, but with the cheapest double costing over F9000 you'd expect a Jacuzzi. Reservations not always necessary. Wheelchair access. ⑨

Madou

Map 3, H5. Rue du Congrès 45 ©217 32 74; fax 218 83 75.
Ⓜ Madou.

Not particularly well-placed and verging on the down-at-heel, but this splendidly tatty hotel – a 5min walk from the cathedral – is a good choice if you're on a tight budget. The rooms are clean, you get your own shower and toilet, and the area – particularly around place Madou – is full of small African and Middle Eastern bars. Breakfast not included. ②

Sabina

Map 3, H5. Rue du Nord 78 ©218 26 37; fax 219 32 39. Ⓜ Madou. Spruce, pretty rooms, in a turn-of-the-century house with a beamed and panelled breakfast room. Prices are low for what you get. A short walk from Métro Madou, in a quiet residential area that was once a favourite haunt of the city's nineteenth-century bourgeoisie. It's wise to make a reservation – the place is often fully booked. ②

La Tasse d'Argent

Map 3, H5. Rue du Congrès 48 ©217 32 74; fax 218 83 75. Ⓜ Madou.

A pleasant, family-run hotel, popular with tourists and only a stone's throw away from Métro Madou. The building is pretty impressive and dates back to 1885, although recent renovation means you're not without modern conveniences. A double room – breakfast included – costs a very reasonable F2050. ②

IXELLES AND AVENUE LOUISE

Argus

Map 6, G2. Rue Capitaine Crespel 6 ©514 07 70; fax 514 12 22. Ⓜ Porte de Namur.

Not in the city centre, but a good location nonetheless, close to avenue Toison d'Or. From here you're within easy walking distance of the Grand-Place, the heart of Ixelles, and St Gilles, and are literally round the corner from avenue Louise. Although the rooms are a bit on the small side, the hotel itself is clean and cosy. It's also fairly good value for money – from mid-July to August double rooms start from F2200. ④

Conrad International

Map 6, G3. Av Louise 71 Ⓒ542 42 42; fax 542 42 00. Ⓜ Louise.
Tram #93, #94.

One of the capital's most stylish hotels, the *Conrad International*,
just past place Stéphanie, looks more expensive than it actually
is – although with a standard double during high season costing
F14,000, it certainly ain't cheap. The good news is that on
weekends during July and August the prices are slashed to an
almost affordable F6600 for a double – well worth it if you
have the cash to spare. ⑦

Lloyd George

Map 1, D3. Av Lloyd George 12 Ⓒ648 30 72; fax 646 53 61.
Tram #93, #94.

A small but pleasant hotel close to the beautiful Bois de la
Cambre. Unlike many of the capital's hotels, the Lloyd George
has its own garden to relax in after a hard day sightseeing in the
centre. Special rates for groups, but it's a bargain anyway. ①

Rembrandt

Map 6, H3. Rue de la Concorde Ⓒ512 71 39; fax 511 71 36.
Tram #93, #94.

Quiet, pension-style hotel with clean and comfortable rooms
close to avenue Louise. It's popular with an older clientele, is
well-placed and reasonably inexpensive. ③

ST GILLES

Les Bluets

Map 6, G4. Rue Berckmans 124 Ⓒ534 39 83; fax 534 39 83. Ⓜ Louise.
Small but friendly, pension-style hotel just off chaussée de
Charleroi and round the corner from Métro Louise. Although
out of the city centre, you're less than a 5min walk away from
one of the best restaurants in the capital – *Les Salons de
l'Atlantide* (see p.180). ②

Duke of Windsor

Map 6, F3. Rue Capouillet 4 ©539 18 19. Tram #91, #92.

Small but intimate, five-room pension known for its reasonable prices – F2000 a double – splendid decor and friendly atmosphere. If you're tired of anonymous hotel rooms and crave the personal touch, head here, but remember to book well in advance. ②

B&BS

For those on a tight budget, staying at a B&B can prove a cheaper alternative to a hotel, and the standard of accommodation can be just as good. A short wander around the town centre, particularly around Ste Catherine, will turn up a few viable options. However, if you prefer the tried and tested approach, head for the **tourist office** on the Grand-Place where you can make reservations for free. Alternatively, contact one of the following budget accommodation agencies direct. The rooms are often comfortable although location is sometimes a problem – don't expect to be in the centre of things.

Bed & Breakfast Taxistop

Map 3, E5. Rue du Fossé-aux-Loups 28 ©223 23 10.

One of the best-known B&B agencies, with a wide range of budget accommodation. You are charged a nominal reservation fee; if you book from outside Belgium it costs an extra F500 on the price of the room, whereas if you wait until you're in the country the tariff is reduced to F300.

Bed and Brussels

Map 6, L8. Rue Victor Greyson 58 ©646 07 37; fax 644 01 14.

Has a good reputation and can usually obtain a double for F1500 or under. Although the standards of rooms are usually high, you may find yourself in the outskirts.

B&BS

New Windrose

Map 6, C6. Av P. Dejaer 21a ©534 71 91.

Provides listings of cheap accommodation, and also doubles up
as the central reservation office for au pairs.

YOUTH HOSTELS

If you don't like communal living or the idea of a complete
stranger snoring in your ear all night, don't panic – the
spectre of the traditional **youth hostel** with a potato peel-
ing roster, huge dorms, and lights-out curfew has thankfully
been laid to rest in Brussels. In its place is a new improved
version, still cheap, but more modern, and infinitely more
private – practically all the hostels in the capital have a
majority of comfortable singles, doubles, and rooms for
four. Prices vary slightly, but generally speaking a single
costs around F650, a double F550 and a quad F400 per
person. Most hostels are located either within the petit ring
– Botanique in particular has three good hostels – or just
outside it and close to a métro. If you don't have an **IYHF
membership card** rooms will cost an extra F100. You can
buy a card from any youth hostel for F500.

Auberge de Jeunesse de la Fonderie Jean Nihon

Map 2, A3. Rue de l'Éléphant 4 ©410 38 58; fax 410 39 05.
Ⓜ Comte de Flandre.

You know that youth hostelling has come a long way when
each room in the hostel is fitted with its own shower and
you're given a magnetic swipe card for 24-hour access. That's
what you get at this modern, spacious, hotel-like hostel. The
only drawback is the 1.5km distance from the city centre, but
even then a 10min métro ride from Comte de Flandre will
have you in the centre of the downtown action. Singles cost
F660, doubles F550, quads F450 per person.

Bruegel

Map 3, A3. Rue de Saint Espirit 2 ©511 04 36; Ⓜ Gare Centrale.
This official IYHF hostel, housed in a modern building, has 135 beds and a basic breakfast is included in the overnight fee – F695 for a single room, F570 for a double, F470 for a quad per person, and F405 for a dorm. Dinner costs an extra F275 and sheets will set you back F125. Although it's pretty central, located by the church of Notre Dame de la Chapelle close to the Upper Town, you have to be back by 1am or you may find yourself wandering the streets. Check-in 7am–1pm.

Le Centre Vincent Van Gogh

Map 3, H3. Rue Traversière 8 ©217 01 58. Ⓜ Botanique.
A rambling, spacious, 210-bed hostel with a good reputation and friendly staff, though it can seem a bit chaotic. Prices are fairly standard, singles F685, doubles F570 with shower, and quads F460 per person, but its main advantage is that there's no curfew and you're on the same street as *Au Travers,* one of the best jazz clubs in the capital (see p.213). Breakfast is included and there are sinks in all rooms, but sheets will cost you an extra F120. Good-value meals – spaghetti, pasta, etc – can be purchased from the hostel bar for around F180–220.

Jacques Brel

Map 3, H4. Rue de la Sablonnière 30 ©218 01 87; fax 217 20 05. Ⓜ Botanique.
An official IYHF hostel, modern, comfortable, and with a hotel-like atmosphere, close to Métro Madou and Métro Botanique. Breakfast is included, and the rooms are the standard price. There's no curfew (you get a key), and cheap meals can be bought on the premises. More comfortable than some of the capital's hotels.

New Sleep Well

Map 3, E4. Rue du Damier 23 ©218 50 50; fax 219 13 13. Ⓜ Botanique.

YOUTH HOSTELS

Bright and breezy hostel close to the city centre, only a five-minute walk from Rogier. *New Sleep Well* has almost hotel-style facilities including a bar-cum-restaurant which serves traditional Belgian beers and well-priced local culinary specialities. There's also an excellent information point for tourists and unlike, many of its rivals, the place has full disabled access. Standard prices for rooms.

CAMPSITES

Although there are around **twelve campsites** in the greater Brussels area, only a few make feasible bases for the city. They tend to be used by caravaners trying to escape the hustle and bustle of the capital, as opposed to backpackers trying to save a few pounds on their accommodation costs. The accepted wisdom seems to be that it's just not worth the effort of camping and commuting, especially as the métro, tram and bus services shut down around the same time as the capital's bars, clubs and music venues begin to warm up. However, if you're set on the idea, the following campsites have the best reputations.

Internationale Camping
Autostrade 100, Londerzeel ©230 94 92.
Although outside the city, it has the advantage of being open all year round. Either take the train to Londerzeel and walk 2km, or get the bus – direction Boom – from the Gare du Nord and walk 200m.

Paul Rosmant
Warandeberg 52, Wezembeek-Oppem ©782 10 09.
Only 10km east of the city, *Paul Rosmant* is the closest campsite to Brussels. To get there, either take the métro (#1B Stockel line) to Kraainem and then the #30 bus to St Pietersplein (last bus leaves at 8.21pm) or take the métro to Stockel and then the

#39 tram to Marcelisstraat. Open April–Sept. F80 per tent plus F80 per person.

Veldkant

Veldkantstraat 64, Grimbergen ☏269 25 97.

One of the most popular campsites, the *Veldkant* is about 15km north of the city centre beyond Laeken. From the Bourse take tram #52, #55, #58 or #81 to Gare du Nord and then catch bus #G to the terminus, after which it's a 15min walk. Open Jan–Nov. F300 per tent.

Eating

Although it's generally expensive, Brussels can be a great (and great-value) city in which to eat. There is a huge variety of **restaurants**, and even the most touristy places serve reasonable, and often first-rate, food for prices that are frequently justified by the quality. Apart from the excellence of the native Belgian fare, the city is among Europe's best for sampling a wide range of different cuisines – from the ubiquitous Italian places, through to Spanish, Vietnamese, Japanese, Turkish, Russian, and even Slovakian, restaurants. You can also eat magnificent fish and seafood, particularly along quais aux Briques and aux Bois à Brûler in Ste Catherine.

Restaurants aside, it's worth remembering many **bars and cafés** serve food, often just spaghetti, soups, sandwiches, and *croque monsieur*, although a lot have wider-ranging menus usually consisting of traditional Brussels fare (see Chapter Eleven). There are also plenty of *frites* stands and pitta places around the Grand-Place, notably on rue du Marché aux Fromages, known locally as "Greek Street", and on rue des Bouchers. The rue Franklin in the EU Quarter has several **pizzerias** for those on a budget. **St Josse** is where pitta is king, but you'll also find spicy Turkish pizzas, or *pide*, topped with combinations of cheese, ground meat or even a fried egg, sold at any number of cafés along the chaussée de Haecht and rue de Méridien.

Unfortunately Brussels is lacking when it comes to catering for the **vegetarian** but for the best see the box on p.172. Alternatively, dine at one of the many Middle Eastern restaurants – they also serve a good selection of vegetarian food.

Belgian Specialities

anguilles au vert	eels in green sauce
faisan à la brabançonne	pheasant in butter, white wine, and chicory
carbonnade flamande	beef braised with beer, onions, carrots and sometimes prunes
crevettes roses/grises	red/grey shrimps – appear in salads
croque monsieur	toasted cheese and ham sandwich
dame blanche	ice cream with melted chocolate
kip-kap	jellied meat (often sold in bars)
gaufres au chocolat	chocolate waffles
lammekezoet	fresh herring croquettes
lapin à la kriek	rabbit in cherry beer
poulet à la Bruxelles	chicken stuffed with cheese and basted in beer
poulet à la framboise	chicken in raspberry beer
salad à l'ardennaise	salad with strips of Ardennes ham
steak américaine	raw minced steak
stoemp	mashed potatoes and mashed seasonal vegetables with sausages and/or bacon
waterzooi	stew with eels, fish, or chicken, cooked in a broth enriched with cream

CAFÉS

Indigo
Map 3, C9. Rue Blaes 160 ℰ511 38 97. Ⓜ Porte de Hal.
Bus #20, #48.
Tues–Fri 10am–2.30pm, Sat & Sun 9.30am–4pm. Inexpensive.
Though verging on the bedraggled, this fashionable café is
favoured by youthful expats and Commission types, particularly
on Sundays after the market at the nearby place Jeu de Balle.
The staff seem a little too Bo-em for their own good, but the
breakfasts and brunches – bacon and eggs, vegetarian quiches –
hit the spot, even if they are a tad overpriced.

Le Pain de Châtelain
Map 6, G7. Pl du Châtelain 29 ℰ534 65 95. Tram #81. Bus #54.
Daily 7am–5pm. Inexpensive.
A pleasant café on the corner of place du Châtelain, with simple wooden tables and a French country farmhouse feel. It's
most popular at breakfast time when they serve tasty croissants,
butter, jam, tea or coffee for only F135, or ham and cheese
omelettes for F120. However, there's also a palatable and reasonably priced lunch menu which includes a wide range of
home-made salads, quiches and sandwiches.

Le Pain Quotidien
Map 3, E8. Rue des Sablons 11 ℰ513 51 54. Ⓜ Louise.
Mon–Fri 7.30am–7pm, Sat & Sun 8am–7pm. Inexpensive.
One of an extremely successful chain of bakery cafés serving
simple but delicious home-baked food such as croissants,
quiches and pastries. Expect to find plain wooden decor, and a
whole range of goodies on sale – chocolate cookies, home-
made jams and great coffee. Great food and a relaxing atmosphere. Also at rue Antoine Dansaert 16.

Le Passiflore

Map 6, G6. Rue du Bailli 97 ⓒ538 42 10. Tram #81. Bus #54.
Mon–Fri 8am–7pm, Sat & Sun 9am–7pm. Inexpensive.
A trendy but relaxing café serving light lunches including home-made salmon and spinach quiche, crêpes, and a variety of salads, all for under F300. It's usually packed on Sunday mornings, when hordes of pasty-faced late-twenty something revellers attempt to cure their hangovers with one of the good-value, Continental breakfasts. Overlooks the Baroque church of Ste Trinité.

SiSiSi

Map 6, F5. Ch de Charleroi 174 ⓒ534 12 72. Tram #91, #92.
Mon–Fri 10am–2am, Sat–Sun noon–1am. Inexpensive.
A late-opening café in the St Gilles neighbourhood, with large windows so you can watch the world drift by. It's a good spot for lunch, and has enjoyed something of a renaissance recently with the hip young things in the area.

RESTAURANTS

The **Lower Town** is great for good-quality cuisine that doesn't cost the earth. The newly invigorated and fashionable rue Antoine Dansaert is an excellent place to start and has several fashionable restaurants, as well as a number of low-budget eateries which serve food of a surprisingly high standard. The Lower Town also holds the frenetic rue des Bouchers, a restaurant ghetto well worth checking out. There's another cluster of good restaurants around the lovely place du Grand Sablon in the **Upper Town**, although the food doesn't come cheap and you may find yourself paying extra for the pretty scenery. Out of the town centre, **Ixelles** is home to some of the capital's finest restaurants, particularly at the place Stéphanie end of chaussée de Charleroi, but also close by the attractive place du Châtelain.

RESTAURANTS

CHAPTER TEN

Price Guide

Restaurants are graded into one of four categories, according to the price, serving a starter and a main course, without drinks or dessert.

Inexpensive: under F500   Expensive: F1000–1500
Moderate: F500–1000   Very expensive: over F1500

Generally speaking, most places are open from noon to 3pm and from 7pm to midnight, and a large minority are open as late as 2am. Sundays and Mondays tend to be the quietest days, and some restaurants close down altogether in July and August. Although not always necessary, it's worth making a reservation, particularly on Friday and Saturday nights.

Restaurant **prices** vary depending on where you eat and when. Lunch menus are considerably less expensive than evening menus, whereas the *plat du jour* – the main course meal of the day – is often great value for money and usually available all day. Although service charges are automatically included, it is customary to leave a tip of around 5–10 percent.

THE GRAND-PLACE AND AROUND

Aux Armes de Bruxelles
Map 4, E2. Rue des Bouchers 13 ©511 55 50. Ⓜ Bourse.
Tues–Sat noon–11.30pm, Sun noon–10.30pm. Expensive.
Right in the middle of the restaurant district near the Grand-Place, this polished spot divides into a formal restaurant popular with the pearls-and-blue-rinse brigade, and a simple bistro with wooden benches, both of which serve old-fashioned Belgian cuisine to a very high standard. Very popular for Sunday lunch.

L'Auberge des Chapeliers

Map 4, C6. Rue des Chapeliers 3 © 513 73 38. Ⓜ Bourse.
Mon–Fri noon–3pm & 6pm–midnight, Sat & Sun 6pm–midnight.
Moderate.

Sited just south of the Grand-Place, this long-established eatery
serves well-priced Belgian fare such as salmon steak in white
beer, *stoemp*, and *waterzooi*. It also specialises in mussels prepared
in a variety of ways – *provençale*, *gratinée*, *marinière* and in soups.
Set menus, of three courses, are from F700.

Chez Léon

Map 4, E2. Rue des Bouchers 18–22 ©511 14 15. Ⓜ Bourse.
Daily noon–11pm. Moderate.

A touristy but good-value café-restaurant on the same street as
Aux Armes de Bruxelles. It's well known for serving typical
Belgian meals, including gigantic portions of mussels and *frites*,
and although not the classiest of eateries, it's been serving honest
grub for over a century and is something of a Brussels institution.
Specialities include *moules au vin blanc* and *poulet à la framboise*.

't Kelderke

Map 4, D4. Grand-Place 15 ©513 73 44. Ⓜ Gare Centrale.
Daily 12.30pm–2am. Expensive.

Run by the same people as *La Roue d'Or*, this well-known
restaurant is housed in a boisterous cellar on the Grand-Place
and is often packed out with tourists. There's an impressive
range of Belgian cuisine including *stoemp*, *carbonnade flamande à
la bière*, and *waterzooi*, but the waiters can be a little stuffy.

La Maison du Cygne

Map 4, D4. Grand-Place 9 ©511 82 44. Ⓜ Gare Centrale.
Mon–Fri noon–2.30pm & 7–10.30pm, Sat 7–10.30pm. Very expensive.

The gorgeous location overlooking the Grand-Place is enough
to make this restaurant a real hit, but add to that some awesome
French and Belgian cuisine and you can see why it's regarded as

RESTAURANTS: GRAND-PLACE AND AROUND

Les Quatre Mers

Map 4, D2. Rue de la Fourche 14 ℂ218 81 91. Ⓜ de Brouckère.
Tues–Fri 6–11pm, Sat & Sun 6pm–1am. Moderate.
An unpretentious Chinese restaurant between the Grand-Place
and place de Brouckère. Main meals, such as stir-fried chicken
and vegetables, or Peking duck, come for under F400. There's
also a half-price menu for children. The staff are friendly and
there's a pleasant atmosphere.

La Roue d'Or

Map 4, C6. Rue de Chapeliers 26 ℂ514 25 54. Ⓜ Bourse.
Daily 12.30pm–12.30am. Expensive.
This old brasserie, handily located close to the Grand-Place,
serves generous portions of Belgian regional specialities, such as
poulet à la Bruxelles, and a mouthwatering selection of seafood.
The *plat du jour* is a bargain at only F350 and the three-course
menu, although over F1000, is well worth it.

Tapas Locas

Map 4, B4. Rue du Marché au Charbon, 74 ℂ502 12 68. Ⓜ Bourse
or de Brouckère.
Daily 7pm–1am. Inexpensive.
This Spanish tapas bar bang in the centre of town serves a wide
range of excellent cheap tapas at F80 a portion. Standard tapas
such as tortilla, calamares or chorizo are listed in the menu and
there is a changing selection of more unusual tapas chalked up
on the blackboards. This long, light informal restaurant in a
trendy area attracts a mainly youthful clientele. Spanish wine
and sangria are both F70 a glass, while a beer is F80.

La Taverne du Passage

Map 4, E3. Galerie de la Reine 30 ℂ512 37 32. Ⓜ Gare Centrale.

Daily noon–midnight. Closed Mon & Thurs June–July. Moderate.
Popular with Belgian families, this traditional place is well
known for its excellent Sunday lunches (F1500), and for serving
delicious classic Belgian dishes such as *anguilles au vert*. There's
also a number of vegetarian options including a tasty cheese
fondue for only F275. Their Belgian beer menu is also worth
perusing.

Totem

Map 4, A6. Rue des Grands Carmes 6 ©513 11 52.
Ⓜ Bourse or de Brouckère.
Wed–Sun 2pm–11pm. Inexpensive.
Though hidden away behind the Grand-Place, this small but
fashionable ground-floor restaurant is a hit with Brussels-based
veggies who come for the friendly atmosphere and wholesome
food – organic soups, fresh salads, tofu, and a delicious selection
of cakes and pastries. It's quite cheap too, a main course costing
less than F400, and there's a good choice of organic wines.

THE LOWER TOWN

L'Achepot

Map 3, C4. Pl Ste Catherine 1 ©511 62 21. Ⓜ Ste Catherine or de
Brouckère.
Mon–Sat 11am–midnight. Moderate.
A welcoming, family-run restaurant in the up-and-coming Ste
Catherine district. Vegetarians would probably have a coronary if
they saw the amount of hearty Belgian meat dishes on the menu,
but carnivores will find *L'Achepot* the ideal place for consuming
huge chunks of flesh, especially on cold winter evenings. The
menu is traditional Belgian and French and includes *lapin à la
kriek* as well as a variety of recipes involving tripe.

Al Barmarki

Map 3, E7. Rue des Éperonniers 67 ©513 08 34. Ⓜ Gare Centrale.

RESTAURANTS: LOWER TOWN

Vegetarian Restaurants

Although eating out in Brussels can prove difficult if you're a vegetarian, it's not impossible. The following restaurants serve well-priced vegetarian food, and, with the exception of *Al Barmarki*, all cater for vegans. *Le Paradoxe* and *Totem* are generally regarded as being the best vegetarian restaurants in the capital.

Mon–Sat 7pm–midnight. Moderate.

Not strictly a vegetarian restaurant, but this well-established Lebanese place serves the usual tasty Middle Eastern staples of houmous, falafel and other chickpea-based delicacies. It's a bit pricey – set menus start at F1000 – but the food is yummy and it's conveniently located near the Grand-Place.

Les Ateliers de la Grande Île

Map 2, C5. Rue de la Grande Île 33 ©512 81 90. Ⓜ Bourse.
Tues–Sun 8pm–2am. Closed August. Expensive.

Located in a converted nineteenth-century foundry, this winding, candlelit, Russian restaurant serves large and hearty meat dishes, and a delicious array of flavoured vodkas. You also get to eat, drink and be merry to the accompaniment of live gypsy violin music. It's worth paying a visit simply for the joyous, if a tad eccentric, atmosphere. Only a couple of minutes' walk from place St Géry.

Bonsoir Clara

Map 3, C5. Rue Antoine Dansaert 22 ©502 09 90. Ⓜ Bourse.
Daily noon–2.30pm & 7–11.30pm. Expensive.

One of the capital's trendiest restaurants on arguably the hippest street in Brussels. Although part of a group which includes *Zebra* and *Kasbah*, *Bonsoir Clara* has its own identity – moody, atmospheric lighting, 1970s geometrically mirrored walls and zinc-topped tables. The food on offer, though expensive, is excellent. Expect to find a menu full of Mediterranean, French and Belgian classics and make sure you reserve.

Comme Chez Soi

Map 3, C7. Pl Rouppe 23 ☏512 29 21. Ⓜ Anneessens.
Tues–Sat noon–2pm & 7–10pm. Very expensive.

With its elegant Art Nouveau decor and quality cuisine, *Comme Chez Soi* is widely regarded as one of the best restaurants in Brussels. Gastronomic genius Pierre Wynants will gently massage your taste buds with his red mullet salad, wild mushrooms in a classic French sauce, caviar, and black truffles. There's an excellent lunch and dinner set menu for F2150. Be sure to make a reservation – the place is supremely popular and often booked up days, if not weeks, in advance.

Da Kou

Map 3, C5. Rue Antoine Dansaert 38 ☏512 67 16. Ⓜ Bourse.
Daily 12.30–3pm & 6.30pm–midnight. Inexpensive.

This run-down, cafeteria-style restaurant serves excellent Vietnamese food at remarkably low prices. Often busy – at times completely hectic – the place is a marvel of efficiency and you'll have a huge steaming plate of delicious noodles in no time. It's an ideal place to go if you're on a tight budget and are in a bit of a rush.

H₂O

Map 3, C6. Rue du Marché au Charbon 27 ☏512 38 43. Ⓜ Bourse.
Daily 7pm–2am. Inexpensive.

Good-value and fashionable eatery close to the Bourse, popular with late-twenty something arty types, who come to sample the simple but tasty "world cuisine", and gay couples on the weekend. Some may find the fantasy theme decor – Tolkien-style sculptures and pictures, and aquamarine walls – slightly off-putting, but there's always an upbeat atmosphere, and the service is both friendly and attentive. Reservations are not always necessary.

Iberica

Map 3, C4. Rue de Flandre 8 ℂ511 79 36. Ⓜ Ste Catherine.
Fri–Wed 11.30am–3pm & 6–11pm. Closed August 5–24. Moderate.
Spanish restaurant at the place Ste Catherine end of rue de Flandre, favoured by Spanish families living in Brussels. The decor verges on the tacky – red velvet-like wallpaper and mock Tudor beams – but the paella is second to none. It's fairly good value for money, most tapas costing around F200–300, mussel dishes for F380–470, and smoked salmon for F400.

Kasbah

Map 3, C5. Rue Antoine Dansaert 20 ℂ502 40 26. Ⓜ Bourse.
Daily noon–2.30pm & 7pm–12.30am. Expensive.
Popular with a youthful, groovy crowd, this Moroccan eatery is famous for serving enormous portions of couscous and other North African specialities. It's run by the same people as *Bonsoir*

Romantic Restaurants

An all-important element for that weekend away.

Clara next door, and although equally hip, the lantern-lit decor makes it seem slightly less fashion-conscious and much more welcoming. Vibrant atmosphere. Set menus from F700.

La Marée

Map 3, C4. Rue de Flandre 99 ⓒ511 00 40. Ⓜ Ste Catherine. Mon–Sat noon–3pm & 7–10.30pm. Moderate.

There's another *La Marée* on rue au Beurre, so don't get confused – this one is a pocket-sized bistro specialising in fish and mussels in the Ste Catherine district. Although the decor is pretty basic, it has a cosy feel, and the food is both creatively made and reasonably priced. The menu includes eight different types of mussels dishes from F460, Burgundy snails with herbs of Provence at F295, and steaks from F450.

Neos Cosmos

Map 3, C5. Rue Antoine Dansaert 50 ⓒ511 80 58. Ⓜ Bourse. Mon–Fri noon–3pm & 6pm–midnight, Sat 6pm–midnight. Inexpensive.

This new Greek meze restaurant is a real find. There's a wide variety of tasty dishes on the menu – fried scampi, octopus sticks, bowls of mussels, spinach and cheese turnovers, aubergine fritters – and nothing costs more than F300. If you're in Ixelles, *Ouzerie du Nouveau Monde* – its sister restaurant at 290 chaussée de Boondael – is just as good.

Le Paon Royale

Map 3, C5. Rue du Vieux Marché-aux-Grains 6 ⓒ513 08 68. Ⓜ Ste Catherine.
Tues–Thurs & Sat 11.30am–2.30pm, Fri 11.30am–2.30pm & 6–9.30pm. Inexpensive.

Cheerful bar in the place Ste Catherine locale that serves good, hearty Belgian food at low prices – and supplements this with a fine array of Belgian speciality beers. A good choice of lunch especially, with the *plats du jour* running at under F250.

Le Pré Salé

Map 3, C4. Rue de Flandre 20 ©513 43 23. Ⓜ Ste Catherine.
Tues–Sun noon–2.30pm & 6.30–11pm. Moderate.
Friendly, old-fashioned neighbourhood restaurant just off place
Ste Catherine, and providing a nice alternative to the swankier
eateries of the district. Like many of the restaurants in this area,
there is an extensive mussels menu – pure mussels, mussels in
white wine, mussels in cream – but it also serves a variety of
fish dishes and Belgian specialities. There are daily specials and
a *prix fixe* menu.

Shamrock

Map 3, C6. Rue J. Van Praet 27–29 ©511 49 89. Ⓜ Bourse.
Daily 12.30–3pm & 7pm–midnight. Moderate.
An Indian restaurant often frequented by expats who come for
their weekly fix of chicken korma, alu gobi, or vegetable
biryani. A standard two-course meal with a couple of beers
costs around F1000. Close to place St Géry.

THE UPPER TOWN

Aux Bons Enfants

Map 3, E8. Pl du Grand Sablon 49 ©512 40 95. Tram #92, #93, #94.
Thurs–Tues noon–2.30pm & 6.30–10.30pm. Closed mid-July to
end of Aug. Moderate.
Well-established and cosy old Italian place, housed in a seventeenth-century building on the attractive place du Grand
Sablon. Expect to find rustic-style decor, classical music, and a
menu of simple but tasty Italian dishes – steaks, pasta, hearty
soups, pizza – at reasonable prices.

Au Chat Perché

Map 3, E8. Rue de la Samaritaine 20 ©513 52 13. Tram #92, #93, #94.
Tues–Fri noon–2.30pm & 7–11pm, Sat 7–11pm. Closed mid-July to
mid-Aug. Moderate.

Excellent crêperie but also serves tasty salads and quiches in pleasant, if a tad chintzy, surroundings. It's a good spot for lunch, and ideal in the evenings for an intimate candlelit dinner. Impressive vegetarian selection, and cheaper than some neighbouring restaurants. Occasional live jazz. Just west of place du Grand Sablon.

Le Bermuchet

Map 3, D9. Rue Haute 198 ℗513 88 82. Ⓜ Porte de Hal.
Mon–Fri noon–2pm & 7pm–midnight, Sat & Sun 7pm–midnight. Moderate.

A happening French restaurant with kitsch decor. Popular with a hip and youthful crowd who come for the lively atmosphere, good food, and friendly service. The price-quality ratio is exceptional here, and the tasty main courses – veal, chicken, ravioli – are excellent value. The only problem is it's a bit of a trek to the nearest métro – although with the money you save on your meal, you can get a taxi.

Chez Lagaffe

Map 3, D8. Rue de l'Épée 4–6 ℗511 76 39. Ⓜ Louise.
Mon–Sat 11.30am–2.30pm & 7pm–1am. Moderate.

French restaurant just below the Palais de Justice, with a good traditional menu which also includes several Belgian specialities. The place really comes alive on Tuesday and Saturday when there's a jazz band. Set menus start at F1200, but the *plat du jour* is only F300.

La Grand Porte

Map 3, D8. Rue Notre Seigneur 9 ℗512 89 98. Ⓜ Anneessens.
Mon–Fri noon–3pm & 6pm–2am, Sat 6pm–2am. Moderate.

Long, narrow and cosy old café, whose walls are plastered with ancient posters and photos. The food is good and hearty – *stoemp*, mussels, *carbonnade flamande* – and you're quite free to just go for a drink. Be warned, though, that it can get very crowded, and the food can be very slow to arrive. On the northern edge of the Marolles near Notre Dame de la Chapelle, and not close to the métro.

Lola

Map 3, E8. Pl du Grand Sablon 33 ℗514 24 60. Tram #92, #93, #94. Daily noon–3pm & 6.30–11.30pm. Moderate.

A trendy restaurant in the Upper Town, serving modern and classic French cuisine including a couple of vegetarian options. It's not cheap – main courses around F600–700 – but the food is good and it makes a nice place for a spot of lunch, particularly in the summer.

Au Stekerlapatte

Map 3, C10. Rue des Prêtres 4 ℗502 86 81. Ⓜ Hôtel des Monnaies. Tues–Sun 7pm–1am. Expensive.

A famous old brasserie near the Palais de Justice, frequented by a youngish crowd who come for the typical Belgian cuisine – beef casseroles, grilled pork, *poulet à la Bruxelles* – and friendly atmosphere. Main meals are in excess of F700, but the food is delicious and the original turn-of-the-century bistro decor is an attractive bonus.

EU QUARTER AND ST JOSSE

Bodeguilla

Map 2, J6. Rue Archimède 65–67 ℗736 34 49. Ⓜ Schuman. Mon–Sat 7–11pm. Inexpensive.

Simple Spanish tapas bar hidden away in the basement of the expensive *Le Jardin d'Espagne* restaurant. The place seems to be a second home to legions of Spanish expats, who are no doubt attracted by the home-cooking and cheap prices. Great place for a quick snack before hitting the town.

La Bonne Humeur

Map 2, I4. Ch de Louvain 244 ©230 71 69. Bus #29.
Mon, Thurs–Sun noon–2pm, 6.30–9.30pm. Moderate.
If you want traditional *moules* and *frites* then forget *Chez Léon* and come to this authentic, well-known, family-run restaurant with a great atmosphere.

Au Brabançon

Map 2, G4. Rue de la Commune 75 ©217 71 91. Ⓜ Madou.
Mon–Fri noon–3pm & 7–10pm, Sat 7–10pm. Moderate.
Although the menu reads like something from the script of *Delicatessen*, rampant carnivores love it. Anything from brains, offal, pigs' trotters, and kidneys are served up at this modest Belgian restaurant, and if you fancy a horse meat stew on a cold winter's evening look no further. Not for the faint-hearted.

Sahbaz

Map 2, G2. Ch de Haecht 102–104 ©217 02 77. Tram #92, #93.
Daily 11.30am–3pm & 6pm–midnight. Inexpensive.
This Turkish restaurant is the best in the capital. The food is cheap and delicious, the staff friendly and attentive, and there's usually cheerful crowds all week. Just beyond the northern boundary of St Josse in Schaerbeek – an area reputed for street crime so it may be worth getting a taxi home.

Takesushi

Map 2, I6. Bd de Charlemagne 21©230 56 27. Ⓜ Schuman.
Mon–Fri noon–2.30pm, 7–10.30pm, Sat & Sun 7–11pm. Moderate.
Eurocrats, Belgians and Japanese expats alike gather here in this restaurant in an old town house near the EU institutions. The sushi lunch menu is a particular bargain at F450 and the traditional hot meals are well worth the price.

RESTAURANTS: EU QUARTER AND ST JOSSE

La Table Gourmande

Map 2, H5. Rue des Deux Églises 80 ⓒ230 66 56. Ⓜ Arts-Loi.
Mon–Thurs noon–3pm, Fri & Sat 7–11pm. Moderate.

This good-value restaurant is usually packed with Eurocrats and
other EU-related bodies. Especially full at lunch time when
there's an eat-as-much-as-you-like buffet comprising various
salads, cold meat platters, and tasty pâtés.

ST GILLES

L'Archipel

Map 6, F4. Ch de Charleroi 163 ⓒ538 91 91. Ⓜ Louise. Tram #91, #92.
Tues–Sat 7.30pm–3am. Inexpensive.

A well-priced pasta and quiche joint and bar, not far from place
Stéphanie. The place occasionally hosts poetry readings, contemporary dance, and live classical piano music. Simple main
courses for under F350. A nice relaxed atmosphere to chill in.

Beni Znassen

Map 6, C4. Rue de l'Église St Gilles 81 ⓒ539 17 81. Ⓜ St Parvis
de St Gilles.
Wed–Sun 6.30pm–1am. Inexpensive.

This off-the-beaten-track Moroccan restaurant, just behind the
Parvis de St Gilles, attracts an eclectic crowd united only by
their appreciation of tasty, well-priced North African food.
The decor is a bit on the dingy side, but somehow it adds to its
attraction. Great couscous.

Les Salons de l'Atlantïde

Map 6, F4. Ch de Charleroi 89 ⓒ537 21 54. Ⓜ Louise. Tram #91, #92.
Sun–Thurs 11.30am–3pm & 7pm–midnight, Fri & Sat 7pm–2am.
Moderate.

Voguish Belgian-French restaurant housed in an atmospheric and
stunningly impressive turn-of-the-century building a few minutes' walk from place Stéphanie. The food – pasta, salads, steaks –

is fair to moderate in quality, but it's worth going just for the decor – high ceilings, arches, drapes, mirrors, candles – all the ambience of Paris in the 1900s. Be sure to make a reservation.

Trave Negra
Map 6, C6. Rue Théodore Verhaegen 9 ©539 28 87.
Ⓜ Parvis de St Gilles.
Tues–Sun noon–3pm & 6.30–10.30pm. Closed mid-Aug to mid-Sept. Moderate.

Quiet and simple Portuguese restaurant with an excellent menu and pastoral decor. It's very welcoming too, and if you're lucky you'll get to hear some live Portuguese folk music. Just west of barrière de St Gilles.

AVENUE LOUISE AND IXELLES

L'Amadeus
Map 6, G5. Rue Veydt 13 ©538 34 27. Ⓜ Louise. Tram #91, #92.
Tues–Sun noon–1am, Mon 6.30pm–2am. Closed August. Moderate.

A restaurant and wine bar in the attractive one-time studio of Auguste Rodin. Modern and classic Belgian cuisine are on offer including the delicious guinea fowl with juniper berries (F575) and the house speciality *Burbot waterzooi*. There's also an excellent wine list, which is rotated once a month to highlight different regions, and an eat-all-you-want brunch on Sunday (10am–2pm) for F700. Not far from place Stéphanie, just off chaussée de Charleroi.

La Chaskanawi
Map 6, J5. Ch d'Ixelles 225 ©640 80 54. Ⓜ Porte de Namur. Bus #71.
Tues–Sun 6pm–1am. Inexpensive.

A small South American restaurant, serving Bolivian, Mexican, Peruvian and Brazilian dishes in cheerful, but basic, surroundings. It's not that expensive either: house specialities, such as pork in lime with potatoes, rice, banana and exotic spices, are F410, and starters – nachos and guacamole, lemon prawns and salad, chicken and cheese tortillas – are around F200. There's also live Bolivian music on Friday and Saturday from 11pm onwards. Just up the hill from place Flaget.

Chez Marie

Map 6, E6. Rue de Witte 40 ©644 30 31. Tram #81.
Daily noon–2.30pm & 7.30–10.30pm. Moderate.
Sister restaurant of the immensely successful *Bonsoir Clara*, this well-known and long-established Ixelles haunt serves impressive French and Mediterranean cuisine in lavish, but not snobbish, surroundings. It's not cheap – set menus from F1200 – but you can get an excellent two-course lunch for around F500. Be wise and reserve in advance.

Doux Wazoo

Map 1, E3. Rue de Relais 21 ©649 58 52/649 02 95. Bus #95, #96.
Mon–Fri noon–2.30pm & 7–11pm, Sat 7–11pm. Closed Aug.
Moderate.
Long-established bistro with a friendly atmosphere just west of the ULB University. The decor is 1930s style, with old posters and a collection of small clocks. Classic French cuisine – roast duck and foie gras, Burgundy ham (F350) – is both tasty and good value for money. Set menus from F925.

Le Fils de Jules

Map 6, G7. Rue du Page 35–37 ©534 00 57. Tram #81. Bus #54.
Mon–Thurs noon–2pm & 7–11pm, Fri & Sat 7–11pm. Expensive.
Basque chefs serve up first-class cuisine from southwestern France at this small and pricey Art Deco-inspired restaurant. The setting, in the swankiest part of Ixelles not far from the Musée Horta, is a perfect backdrop to the delightful food. Reservations usually necessary, particularly on weekends. Recommended.

Gioconda' Store Convivio

Map 6, G7. Rue de l'Aqueduc 76 ℂ539 32 99. Tram #81. Bus #54.
Mon–Sat noon–2.30pm & 6.30–10.30pm. Inexpensive.

This bright, wedge-shaped wine and pasta shop doubles up as a restaurant and is a great place for a spot of lunch or an evening meal. The prices are fairly cheap, and the food – mainly Italian pasta dishes – is nice and tasty. There's usually an upbeat, chatty atmosphere, and the entertainment is provided by the amusingly manic Italian waiting staff. Good for vegetarians.

Le Macaron

Map 6, H7. Rue de Mail 1 ℂ537 89 43. Tram #81. Bus #54.
Tues–Fri, Sat 6.30pm–1am, Sun noon–2.30pm & 6.30pm–1am.
Inexpensive.

Charming French restaurant just off place du Châtelain on the corner of rue de Mail. The convivial ambience, homely surroundings, and cheap fish, meat and pasta dishes – main meals under F350 – mean the place is often packed to bursting, even on weekdays. Admittedly the food can be a bit bland, but the place is cheap, and more than cheerful. Reservations advised.

Ô-Chinoise-Riz

Map 6, G7. Rue de l'Aqueduc 94 ℂ534 91 08. Tram #81. Bus #54.
Mon–Fri noon–2.30pm & 6–11pm, Sat & Sun 6–11pm. Inexpensive.

This small restaurant, just round the corner from place du Châtelain, is where the Chinese come to eat Chinese food. The food is excellent and you get the spectacle of frantic cooks boiling and sizzling your meal in the open-plan kitchen. It's also remarkably cheap by Brussels standards. Starters are under F200 and a main meal costs between F200 and F400. Check out the dim sum – they're delicious.

Pablo's

Map 2, E7. Rue de Namur 51 ℂ 502 41 35. Ⓜ Porte de Namur. Bus #71.
Mon–Sat noon–3pm & 6pm–midnight, Sun noon–3pm. Moderate.

Tex-Mex joint just across the road from Métro Porte de Namur. Although there's always a good atmosphere, the food – spare ribs, steaks, tacos – is pricey for what you get. On the plus side, the desserts, especially the cheesecakes, are delicious, and there's a long bar serving interesting, but lethal, cocktails.

Le Paradoxe

Map 6, J5. Ch d'Ixelles 329 ©649 89 91. Ⓜ Porte de Namur. Bus #71. Mon–Fri noon–2pm & 7–10pm, Sat noon–2pm. Inexpensive.
A Buddhist-run, wholefood restaurant and tearoom, with an ascetic feel, and an eclectic programme of live folky/Eastern music on most Friday and Saturday evenings. Set menus start at F500 and *plats du jour* are F350. It's also a peaceful place to retreat during the day for a herbal tea and toast.

La Quincaillerie

Map 6, G7. Rue du Page 45 ©538 25 53. Tram #81. Bus #54. Mon–Fri noon–2pm & 7pm–midnight, Sat & Sun 7pm–midnight. Very expensive.
The chic, stylish and downright loaded make their way to this delightful restaurant, which is well known for serving mouth-watering Belgian and French cuisine, and occupies the premises of an old hardware shop. Specialities include fish and fowl, often cooked up in imaginative ways. There's normally a reasonably priced *plat du jour* (under F500), but the à la carte is very pricey. A couple of streets from Musée Horta. Highly recommended.

Touch and Go

Map 6, I2. Rue St Boniface 12. Ⓜ Porte de Namur. Mon–Sat noon–2.30pm & 6.30pm–12.30am, Sun 6.30pm–12.30am. Inexpensive.
A cheap and trendy pitta chain – ideal if you want to catch a tasty snack and you're in a hurry. Although more upmarket than the average fast-food joint, the turnover is almost as rapid and the food – exotic pitta fillings and salads – is scrumptious.

Other branches are at avenue Paul Héger 20, and rue de
Livourne 131.

Tsampa

Map 2, E9. Rue de Livourne 109 ℂ647 03 67. Ⓜ Louise.
Daily noon–2pm & 7–10pm. Moderate.
Congenial restaurant at the back of a health-food shop just off
avenue Louise. The menu is fairly wide-ranging – Indian,
Vietnamese and Thai dishes are usually available – and it's not
at all costly. The *plat du jour* is under F500, and set menus start
from F600. Organic wines are available, and if there's good
weather it's nice to eat outside on the pretty terrace.

Tutto Pepe

Map 6, G6. Rue Faider 123 ℂ534 96 19. Tram #81.
Mon–Fri noon–2.30pm & 7–11pm, Sat 7–11pm. Moderate.
Located just off rue du Bailli, this intimate eight-table Italian is
romantic without being clichéd. *Tutto Pepe* combines tasteful
rustic-style decor, a background soundtrack of Italian opera,
and a simple menu of tasty Italian staples such as tagliatelle,
spaghetti and bruschetta.

Yamato

Map 6, H2. Rue Francart 11 ℂ502 28 93. Ⓜ Porte de Namur.
Mon–Sat noon–2pm & 7–10pm. Inexpensive.
Japanese restaurant with minimalist decor, just round the corner from place St Boniface. It's busiest at lunch times when the
capital's Japanese community descend on the tiny premises to
eat noodles at the plain wooden counter. If you like authentic
Japanese food this noodle bar is the place to come – it's fairly
cheap (F300 for a main) and full of character. Currently being
refurbished.

Drinking

Drinking in Brussels, as in the rest of the country, is a joy. The city has an enormous variety of bars and cafés: sumptuous Art Nouveau bars sit alongside swanky, Parisian-style terraced cafés; traditional drinking dens with ceilings stained by a century's smoke nestle next to hi-tech cyber bars; and speciality beer bars offering hundreds of different types of ale co-exist quite happily with bizarre theme pubs set up for no other reason than that the owner happens to have a penchant for Jacques Brel, the American Civil War, the occult...

Most of the best places can be found in the centre, particularly in the Lower Town around the Grand-Place, the Bourse, place de la Monnaie, and in the Marolles quarter. In recent years the area west of the Bourse, particularly place St Géry, has seen a proliferation of trendy bars where the fashion-concious youth of Brussels drink beer, cocktails and flavoured vodkas until the wee small hours. This makes for an amazingly upbeat ambience, particularly if the weather allows for the crowds to spill on to the *terrasses* and streets, but it's unfortunately to the detriment of the rest of town which can seem eerily empty during midweek. Although the Upper Town doesn't have as much to offer, there are a few exceptions scattered around the attractive place du Grand Sablon, and the gilded youth are extending their haunts in this direction towards St Gilles. Generally speaking, "typically Bruxellois" bars are often frequented by tourists and expats, but in areas like Ste Catherine, or even tucked away in the narrow side streets of the Grand-Place, there are places which remain refreshingly local. Venturing out of the petit ring can also be worthwhile, especially if you head to the laid-back Ixelles or St Gilles, where you'll find a selection of trendy bars and cafés and an almost inexhaustible supply of small local hangouts untouched by tourism. The EU Quarter, particularly around Schuman, isn't too exciting, but it's the place to go for Irish- and English-style pubs.

Belgians make little or no distinction between **bars** and **cafés**, and the two words tend to be used interchangeably; most bars serve food, and practically all cafés serve beer and other types of alcohol – cafés often have a terrace, but then again so do many bars.

For DJ-bars or bars with small dance floors, see p.210.

As **opening hours** in Brussels are not officially restricted, bars and cafés can stay open as long as they want, usually until the last soaks slide out. In practice most close around 2am, although on a weekend it's often much later.

Prices for drinks can vary hugely depending on where you are. As a general rule you pay above the odds for the privilege of drinking around the Grand-Place, though not necessarily in the streets around it. If you're paying more than F130 for a pint, or F100 for a traditional bottled beer, you're paying too much. Spirits are relatively expensive, and a gin and tonic can cost you between F200 to F250, though the measures are often generous. There's a good selection of reasonably priced wines (especially white and red Burgundy) available by the bottle or glass. **Food** is served in most places, ranging from sandwiches and *croque monsieur*, to more exotic fare, and is often better value than eating in a restaurant.

DRINKING

THE GRAND-PLACE AND AROUND

À la Bécasse

Map 4, C2. Rue de Tabora 11. Ⓜ de Brouckère.

Mon–Thurs 10am–midnight, Fri–Sun 11am–2am.

Run by the same people as *À l'Imaige Nostre Dame*, this ancient bar has long wooden benches, beer served in earthenware jugs, and heavy Moorish architecture. There's also an excellent beer menu, and the food on offer, though simple, is tasty and relatively cheap.

Au Bon Vieux Temps

Map 4, D3. Rue du Marché-aux-Herbes 12. Ⓜ de Brouckère.

Daily 1pm–12.30am.

Cosy old place tucked down an alley and only a minute's walk from the Grand-Place, with tile-inlaid tables and a seventeenth-century chimneypiece. The building dates back to 1695 and the stained-glass window depicting the Virgin Mary and St Michael was originally in the local St Guoliche parish church. Popular with British servicemen just after the end of World War II, the bar still has comforting old-fashioned signs advertising Mackenzies' Port and Bass pale ale. A great place for a quiet, contemplative drink.

Au Brasseur

Map 4, C6. Rue des Chapeliers 9. Ⓜ Bourse.

Daily noon–5am.

Although this simple, unpretentious bar won't set the pulse racing, it's ideal for late-night drinks and often stays open until first light. The beer is also relatively cheap and you can usually find a table. Just off the Grand-Place.

Le Cercueil

Map 4, D3. Rue des Harengs 10–12. Ⓜ Bourse.

Mon–Thurs 11am–3am, Fri & Sat 11am–5am.

If you fancy a night out in a funeral parlour, then you'll really dig this. This bizarre concept bar, just off the Grand-Place, has coffins for tables, UV lighting, and music that alternates between Gregorian chant and Chopin's Funeral March, not forgetting the fact that your beer will be served up in a skull. As the prices suggest, *Le Cercueil* is clearly for tourists, but it's good fun nonetheless.

La Chaloupe d'Or
Map 4, D4. Grand-Place 24–25. Ⓜ Bourse.
Daily 9.30am–2am.
This famous Grand-Place bar, formerly the tailors' guildhouse, is home to large groups of snap-happy tourists. Nevertheless it's still a pleasant spot, especially during the summer, when you can sit on the terrace with a beer or a café au lait and people-watch. A buffet of cold meats and salads is available from noon to 2pm.

Le Cirio
Map 4, B2. Rue de la Bourse 18. Ⓜ Bourse.
Daily 10am–1am.
Established in 1886, this airy bar is lavishly decorated in fin-de-siècle-style, with wood-panelling and scattered aspidistras. Popular with an older clientele, it is also said to have been frequented by Jacques Brel. The olde worlde decor and relaxed atmosphere make this a great place to escape from the hustle of the city.

Le Cygne Café
Map 4, D4. Grand-Place 9.
Mon–Fri 12.15–2pm, 6.30pm–1am, Sat 6.30pm–1am.
Believe it or not, this venerable establishment on the Grand-Place used to be Karl Marx's local. In fact historians insist Marx polished off the *Communist Manifesto* at meetings of exiled German socialists here. The only reminder today is a plaque on the wall commemorating the founding, in April 1885, of the Belgian Socialist Party. Also serves capital food (see "Restaurants", p.169) and is nice for a quiet drink, but probably a bit too bourgeois now for Karl.

Le Falstaff

Map 4, B3. Rue Henri Maus 17–23. Ⓜ Bourse.
Sun–Thurs 11.30am–2am, Fri & Sat 11.30am–4am.

This hugely impressive Art Nouveau bar, conveniently close to the Bourse, attracts a mixed bag of tourists, Eurocrats and bourgeois Bruxellois, and is a great place to sit back and soak up some atmosphere. It's also surprisingly good value and serves a three-course *menu du jour* for F370 or a main course for F260. Belgian specialities include sumptuous beef stewed the Flemish way (with fried potatoes) and there's a mouthwatering selection of Flemish cakes and tarts. The entertainment is provided by the amusingly po-faced staff.

Hallowe'en

Map 4, A6. Rue des Grandes Carmes 10. Ⓜ Bourse.
Mon–Thurs noon–1am, Fri noon–3am, Sat 4pm–3am.

This Gothic theme bar-bistro, close to the Manneken Pis, has barmen dressed in monks' habits and decor straight out of a horror props department. Everywhere you look there's a sculptured monster or a bust of Beelzebub, and if you're there at midnight on a Saturday you'll see a pseudo-priest exorcise the place. Mainly frequented by students and tourists who come for the good food and carnivalesque ambience.

À l'Imaige Nostre Dame

Map 4, D3. Impasse de Cadeaux 3. Ⓜ Bourse.
Daily 11.30am–1am, Sundays from 4pm.

Hidden down an alleyway just off the Grand-Place, this traditional drinking den is frequented by a mixed bag of Eurocrats, Bruxellois and stray tourists. The building dates back to 1664, but it still feels a bit like an English steakhouse. Bar food available.

La Rose Blanche

Map 4, D4. Grand-Place 11. Ⓜ Bourse.
Daily 10am–3am.

Next door to the Musée de la Brasserie, this classic Grand-Place bar has an open fire and traditional menu including the delicious breast of duck in a sweet southern Belgian beer. You also get a great view of the square, especially from the comfortable terrace out front, but don't expect to meet many Belgians and expect to pay tourist prices.

Le Roy d'Espagne

Map 4, C3. Grand-Place 1. Ⓜ Bourse.
Daily 10am–1am.

Housed in a sevententh-century guildhouse (the bakers'), this popular tourist bar combines Baroque facades, wicker lampshades, pigs' bladders, hanging marionettes, and a bust of Charles II. A slightly macabre large stuffed horse also adds to the Bruegelian atmosphere. The fine views of the Grand-Place from the rooms upstairs and the terrace, and the reasonable bar prices, mean it's often packed, especially in the summer. Overpriced sandwiches and a hot and cold buffet of meats, salads and soups are available.

Au Soleil

Map 4, A5. Rue de Marché au Charbon 86. Ⓜ Bourse.
Daily 10am–2.30am.

Formerly a men's clothing shop, this trendy café on the laid-back rue de Marché quenches the thirst of young arty Brussels types writing poetry as well as stray tourists who've wandered down from the Grand-Place. Cheap bar snacks are on offer – soup of the day is only F90 – and there's a pleasant terrace where you can while away the day over a coffee or something a little stronger. A good atmosphere, but it's often difficult to get a seat come nightfall.

GRAND-PLACE AND AROUND

Théâtre de Toone

Map 4, D3. Impasse Schuddeveld 6, petite rue des Bouchers.
Ⓜ de Brouckère.
Daily noon–midnight.

This congenial bar belonging to the Toone puppet theatre is just north of the Grand-Place but quite difficult to locate, hidden away as it is down an alleyway in the heart of the fish restaurant quarter. When you eventually get there you'll find two small rooms with old posters on rough plaster walls, a reasonably priced beer list, a modest selection of snacks, and a soundtrack of classical and jazz.

THE LOWER TOWN

Beursschouwburg

Map 3, C6. Rue Auguste Orts 20–28 ℗513 82 90. Ⓜ Bourse.
Thurs–Sat 7.30pm–4am.

Hip and happening to the extreme, this large industrial-space café-bar regularly serves up a mixture of bangra, drum 'n' bass, acid jazz, and funk, for the Love Parade generation. The clientele is mostly cool, artsy Flemish types that you don't see anywhere else. Get there before 11pm if you want a table at the weekend or the chance to catch a live band or DJ set. For listings check out their freebie *Beursschouwburg* available in most of the trendy bars and cafés in the area.

Bizon

Map 3, C5. Rue du Pont de la Carpe 7. Ⓜ Bourse.
Daily 6pm–5am.

A small, Flemish-run bar on two levels which serves excellent cheap beer and speciality *genièvres* – highly recommended Belgian fruit liqueurs. The blue-lit decor is eclectic, with South American slide shows projected onto a screen above the bar, an Arizonian bull head, and a motorbike. Late-closing every night attracts a few barflies. Live blues-style music on Thursdays at 10pm with no cover charge.

Café Métropole

Map 3, D4. Pl de Brouckère 31. Ⓜ de Brouckère.
Daily 9am–1am.

Sumptuously ritzy fin-de-siècle café, belonging to an equally opulent hotel with exquisite Renaissance decor including stained-glass windows and ornate candelabras. This place seems to have instant stress-relieving properties and after five minutes of sipping coffee in utter luxury you feel like the world's a pretty civilized place after all. If you've cash to spare, indulge in a brunch of smoked salmon or caviar.

Coasters

Map 3, C6. Rue des Riches-Claires 28. Ⓜ Bourse.
Daily 8pm–8am.

This cosy, two-roomed bar around the corner from *Java* is where students come to play table football and take advantage of the very generous happy hour (8–11pm). However, in the early hours, especially on weekends, the place becomes a pulsating mass of nubile young bodies when clubbers, not quite ready for their cocoa, pile in to dance to the latest tracks.

Le Corbeau

Map 3, E4. Rue St Michel 18. Ⓜ de Brouckère.
Sun–Thurs 9.30am–12.30am, Fri & Sat 9.30pm–2am.

During the day this tavern, just off rue Neuve, is a little sleepy to say the least but by evening, especially on weekends, the place is taken over by students and drinking competitions. Table-dancing is not unheard of.

Fin de Siècle

Map 3, C5. Rue des Chartreux 9. Ⓜ Bourse.
Daily 5pm–3am; kitchen open till 1am.

LOWER TOWN

This charming and civilized café-bar is home to a young arty twenty- and thirty-something crowd who come for the vibrant atmosphere and top-class Italian, Greek, and Iranian food. The decor's pretty impressive as well, especially the original Art Nouveau facade and stained-glass windows. On the downside you often have to wait for a place at one of the long stripped-wood tables.

La Fleur en Papier Doré

Map 3, D7. Rue Alexiens 55.
Sun–Thurs 11am–2am, Fri & Sat 11am–4am.
One of the capital's most eccentric bars, this mad temple of surrealism has walls covered with doodles and poems, deer antlers hanging from the ceiling, and enough bric-à-brac to start a junk shop. Legend has it Magritte and the Dadaists used to get tanked-up here in the 1920s and apparently it was also the chosen venue for the novelist Hugo Claus' second wedding reception. The place is still frequented by artistic and literary types as well as amiable local lunatics who seem to drink Leffe Triple (see p.299) from dusk till dawn. Just south of the Grand-Place near the bowling alley.

Goupil Le Fol

Map 3, D6. Rue de la Violette 22. Ⓜ Gare Centrale.
Daily 7.30pm–6am.
This unusual bar, between the Grand-Place and the Manneken Pis, should not be missed, especially if you are interested in traditional French singing of the likes of Edith Piaf or Belgium's very own Jacques Brel. Every surface is covered with *chanson française* memorabilia and it lives up to its reputation as a former brothel with three floors of cosy corners, sink-into sofas, and dimmed red lights. It's worth a visit simply for the flea-market-style decor, if not for the delicious and extremely potent fruit wines which come in a variety of combinations at a slightly pricey F200.

Le Greenwich

Map 3, C5. Rue des Chartreux 7. Ⓜ Bourse.
Daily noon–1am.
An oasis of calm in a commercial storm, this smoky traditional chess bar, next door to *Fin de Siècle*, has been patronised by generations of chess and backgammon enthusiasts including, according to the locals, Magritte. Although a little down-at-heel, the cheap beer and get-away-from-it-all atmosphere easily make up for it.

Le Java

Map 3, C6. Rue St Géry 31. Ⓜ Bourse.
Daily 3pm–3am.
Close to the attractive place St Géry, this small triangular bar seems perpetually thronged with city slickers and funksters living it large on schnapps and cocktails. If you like Gaudí-inspired decor, groovy music, and a kicking atmosphere – you're home.

La Lunette

Map 3, E5. Pl de la Monnaie 3. Ⓜ de Brouckère.
Sun–Thurs 8am–1am, Fri & Sat till 2am.
This traditional bar-brasserie serves inexpensive bar snacks and has a relaxing terrace ideal for people-watching. Best known for the huge stemmed glasses – *lunettes* – in which it serves its beer. Light meals of spaghetti, soup and *croque monsieur* are served.

Mappa Mundo

Map 3, C5. Rue du Pont de la Carpe 2 Ⓒ 514 35 55. Ⓜ Bourse.
Mon–Fri 8am–4am, Sat & Sun 10am–5am.
The latest bar on the scene from the French entrepreneurs who have reinvigorated Brussels nightlife with *Zebra*, *Bonsoir Clara* and *Kasbah*. This is an oak-lined pub where people come for some serious drinking. They serve a copious breakfast all morning and there is a brunch on Sundays for which you have to reserve. The rest of the food consists of bagels, pittas, salads, soups and is

LOWER TOWN

served from 11am to 3pm and from 6pm to 1am. Watch the building on the corner directly opposite for their next venture.

À la Mort Subite

Map 2, E4. Rue Montagne aux Herbes Potagères 7. Ⓜ Gare Centrale.

Daily 11am–1am.

Twenties bar that borrowed its name from a widely available bottled beer. Expect to find a long, narrow room with nicotine-stained walls and mirrors, a thirtysomethingish clientele and an animated atmosphere, not forgetting the surliest bar staff in Brussels. Snacks served, or just order a plate of cheese cubes to accompany your beer. Just northeast of Grand-Place.

Pathé Palace Café

Map 3, C6. Rue J. Van Praet 28. Ⓜ Bourse.

Mon–Thurs noon–1am, Fri–Sun noon–2am.

Outrageously popular with the chic and stylish, this jaunty Parisian-style café (known as PPs), is located in a converted cinema, crammed at weekends and lively every night. The great decor, upbeat jazzy atmosphere, and reasonably priced tasty cuisine (served till midnight), make it a top spot to wine and dine, although you might have difficulty getting a seat after 10pm on a weekend. A great place to start the evening, although don't be put off by the unfriendly service.

Plattesteen

Map 3, C6. Rue Plattesteen 41. Ⓜ Bourse.

Daily 11am–midnight.

Traditional Belgian café which attracts a lot of people-watchers, particularly in the summer for the south-facing pavement *terrasse*. The atmosphere is such that drag queens and pensioners alike frequent this indefinably special café. There's a good selection of traditional food, such as steak and *frites*, pasta or soups, which is served from noon to 3pm and from 6 to 10pm.

Postiers

Map 3, E5. Rue Fosse aux Loups 14. Ⓜ de Brouckère.
Daily 8am–midnight.

This unpretentious, nineteenth-century Brussels tavern, close to place de la Monnaie, used to be the post office workers' local (hence its name) and was no doubt the scene of many an evil plot to redirect your mail. Although not the most exciting of places, the bar food is relatively cheap and there's an impressive beer menu which features over forty types of Belgian beer.

O'Reilly's

Map 3, C6. Pl de la Bourse 1. Ⓜ Bourse.
Sun–Thurs 11am–1am, Fri & Sat till 2am.

This large Irish theme bar directly opposite the Bourse is the unofficial venue for Irish supporters when there's an Irish rugby or football game on (see p.250). It's also the only bar in the centre which screens live English Premiership football. Although nothing to write home about, it's a handy enough meeting place, except on Friday and Saturday nights when the bar is mobbed with drunken revellers. Food (fries, baked potatoes, Irish stew, salmon, chicken) is available from 11am till 10pm.

Zebra

Map 3, C5. Pl St Géry 33–35. Ⓜ Bourse.
Mon–Thurs noon–2am, Fri–Sun till 3am.

This small but trendy bar on the corner of place St Géry was the first venture of the French crew who own *Kasbah* and *Mappo Mundo*. It is still the supreme location – anyone who is anyone has been here at some point – and attracts a young chic crowd who come for the upbeat atmosphere, groovy music and cheap bar snacks (under F200). It's also terrifically popular in the summer when all and sundry come out to read their newspapers on the large terrace.

LOWER TOWN

Top Ten Bars

THE UPPER TOWN

Le Bier Circus

Map 3, G5. Rue de l'Enseignement 89. Ⓜ Gare Centrale.
Mon–Fri noon–2.30pm & 5pm–midnight, Sat noon–midnight.
Close to the Cirque Royal theatre in the Parliament district,
this homely bar is best known for serving a vast array of traditional Belgian beers including a number of rare brews from
Wallonia. The front room has plain wooden decor, but the
innermost bar cheerfully celebrates cartoon art with pictures
of Astérix and Tintin.

Le Perroquet

Map 3, D8. Rue Watteau 31. Ⓜ Gare Centrale.
Daily 10.30am–1.30am.
This small, semicircular café-bar, a 2min walk from place
du Grand Sablon, has stained-glass windows, Art Nouveau
decor and a pleasant terrace out front. Young and old rub
shoulders over cheap salads and pittas, whilst those of a
more dipsomaniacal disposition work their way through the
long list of speciality beers. Although it's often difficult to
get a seat on a Friday or Saturday night, it's worth the
hassle.

La Puce

Map 3, C10. Pl du Jeu de Balle 12. Ⓜ Porte de Hal.
Tues–Sun noon–2am.

For those who like to drink in unpretentious, no-frills surroundings, this one-roomed working-class bar, opposite the
market square in the Marolles quarter, might prove ideal.
Cheap beer, simple decor, and a lively, if at times boisterous,
atmosphere make it a refreshing change from some of the capital's more fashion-conscious hangouts.

De Skievers Architeck

Map 3, C10. Pl du Jeu de Balle 50. Ⓜ Porte de Hal.
Daily 6am–1am.

The smartest place on the square, this high-ceilinged, airy café-
bar has an impressive traditional beer menu, newspapers to
browse, and serves a wide range of cheap but tasty meals and
snacks. "The Slanted Architect" is named after its designer,
Joseph Poelaert, who also put up the Palais de Justice and
cleared more than a hundred small working-class houses in the
process. The locals gave him his disparaging nickname because
when viewed from the Marolles quarter the Palais looks like it
slopes to one side. Often busy on Sunday afternoons after the
market at Jeu de Balle.

De Ultieme Hallucinatie

Map 3, H3. Rue Royale 316. Ⓜ Botanique.
Mon–Fri 11am–2am, Sat & Sun 5pm–3am.

On the outskirts of the city centre close to Métro Botanique,
this well-known and fancifully ornate Art Nouveau bar is done
up like an old 1920s train car and is popular with a youngish
crowd who come for the excellent choice of beers and reasonably priced food – omlettes, lasagne, etc. The lavishly decorated restaurant in the front also comes highly recommended,
although on the downside the area has a bad reputation for
street crime.

UPPER TOWN

IXELLES

L'Amour Fou

Map 6, I3. Ch d'Ixelles 185. Ⓜ Porte de Namur.

Sun–Thurs 9am–2am, Fri & Sat till 3am.

Upbeat café off place Fernand Cocq, where you can drink a delicious selection of vodkas, mezcal and tequila while taking in the latest works of unknown European artists which decorate the walls. The food is pretty good as well, with a main meal (pasta, quiche) for F250–350, a large salad for F280, and bar snacks (mushrooms on toast, *croque monsieur*) for under F200. The kitchen is open from 11am till 1am. Open late and often busy – and useful for checking your emails whilst you're there.

Nashville

Map 6, I2. Ch de Wavre 100. Ⓜ Porte de Namur.

Daily 5pm–2am.

Filled with "Confederate" memorabilia ranging from old photographs to a life-size plastic General Lee on horseback, this pool bar has the dubious distinction of being Brussels' only shrine to the American Civil War. It also sells remarkably cheap beer (F85 per pint) and has excellent pool tables, but beware of the management who may try to press-gang you into re-enacting battles on a Saturday morning somewhere out in the sticks.

L'Ultime Atome

Map 6, I2. Rue St Boniface 14. Ⓜ Porte de Namur.

Sun–Thurs 8am–2am, Fri & Sat 10am–2am.

A large selection of beers and wines, simple but tasty cuisine (open till 12.30am), and late opening hours, make this funky café-bar a hit with the hip Ixelles crowd weekdays and weekends alike. Its location, on the laid-back rue St Boniface, also makes it a great place to sit outside with a newspaper in the summer.

Volle Gas

Map 6, I3. Pl Fernand Cocq 21. Ⓜ Porte de Namur.
Daily 11am–2am.

On the place Fernand Cocq, this traditional bar-brasserie serves classic Belgian cuisine in a friendly, family atmosphere. The Brussels specialities on offer include the delicious *carbonnades de boeuf à la Gueuze* – beef in beer. There's also occasional live jazz, although when there is a band playing the bar prices tend to go through the roof.

AVENUE LOUISE AND AROUND

Le Châtelain

Map 6, G7. Pl du Châtelain 17. Tram #81.
Mon–Sat 10.30am–2am.

Cheerful café serving all the Belgian classics including *chicons au gratin* and the delicious *stoemp saucisse et lard* – mashed potatoes, carrots and bacon. Although a tad pricey (main meals F400–500 and served till 1am), the friendly atmosphere and great location make up for it.

Conways

Map 2, E7. Av de la Toison d'Or 10. Ⓜ Porte de Namur.
Mon–Wed noon–2am, Thurs–Sat noon–4am, Sun 6pm–2am.

Lively, late-night Irish-American bar frequented by the young, free, and extremely desperate. If you want to get drunk and stand on a barstool playing air-guitar, this is the place to come. But be warned, it's a bit of a meat market.

Cybertheatre

Map 2, E7. Av de la Toison d'Or 415. Ⓜ Porte de Namur.
Daily 11am–2am.

This huge, hip and hi-tech café-bar wouldn't look out of place on the Starship Enterprise. Futuristic decor, ambient dance music and ultra-modern visuals (including a live link with the *Café Trésor* in Paris) combine to create a weirdly relaxed atmosphere. Free Internet access, screenings of cult films and occasional live DJ sets.

Tierra del Fuego
Map 6, G4. Rue Berckmans 14. Ⓜ Louise.
Sun–Thurs 5pm–12.30am, Fri & Sat 6.30pm–2am.
Just off chaussée de Charleroi, this largely undiscovered Latin American resto-bar in the Maison de l'Amérique Latine is definitely worth a visit. Delicious food and wine, tasteful decor, a lovely candlelit garden and a Moorish ceramics *terrasse* out back make this one of the capital's most relaxing retreats. Live music and barbecues in the summer.

EU QUARTER

Hermans
Map 2, I6. Rue Stévin 14. Ⓜ Schuman.
Daily 10pm–5am.
This scuzzy but lively, late-night/early-morning Irish drinking den, close to Schuman, is often the next port of call for *stagiaires* and other EU-related bodies after *The Wild Geese* closes. Relatively cheap beer and a Brit-Pop soundtrack make it just about tolerable, but it's a bit on the last-chance-café side of things.

The Wild Geese
Map 2, I5. Av Livingstone 2–4. Ⓜ Schuman/Madou.
Sun–Wed 11am–1am, Thurs 11am–2am, Fri & Sat 11am–3am.
This enormous Irish theme pub is the preferred watering hole of the EU crowd, especially Thursday nights when the Euro-youth strut their stuff en masse. It also serves good-value bar food including large baked potatoes with salads and fillings for under F200. Occasional live music.

James Joyce

Map 2, J6. Rue Archimède 34. Ⓜ Schuman.

Mon–Fri 11am–2am, Sat & Sun 11.30am–2am.

Within staggering distance of the Centre Berlaymont building, this cliquey Irish hangout is sometimes a bit on the boisterous side, although it's still popular with Commission types and expats. Unless you have a peculiar penchant for over-priced stodgy Irish food eat elsewhere, but the bar is worth the excursion on Tuesday from 8.30pm for the good traditional Irish folk music.

Kitty O'Shea's

Map 2, I6. Bd Charlemagne 42. Ⓜ Schuman.

Mon–Sat noon–3am, Sun noon–3pm.

This large Irish bar, opposite the Centre Berlaymont, is the place to come for Irish food and draught Guinness. Although it gets a bit rowdy when there's a football or rugby international, it's one of the more palatable bars in the area and attracts a rather more middle-aged crowd than the *Joyce*.

Papa Joe's

Map 2, J6. Rue Archimède 55. Ⓜ Schuman.

Daily noon–1am.

One of several unremarkable pubs on this street, a bit on the dark and poky side, but distinguished by the fact that it has a small beer garden round the back and holds barbecues in the summer. Can sometimes get a bit rough and ready late at night when the rugby lads have had one too many.

ST GILLES

À Malte

Map 6, F4. Rue Berckmans 30. Ⓜ Louise.

Daily 10am–3am.

Just off chaussée de Charleroi, this eccentric place is more of a restaurant than a bar, but it's a great spot for a bottle of wine or a few beers late at night. Dark and atmospheric, the interior looks more like the home of an odd Victorian traveller with wall-to-wall *objets d'art* including old portraits, twisted figurines, and African sculptures. If you prefer to come during the day there's an excellent brunch available and a summer garden round the back.

Chez Moeder Lambic

Map 6, C7. Rue de Savoie 68. Ⓜ Horta.
Daily 4pm–3am.
Small bar in a down-at-heel part of St Gilles, just behind the *commune*'s Hôtel de Ville, that has over 1000 beers available, including 500 Belgian varieties. Not at all expensive and ideal for a quiet drink, although the rest of the neighbourhood doesn't have a great deal to offer.

La Porteuse d'Eau

Map 6, C4. Av Jean Volders 48a. Ⓜ Porte de Hal.
Daily 10am–1am.
This refurbished Art Nouveau café, on the corner of rue Vanderschrick, is one of the few signs of gentrification in this run-down section of St Gilles. The food is not cheap, but it's worth the price of a beer to see the airily ornate interior.

SiSiSi

Map 6, F5. Ch de Charleroi 174. Tram #91, #92.
Mon–Fri 10am–2am, Sat & Sun noon–2am.
Youthful, laid-back bar offering a splendid range of cheap salads and stuffed pittas. Especially popular at lunch times. Located in the eastern – and more prosperous – part of St Gilles, a 10min walk north of the Musée Victor Horta, close to place Paul Janson. Food served noon–3pm & 6pm–midnight.

Clubs and
live music

After a slow start, **club** culture seems to have finally taken hold in Brussels, with the arrival of a number of trendy clubs ranging from the throbbing *Fuse* with its regular line-up of big-name house DJs, to the sassy *Who's Who Land*, which often sees crowds of over 1500 and attracts people from as far away as Paris and Amsterdam. Although you couldn't call the club scene cutting edge, Brussels does draw favourable comparisons with many of its European counterparts.

Most clubs, and practically all of the best ones, can be found in the **Lower Town**, especially in the area between place St Géry and the Manneken Pis, or in the scruffily hip **Marolles** quarter just southeast of the Grand-Place. The **Upper Town** has little of interest except *Bazaar* and *Pitt's Bar*, but there are a couple of places beyond the petit ring worth the trip. If you do venture out of the centre, don't forget that the **public transport** system finishes at 12.30am and starts up at 5.30am so you may have to get a taxi home. Night **buses** are fairly infrequent.

As a general rule **clubs open** Thursday to Saturday from 11pm until as late as 6am, but it is possible to club every night. **Entry prices** are fairly low: you rarely have to pay more than F400, and many of the smaller clubs have no cover charge at all, although you have to tip the bouncer a nominal fee (F20 or so) on the way out.

The cost of **drinks** vary depending on where you are, although shorts and cocktails are expensive across the board. If you're on a limited budget it's worth remembering that the bars which morph into clubs on a weekend, such as *Le Sud* and *Acrobat*, tend to have cheaper drinks than ordinary clubs.

Although the city just about holds its own on the club and disco scene, Brussels fares better as a place to catch **live music**. The capital has a vibrant **jazz scene**, with many bars, both in the centre and on the outskirts, playing host to local and international acts. Jazz buffs in particular will be pleased to learn that live jazz has been popular in Brussels since the 1920s – a tradition kept alive today by small atmospheric venues such as *Sounds*, *Au Travers*, and *L'Archiduc*, and by the annual Brussels Jazz Festival (see p.274) – widely regarded as being one of the best in Europe.

Unfortunately the local **rock** and **indie** scene isn't particularly kicking, although if you are prepared to go off the beaten track you can still catch some excellent live music at the *Fool Moon*, *Magasin 4* and *VK*. The good news for mainstream gig-goers is that Brussels is a regular stop on the European tours of major and up-and-coming artists. The biggest gigs are held in *Forest National*, although many medium-sized gigs are held in *Botanique*, *Cirque Royal* and *Ancienne Belgique*. It's also worth considering going to one of the music festivals held regularly outside Brussels, which usually attract a good line-up of rock bands mixed with dance DJs. The Torhout-Werchter Festival (see p.272), held in early July, is the biggest, and has played host to the likes of The Verve, Garbage, The Beastie Boys, Sonic Youth, Underworld, Björk and Nick Cave.

For classical music listings, see p.221.

For **listings** of concerts and events, check the "What's On" section of the weekly *Bulletin* or the Wednesday pull-out section of *Le Soir*. **Flyers** for most clubs and raves can be picked up in the trendy bars and cafés in the centre, particularly in the *Beursschouwburg* – which also has its own events list – *Zebra*, and *Au Soleil*. **Tickets** for most things are available from Fnac in the City 2 complex, on rue Neuve (©219 29 07), the Free Record Shop next to place de la Monnaie (©217 88 99) (see p.243) or from the booking office at the **tourist office** on the Grand-Place.

CLUBS

THE GRAND PLACE AND AROUND

Drum Beats
Map 4, D3. Rue des Harengs 14. Ⓜ Bourse.
Tues–Sun 11pm–4am, Fri & Sat 11pm–6am.
A tiny, three-floored bar-cum-club next door to the *Le Cercueil*, where the music alternates between drum 'n' bass, trip-hop, electrowave, techno and acid house. Popular with ravers, who use it as either a pre-club warm-up or post-club chill-out.

THE LOWER TOWN

The Fuse
Map 3, C9. Rue Blaes 208. Ⓜ Porte de Hal.
Sat 10pm–7am.
Not for those with a history of cardio-pulmonary disease, this pulsating dance club has played host to some of the best DJs in Europe including The Orb, Daft Punk, Carl Cox and Dave

Angel. Expect to find three floors of techno, house, jungle and occasional hip-hop, as well as the usual staple of chill-out rooms and visuals. The acts are a slightly orientated towards Belgian DJs but the big international guests are still being pulled in. Entrance is free before 11pm but F300 after, although the price goes up if there's a big name spinning the discs.

Who's Who Land
Map 3, C8. Rue du Poinçon 17. Ⓜ Anneessens.
Thurs–Sat 11pm–6am.
One of the capital's runaway success stories, this trendy house club (with occasional foam parties) often sees enormous teenage crowds, even from abroad. Fridays and Saturdays are the busiest nights as legions of young latex-wearing revellers pile through the doors and make a beeline for the main dance area where drum 'n' bass and classic house anthems are blasted out until the early hours. Thursdays is rap and ragga night. Expect to pay F300 entrance on a weekend and about the same for a short, whereas a beer is about F100.

THE UPPER TOWN

Le Bazaar
Map 3, C9. Rue des Capucins 63. Ⓜ Porte de Hal or Louise.
Thurs–Sat 10pm–5am.
Le Bazaar is where the Eurotrash Brussels crowd live it up on the weekend. Upstairs there's a dimly lit bar-restaurant serving so-called "cuisine de monde", whereas downstairs you can dance the night away to a mixture of funk, soul, rock and indie. Not far from rue Haute, down from the Palais de Justice, but not near a métro.

Pitt's Bar
Map 3, D9. Rue des Minimes 53. Ⓜ Louise.
Tues–Sun 8pm–3am.

A popular (it's free) student hangout close to the Palais de Justice, where the music alternates between techno, garage, house and bangra as well as a regular DJ set at 10.30pm. It's a bit of a walk (about ten minutes) from the nearest métro.

EU QUARTER AND ST JOSSE

Mirano Continental
Map 2, H4. Ch de Louvain 38. Ⓜ Madou.
Sat 11pm–5am.
A large, trashy club within staggering distance of Métro Madou, popular with wannabe jet-setters and preppy yuppies. Inside it's more like a second division catwalk than a house club, with teams of insalubrious, fashion-conscious posers strutting round the place in designer-wear. For sheer tackiness value, the revolving dance floor is worth a go. Entrance will set you back somewhere in the region of F400 and, needless to say, the door policy doesn't favour mere mortals.

KOEKELBERG

Tour & Taxi
Map 1, C2. Rue Picard 5. Ⓜ Belgica.
Fri & Sat 11pm–5am.
This huge, industrial, hi-tech dance club is not quite in the same league as *The Fuse*, but it's good nonetheless. DJs spin a mix of progressive house and ambient dance through the night and the reasonably priced bar (beer F100, shorts F200) means buying a few rounds won't break the bank. Entrance is free before midnight or F300 after. The drawback is that it's in a slightly dodgy area so it's worth getting a taxi.

DJ-BARS

Acrobat
Map 3, C5. Rue Borgval 14. Ⓜ Bourse.
Daily 10pm–6am.
A slightly scruffy bar, just round the corner from *Zebra*, which becomes a small club on the weekend (Fri & Sat 10pm–6am). DJs spin disco-house and funk for a clientele who uninhibitedly dance the night away in Latin American kitsch surroundings brightened by fairy lights. There's a great atmosphere, reasonably priced drinks and no entrance fee.

Canoa
Map 3, C6. Rue du Marché au Charbon 53. Ⓜ Bourse.
Tues–Sun 9.30pm–5am.
This lively Latin American bar, close to *Au Soleil*, mutates into a club on the weekend. It's popular with the post-party crowd and other drunken revellers who come to salsa and samba the night away on the small dance floor. If it gets too hectic, head for the small bar at the back where you can down a few delicious Caipirinhas –typical Brazilian cocktails of cachaça (white rum), lemon and sugar. No cover charge, but all the cocktails cost around F300.

Cartagena
Map 3, C6. Rue du Marché au Charbon 70. Ⓜ Bourse.
Fri–Sat 11pm–4/5am.
This enjoyable downtown club is opposite *Canoa*, and offers arguably the best and certainly the widest range of South American and Latino sounds in town. Attracts the late twenties age-range, and only really gets going around midnight.

Pablo's Disco Bar

Map 3, C6. Rue du Marché au Charbon 60. Ⓜ Bourse.
Mon–Thurs 7pm–1am, Fri–Sat 7pm–3/4am.

Small, trendy Parisian-style DJ-bar. Good for DJ-spotters who want to admire the techniques. They generally play easy listening, salsa-Latino, house or drum 'n' bass. The garden terrace is a pleasant chilling area in the summer. The regular crowd is slightly overly trend-conscious, but it's welcoming enough if it's not too packed.

Le Sud

Map 3, E5. Rue de l'Écuyer 43–45. Ⓜ de Brouckère.
Thurs–Sat 10pm–6am.

A large, maze-like hangout with Arabic decor, and a slightly Bohemian feel as it used to be a squat. The front room has a long bar serving the delicious but lethal *vodka citron* (F550 a bottle) especially imported from Bombay, and if you follow the dark and twisting corridors you'll find a DJ pumping out a mixture of rap, jungle and dance. Membership is F100 for a year, although if there's a live band (occasionally on Thurs) or guest DJ, you may have to pay more on the door.

LIVE MUSIC VENUES

THE LOWER TOWN

Ancienne Belgique

Map 3, C6. Bd Anspach 110 ©548 24 24. Ⓜ Bourse.
See local listings. Closed July & Aug.

The capital's premier rock and indie venue with a seating capacity of 2000 (plus 750 standing) and a reputation for showcasing local bands and international acts who perform either in the main auditorium or the smaller space on the first floor (capacity around 400). There are usually around four gigs a week and visiting artists to the *AB*, as it is known, have included Echo and the Bunnymen, Super Furry Animals, Ray Davies and Judas Priest. Also open Wednesdays noon–2pm for the "Brootje club" where you can see up-and-coming Flemish bands for F100 with free sandwiches thrown in for good measure. Concert tickets cost around F650.

L'Archiduc

Map 3, C5. Rue Antoine Dansaert 6 ©512 06 52. Ⓜ Bourse. Daily 4pm–4/5am.

A famous Art Deco jazz café, close to place St Géry, full of thirty-somethingish media types tapping their fingers and wiggling their toes to Blue Note and post-1960s modern sounds. Legend has it Nat King Cole once played here, and music fans will be pleased to learn the quality of the acts is still high. Live jazz can be heard every Saturday from 1 to 5pm for free and most Sunday evenings from October to April at 5pm with an entrance fee of around F500–600.

Beursschouwburg

Map 3, C6. Rue Auguste Orts 20–28 ©513 82 90. Ⓜ Bourse. See local listings.

A great venue next door to and part of the café of the same name (see p.192). It occasionally features live bands and DJ sets, although it's better known for specialising in "the spoken word" – stray musicians give esoteric readings on life, the universe and everything else in between. It's also the annual meeting place of the Belgian hip-hop convention. Look for the *Beursschouwburg* events calendar available in most of the trendy bars in the area or pay a visit to their events desk. Entrance fees vary, but tend to be under F300.

Magasin 4

Map 2, D2. Rue du Magasin 4 ©223 34 74. Ⓜ Yser.

This small converted warehouse is a great place for catching new punk-rock, indie or rap/hip-hop bands and has a reputation for featuring "the next big thing". It's usually worth checking the listings pages and flagging down a taxi. Alternatively head for Métro Yser and walk south until you find a turning off rue des Commerçants. Entrance usually sets you back around F300.

Phil's Café

Map 3, D9. Rue Haute 189 ⊘513 95 88. Ⓜ Porte de Hal.
Mon–Thurs 6.30pm–2am, Fri–Sun 10.30pm–5am.

Although it might attract a few too many Eurocrats, this small, relaxed bar, not far from Jeu de Balle, is a safe bet if you want to catch some cool vibes in the city centre. Soul, funk, jazz and blues can be heard (from Tues to Sun for free, with a mellow night on Mondays). The music usually starts around 10pm, but be there by 9pm to get a table. Take a peek at their Web site: *www.phils-jazz.com*.

THE UPPER TOWN

Au Travers

Map 3, H3. Rue Traversière 11 ⊘218 40 86. Ⓜ Botanique.
Daily 8pm–3am; Mon & Tues free, Wed–Sun F300.

A small, rather down-at-heel kind of place, but it's still popular with students and jazz buffs and excellent live jazz can be heard here every night of the week. A good night to go is Monday when jam sessions can go on way into the wee small hours.

Le Botanique

Map 3, G3. Rue Royale 236 ⊘226 12 11. Ⓜ Botanique.
Housed in the 150-year-old conservatory of the Parc du Jardin Botanique and includes an art gallery, two theatres, and a small cinema. Frequent rock and pop concerts, and some good, mostly contemporary, theatre. Tickets F300–600.

LIVE MUSIC VENUES: THE UPPER TOWN |

Le Cercle

Map 3, E8. Rue Ste Anne 20–22 ℂ514 03 53. Ⓜ Gare Centrale.
Daily 8pm–2am.

Small, unremarkable venue in itself, but people come here for the
live music which is on three or four times a week and ranges
from jazz and Latino to *chanson française*. The place is not cheap –
entrance usually costs at least F300 and a small beer will set you
back F80 – but there's a relaxed atmosphere and the bands are
usually very good. If you have any brain cells left from Saturday
night, you might want to pop in on Sunday at 6pm for *Le Cercle*'s
regular philosophy discussion. Just off place du Grand Sablon.

Palais des Beaux Arts

Map 3, F7. Rue Ravenstein 23 ℂ507 82 00. Ⓜ Gare Centrale.
With a concert hall holding around 2000, as well as some
smaller theatres, the Palais is used for anything from contemporary dance to Tom Jones, though the majority of performances
are of classical music – the place is the home of the Orchestre
National de Belgique (see p.217).

IXELLES

New York Jazz Café

Map 6, G3. Ch de Charleroi 5 ℂ534 85 09. Ⓜ Louise.
Fri–Sat 10pm–1.30am.
Upmarket bar-bistro just off place Stéphanie where quality live
jazz can be heard Friday and Saturday in the club behind.
There's no cover charge and usually a good atmosphere, but the
price of booze soars when there's a live band playing.

Sounds

Map 6, I3. Rue de la Tulipe 28 ℂ512 92 50. Ⓜ Porte de Namur.
Mon–Sat noon–4am.
Strangely enough this atmospheric jazz café, close to the place
Fernand Cocq, has remained largely undiscovered despite the

fact it has been the haunt of both local and internationally renowned jazz acts every weekend for the last twenty years. Saturday seems to be the day for the big names and you'll only be charged F200–300 entrance fee, although if you pop in midweek it's free and the music is often just as good.

MOLENBEEK

Fool Moon
Map 1, C2. Quai de Mariemont 26 Ⓒ410 10 03. Ⓜ Gare de l'Ouest. Tram #18.

Great venue for live music and parties, particularly if you like soul, dub, Latino sounds 'n' drum 'n' bass, but also good for rock and indie bands. Entrance is around F300, there are reasonably priced drinks, a good cutting-edge ambience and usually a fair-sized crowd. The upstairs bar with its comfortable sofas is a great place to chill out. The only drawback is the out-of-the-way location.

VK
Map 2, B3. Rue de l'École 76 Ⓒ414 29 07. Ⓜ Comte de Flandre. One of the best cutting-edge "alternative" venues in the capital, *VK* regularly features top-class hip-hop, ragga, rock and indie acts and occasionally puts on the odd punk band. The only problem is it's in an area renowned for street crime, so don't hang around after the gig. It's best to get a taxi or one of the shuttle buses which run to the Bourse on the way back. Entrance F300–400.

FOREST

Cirque Royal
Map 1, C3. Rue de l'Enseignement 81 Ⓒ218 20 15. Ⓜ Madou. Formerly an indoor circus, this venue has been host to the likes of David Byrne and Lou Reed down the years, although live gigs are randomly scheduled.

LIVE MUSIC VENUES: MOLENBEEK, FOREST

Forest National

Av du Globe 36 ℂ340 22 11. Tram #18. Bus #54.

Brussels' main arena for big-name international concerts, holding around 11,000 people.

The performing arts and film

Despite its reputation as the grey city of Europe, when it comes to the city's cultural scene, Brussels answers, if not confounds, its critics. Domestic talent flourishes, particularly on the **theatre** scene, which is home to a new generation of young playwrights including Philippe Blasand and Jean-Marie Piemme, and in the **modern dance** arena, where Wim van Dekëybus, artist in residence at Koninklijke Vlaamse Schouwberg, has gained international acclaim for his cutting-edge choreography. Although the domestic **classical music scene** has suffered from serious underfunding in recent years, it remains strong – the Orchestre National de Belgique continues to thrive under Yuri Simonov, and there are a number of excellent classical music festivals and concerts organised by the Philharmonic Society (see "Palais des Beaux Arts"). Sadly, despite Belgians being avid **cinema**-goers, home-grown film-makers seem something of an endangered species, though, more promisingly, there are a number of first-rate **film festivals**.

Listings of theatre and dance performances, concert recitals, and films showing, can be found in the "What's On" section of the weekly *Bulletin*, or the Wednesday pull-out section of *Le Soir*. For tickets and information go to either the tourist office on the Grand-Place or the Fnac store in the City 2 shopping complex at rue Neuve.

THEATRE AND DANCE

Despite years of underfunding, the Brussels **theatre** scene still remains strong. The city currently has more than thirty theatres staging a variety of productions ranging from Shakespeare to Stoppard. Most theatre is performed in French and Flemish, yet the various American, Irish and British theatre groups frequently put on high-quality amateur productions (check *The Bulletin* for details).

Being at the centre of Europe, the city is a stop-off point for many **international dance** and **theatre** groups – including the RSC, the Comédie Française and the Israeli dance group Badsheva – and it's quite common for the capital's theatres to stage joint-productions with other European theatre companies.

Brussels' **dance** tradition has been impressing visitors ever since Maurice Béjart brought his classical Twentieth Century Ballet here in 1959. However, the city still lacks a proper dance venue and unfortunately companies have to make do with stages – the Palais des Beaux Arts, Théâtre de la Monnaie, and the Cirque Royal – better suited to plays and concert recitals. But the innovative legacy of Béjart lives on, with his old company (now called Rosas) regularly performing at La Monnaie.

Ticket **prices**, for dance and theatre, vary depending on the venue. However, generally speaking, a good seat costs around F700–1000.

Cirque Royal

Map 2, F5. Rue de l'Enseignment 81 ©218 20 15. Ⓜ Madou.
This former indoor circus has the most eclectic programme of
any of the city's major venues (see "Live Music", p.215).
Although well-known as a classical music and dance venue – it
recently played host to the Vienna State Opera and Ballet – it
has, in the past, also acts ranging from David Byrne to the
Chippendales. It's also a good venue for musicals and operettas.

Koninklijke Vlaamse Schouwberg

Map 2, B3. Rue de Laeken 146 ©217 69 37. Ⓜ Yser.
This Flemish-language theatre is housed in a converted nineteenth-century arsenal, and has a good reputation for showcasing the works of up-and-coming young playwrights, as
well as staging modern classics by the likes of Chekhov,
Pinget and Beckett. It's also an excellent place to catch some
innovative dance.

Palais des Beaux Arts

Map 3, F7. Rue Ravenstein 23 ©507 82 00. Ⓜ Parc.
Their resident theatre company – Rideau de Bruxelles – has
been putting on modern theatre productions since its incep-
tion in 1943. Performances are in French, and the most
recent playwrights to have their work performed include
David Hare, Paul Willems and Jean Sigrid. The Palais des
Beaux Arts is also an excellent venue for modern dance and
classical ballet, and it is often one of the first ports of call for
touring dance companies – however, tickets can rise to F2000
for these performances.

Théâtre National

Map 3, F3. Centre Rogier, pl Rogier ©203 53 03. Ⓜ Rogier.
This French-only theatre performs high-quality productions
ranging from Molière to Brecht, and it's popular with a wide
range of visiting theatre companies including the RSC, the

THEATRE AND DANCE

Parisian Théâtre Odéon and the Berlin-based Berliner Scubuhne – who perform classics from their country of origin in the original language.

Théâtre-Poème

Map 6, E3. Rue d'Écosse ©538 63 58. Ⓜ Hôtel des Monnaies.
A small, avant-garde theatre group, best known for dramatizing excerpts from novels and poems. It's also a place where authors, poets, playwrights and philosophers come to discuss their work – the most notable guest speaker being post-modernist guru Jacques Derrida.

Théâtre Public

Map 2, H4. Rue Braemt 64–70 ©223 29 66. Ⓜ Madou.
The only private theatre in Brussels, *Théâtre Public* is deservedly acclaimed for bringing the works of young Belgian French-language playwrights – Jean-Marie Piemme and Philippe Blasand to name but two – to the stage, although Chekhov, Molière and Brecht also get a look-in from time to time. Tickets usually cost F750; however, for F1300 you also get wined and dined before the performance at the theatre's very reasonable French restaurant.

Théâtre Royal du Parc

Map 3, G6. Rue de la Loi 3 ©512 23 39. Ⓜ Arts-Loi.
Stage productions are in French only, but even if you don't fancy a play it's worth visiting this glorious theatre for the beautiful architecture alone – the actual building dates back to 1782. The programme consists mainly of French burlesques, and modern classics – Ionescu, Brecht, Camus – but they also stage more modern pieces, and have been known to put on the odd bit of Shakespeare.

CLASSICAL MUSIC AND OPERA

Fans of **classical music** will be pleased to learn the concert scene in Brussels is impressive. The main classical music venue is the Palais des Beaux Arts, while the Conservatoire Royal de Musique has an excellent reputation for its programme of chamber music and song recitals. **Annual events** include the recently established Ars Musica, held in March, and the prestigious Concours International Musical Reine Elisabeth de Belgique, a competition for piano, violin or voice in May (see p.270), which numbers among its prize-winners Vladimir Ashkenazy, David Oistrakh and Gidon Kremer.

Lovers of **opera** need go no further than the beautiful and historic Théâtre de la Monnaie, which has enjoyed something of a renaissance of late, first under the musical direction of Gérard Mortier, but more recently with the inspired conductor Antonio Pappano.

Tickets can be bought for concerts and opera from as little as F300–500 but can zoom up to as much as F6200 for a first night at La Monnaie.

Conservatoire Royal de Musique

Map 3, E8. Rue de la Régence 30 Ⓒ507 82 00 or 511 04 27. Ⓜ Gare Centrale.

Although the Orchestre National de Belgique sometimes plays here, it's more suited to chamber music and song recitals. The acoustics are second to none and there is an impressive, at times highly innovative, programme interspersed with the early rounds of the Concours Musical International Reine Elisabeth de Belgique competition.

Palais des Beaux Arts

Map 3, F7. Rue Ravenstein 23 Ⓒ507 82 00. Ⓜ Parc.

The jewel in the crown of the capital's classical music scene, the Palais des Beaux Arts is not only the home of Belgium's national orchestra, but also the Philharmonic Society who organize classical music performances throughout the city. Visiting orchestras have included the Los Angeles Philharmonic and the Chicago Symphony Orchestra. The season runs from September to June, and the Palais hosts in excess of 350 concerts each year.

Théâtre de la Monnaie

Map 3, E5. Pl de la Monnaie ©229 12 11. Ⓜ de Brouckère.

This is Belgium's premier opera house. Renowned for its adventurous repertoire and production style, it has earned itself glowing reviews over the years. Its policy of nurturing promising singers rather than casting the more established stars ensures that it's a good place to spot potential. It's also of great historical significance. Following the staging of Auber's *The Mute Girl of Portici* in 1830 – an opera based on a revolution – an inspired audience charged out of the building and held an impromptu protest. Belgian independence was declared one month later. Book well in advance: tickets are always difficult to obtain as the house contains only 1200 seats.

CINEMA

Although Belgium's contribution to world cinema is modest – *The Sexual Life of the Belgians*, *Man Bites Dog* and the "Muscles from Brussels" himself, Jean-Claude van Damme – cinema-going, particularly in the capital, flourishes. The city's main commercial **cinemas** are UGC De Brouckère, UGC Acropole and Heysel's Kinepolis, all of which devote their screens to the big US blockbusters. However, the sheer number of cinemas in Brussels means there's a good range of art house or classic films showing continually.

The city's annual **film festivals** (see "Festivals", p.267) are held in the spring and are highly recommended. They include the impressive Brussels Film Festival in January, and the bizarre, but wonderful, Brussels Festival of Fantasy Film, Science Fiction and Thrillers in March.

Somewhat surprisingly, about half the films shown in Brussels' cinemas are in English (coded "VO" or *version originale*); subtitles for non-French or Flemish films are in French and Flemish. *The Bulletin* is the best source for **listings** of the week's movies, which usually change their programmes on Wednesday. **Prices** tend to be F200–250, except on Monday when they are F150–190.

Actors Studio
Map 2, D4. Petite rue des Bouchers 16 Ⓒ512 16 96. Ⓜ de Brouckère.

This small cinema is probably the best place in the centre to catch art house or independent films. It's also one of the leading venues for the Brussels Flm Festival.

Arenberg Galleries
Map 4, D4. Galerie de la Reine 26 Ⓒ0900 29 550. Ⓜ Gare Centrale.
Best known for it's "Sneak Previews", where you get to see a new film before its official release date. Occasionally they take a poll to gauge audience reaction to the film. They also screen an adventurous variety of world films. The cinema itself is a beautiful Art Deco building converted from a theatre.

UGC De Brouckère
Map 3, D4. Pl de Brouckère 38 Ⓒ0900 29 930. Ⓜ de Brouckère.
A ten-screen cinema showing the usual Hollywood fare. If you go on Sunday morning you get a coffee and croissant in the price of the ticket. Its sister cinema, the UGC Acropole at Galerie de la Toison d'Or 17, screens the same sort of stuff. Both cinemas usually screen in English.

Kinepolis
Map 5, C2. Av du Centenaire 1 Ⓒ474 26 04. Ⓜ Heysel.

CINEMA

A hi-tech cinema complex with 27 auditoriums and the largest IMAX screen in Europe. The line-up is pretty commercial but the choice of films is unrivalled.

Movy Club

Map 6, A5. Rue des Moines 21 ©537 69 54. Tram #18. Inconveniently located, but it usually offers a wide range of films in English. The line-up includes modern classics and popular films released within the last year.

Musée du Cinéma

Map 3, F7. Rue Baron Horta 9 ©507 63 70. Ⓜ Gare Centrale. This small museum-cum-cinema is popular with film buffs who come to watch an excellent selection of old silent movies with piano accompaniment. The museum is pretty interesting as well, especially the early attempts at moving pictures such as the mutoscope and kinetoscope. Children under 16 not admitted. See p.48 for a review of the museum.

Nova

Map 4, E4. Rue d'Arenberg 3. ©511 27 74. Ⓜ de Brouckère. A small, one-screen cinema, popular with students who favour the cheap price (students F150, adults F200) and the art house programme – anything from obscure Eastern European offerings to Portuguese classics. English-language films are sometimes screened; however, if it's not originally in English, the subtitles will be in French and Flemish. Only two showings per day – 8pm & 10pm.

Styx

Map 6, G3. Rue de l'Arbre Bénit 72 ©0900 29 969. Ⓜ Porte de Namur. A tiny, two-screen repertory cinema, with old moth-eaten chairs, and a smoky atmosphere. Most films are in the original language and there's usually a good selection of English language movies, as well as midnight screenings.

Vendôme

Map 6, H1. Ch de Wavre 18 ℭ502 37 00. Ⓜ Porte de Namur.
A trendy, five-screen cinema well-known for showing a wide
selection of arty films – *The Ice Storm*, *Kundun* – as well as
more mainstream stuff like *Titanic* and *Scream*. They usually
have at least two English-language films showing at the same
time.

Shopping

Brussels has a wide range and variety of goods on offer although it's certainly not a cheap place to **shop**. There are two main shopping areas in the city, the city centre around the **Grand-Place** and the south part of the **Upper Town**. The city centre's main shopping street is **rue Neuve**, which has just been revamped and is home to City 2, the ultimate inner-city shopping mall.

Not far from the Grand-Place, **Galeries St Hubert** accommodates a smattering of conservative boutiques in stark contrast to the **Galerie Agora**, which peddles cheap leather jackets, incense, piercing jewellery and ethnic goods directly opposite. Behind the Bourse, **rue Antoine Dansaert** caters for young, cutting-edge fashion-groupies, housing a number of young designers as well as shops selling clothing ranging from the internationally known to such Belgians as the Antwerp 6 and Raf Simons. Neighbouring **St Géry** contains rue des Riches, Claires and rue du Marché au Charbon which have streetwear shops and vintage stores.

Uptown, the **chaussée d'Ixelles** has most of the big stores and a lively feel in the African quarter around the Galerie d'Ixelles. The label-conscious will want to shop at the smartest addresses on avenues Louise and de la Toison d'Or, where shops offer everything from DKNY to Giorgio Armani, as well as Belgian designers.

Shopping Contents

The Grand Sablon has a weekend **antiques market** and the surrounding area has a good selection of similar shops. For bric-à-brac, it's best to wander down to the Marolles district – the closest Brussels gets to New York's Lower East Side – and the daily **flea market** at the place du Jeu de Balle. There is a labyrinth of old books in the stores of the **Galerie Bortier** near Gare Centrale.

Belgian beer, chocolate and lace – though found throughout the city – are highly concentrated in the tourist areas around the Grand-Place. Shops catering to another national passion, the comic strip or "bande dessinée" (BD), can be found a little further afield near the Bourse and on the chaussée d'Ixelles near place Fernand Cocq.

ART AND ANTIQUES

Costermans

Map 2, D6. Pl du Grand Sablon 5. Tram #92, #93, #94.
Mon–Fri 9am–6pm, Sat 10am–noon & 2–6pm.
Famous Grand Sablon antiques shop, established in 1839 and

now run by Marc-Henri Jaspar-Costermans. Its speciality is eighteenth-century furniture and *objets d'art* as well as paintings and beautifully crafted clocks. There's also an impressive range of old fireplaces and wrought ironwork. Prices are mostly prohibitive to purchasing but it's a lovely place to look around nonetheless.

De Leye
Map 2, D6. Rue Lebeau 16. Tram #92, #93, #94.
Tues–Sat 10.30am–12.30pm & 2.30–6.30pm.
Just off place du Grand Sablon, this newly established shop specialises in high-quality seventeenth- and eighteenth-century silverware and everything from silver candlesticks to serving ladles, mirrors, statuettes, teapots and gravy boats. Excellent selection and competitive prices.

Kanal 20
Map 2, B4. Bd Barthélemy 20. Ⓜ Comte de Flandre.
Wed–Sat 2–6pm.
Kanal 20 is six galleries dedicated to exhibiting contemporary art. Particularly interesting is the Crown Gallery which shows young Belgian and foreign artists as well as more established artists like Liam Golub and Nancy Spero. H&R Projects (linked to the Hussenot Gallery in Paris) shows Belgians, French and Americans such as 1960s artist Alain Jacquet or the more contemporary Gregory Crewdson, Karen Kilimnik and George Pardo.

Kenulf Van Bockstade
Map 2, D6. Pl du Grand Sablon 9. Tram #92, #93, #94.
Thurs–Fri 2–6pm, Sat 10.30am–6pm, Sun 10.30am–2pm.
Long-established and popular fine art gallery specializing in romantic paintings dating from the nineteenth century and early twentieth-century Impressionist paintings. Full of portraits, rustic landscapes and seascapes.

Opening Hours

Shops are generally open from 10am to 6–7pm from Monday to Saturday. On Friday, department stores stay open until 8pm. In some districts, certain shops – mainly those selling booze, news, cigarettes and food – also open at night and/or on Sunday. For instance, the corner shops in St Josse stay open till around 10–11pm. The Grand-Place and the Bourse and St Géry areas have night shops staying open till between 2–5 am. The White Night chain has central branches at rue du Lombard 8, rue E. Allard 3 and place du Châtelain 43, as well as branches in the outskirts, and these are open Sun–Thurs 6pm–1am and Fri–Sat 5pm–2am.

Sabine Wachters
Map 2, B7. Av de Stalingrad 26. Ⓜ Lemonnier.
Tues–Sat 11am–7pm.
A gallery specializing in young unknown artists as well as the big names on the scene such as Andy Warhol, Donald Judd and Daniel Spoerri.

BOOKS AND COMICS

Le Bande des Six Nez
Map 6, J2. Ch de Wavre 179. Ⓜ Schuman.
Stocks a variety of new comics, as well as original editions from the 1940s and 1950s. It also sells original drawings, and those who think cartoon art is kid's stuff might be surprised to learn they recently sold a 1930s sketch of Tintin for F1,000,000. Fortunately the comics come a little cheaper – anything from F60 to F6000 – and there's a modest, but interesting, English-language section.

Brüsel

Map 3, C6. Bd Anspach 100. Ⓜ Bourse.
Mon–Sat 10am–6.30pm.

This well-known comic shop stocks more than 8000 new issues and specializes in French underground editions – *Association*, *Amok* and *Bill* to name but a few. You'll also find the complete works of the famous Belgian comic-book artist Schuiten, most popularly known for his controversial comic *Brüsel*, which depicts the architectural destruction of a city (guess which one) in the 1960s. Calvin and Hobbes make an appearance, as does Tintin in a babel of language versions. The shop is particularly worth visiting when it hosts a pop-art or comic-book exhibition.

La Boutique Tintin

Map 4, D4. Rue de la Colline 13. Ⓜ Bourse.
Mon 11am–6pm, Tues–Sat 10am–6pm, Sun 11am–5pm.

Set up, no doubt, by someone with an unhealthy obsession with Hergé's quiffed hero. Expect to find anything and everything to do with Tintin – comic books, postcards, stationery, figurines, T-shirts and sweaters – and all Hergé's other cartoon creations, such as Quick & Flupke. Just off the Grand-Place.

Centre Belge de la Bande Dessinée

Map 3, F4. Rue des Sables 20. Ⓜ de Brouckère, Botanique or Rogier.
Tues–Sun 10am-6pm.

This museum bookstore (see p.38) is definitely worth a visit even if you haven't been to the museum – it contains a wide range of new comics.

Fil à Terre

Map 6, J2. Ch de Wavre 198. Ⓜ Porte de Namur.
Daily 11.30am–8pm.

A comic shop with a fairly wide selection – there are over three thousand – of Belgian and French comics. Fil à Terre also provides customers with a bar in which to read their latest purchase.

BOOKS AND COMICS

Librairie des Étangs
Map 6, J5. Ch d'Ixelles 319. Bus #71.
Mon–Sat 10am–7pm, Sun 10am–2pm.
More than 3000 English-language titles, as well as a good selection of Asian and Caribbean works. They also have occasional prose readings in the basement, and when you get tired of browsing the bookshelves there's a tearoom at the back serving refreshments and a small gallery to wander in.

Nijinski
Map 6, G7. Rue du Page 15. Tram #93, #94.
Mon, Wed–Sat 11am–6pm, Tues 11am–9pm.
Although it's mainly a French-language bookshop, this second-hand shop near place du Châtelain has an excellent selection of twentieth-century English-language fiction – Graham Greene, Gore Vidal, Anthony Burgess – and the prices, often under F200 a book, are reasonable.

Pêle-Mêle
Map 2, B6. Bd Maurice Lemonnier 55. Ⓜ Annessens.
Mon–Sat 10am–6.30pm.
A maze-like shop with a jumble of second-hand books stacked up against the walls. Thrillers, classics, comics, magazines and even CDs retail at some of the lowest prices in Brussels: a Balzac or a Camus will cost around F20. The whole wall devoted to English-language titles (including an unhealthy number of self-help books) houses novels selling at F45–60. A good place to unload any unwanted books as they also buy.

Sterling Books
Map 2, D4. Rue du Fossé aux Loups 38. Ⓜ de Brouckère.
Mon–Sat 10am–7pm, Sun 12–6.30pm.
This newly established, large English-language book shop has more than 50,000 UK and US titles, including a large selection of magazines and is much cheaper than Waterstone's – they sell

BOOKS AND COMICS

books at the cover price, converted at the day's exchange rate, plus six percent VAT. You can also pay directly in pound sterling.

Waterstone's

Map 2, E3. Bd Adolphe Max 71–75. Ⓜ de Brouckère or Rogier.
Mon–Thurs 9am–6.30pm, Fri–Sat 9am–7pm.

The Brussels branch of the British parent company, selling over 70,000 English-language titles. The premises are a bit cramped, making it far from ideal for browsing, but there's an excellent selection of books and magazines and a good ordering service.

CHOCOLATE

Léonidas

Map 2, C5. Bd Anspach 46. Ⓜ Bourse.
Daily 9am–7pm.

Léonidas remains one of the most popular – and cheapest – widespread outlets for Belgian chocolates and pralines, although like some other choc chains they are straight off the production line. They are rather sickly-sweet in comparison to the others but no one will notice the difference back home. Branches all over.

Mary's

Map 2, F5. Rue Royale, 73. Tram #92, #93, #94.
Tues–Fri & Sun 9am–6pm, Sat 9am–12.30pm & 2–7pm.

A very exclusive and pricey shop, with beautiful period decor, selling handmade chocolates. You can instantly taste the difference between these and those of the chains: these pralines are top-notch, melt-in-the-mouth gourmet delicacies.

Neuhaus

Map 4, C4. Grand-Place 27. Ⓜ Gare Centrale.

A chocoholic's paradise, this ludicrously expensive shop stocks the best that Belgium has to offer in the chocolate depart-

CHOCOLATE

ment. Check out their specialities – the handmade Caprices, which are pralines stuffed with crispy nougat, fresh cream and soft-centred chocolate, and the delicious Manons, stuffed white chocolates, which come in fresh cream, vanilla, and coffee fillings. They have branches all over the town, but other central ones are in avenue de la Toison d'Or 27 and in the Galerie de la Reine.

Planète Chocolat

Map 2, D5. Rue du Lombard 24. Ⓜ Bourse.
Tues–Sat 10am–6.30pm, Sun 1–6.30pm.
Sells standard boxes of delicious Belgian chocolates as well as a whole range of strangely shaped ones. You also get to see how the bonbons are made in their mini-chocolate museum. When you've had enough of that, pay a visit to the tearoom in their new spacious premises.

Wittamer

Map 3, E8. Pl du Grand Sablon 6 & 12. Ⓜ Gare Centrale.
Mon 8am–6pm, Tues–Sat 7am–7pm, Sun 7am–6pm.
Brussels' most famous patisserie and chocolate shop, established in 1910 and still run by the Wittamer family, who sell gorgeous if expensive light pastries, cakes, mousses, and chocolates. Also serves speciality teas and coffees in their tearoom at no. 12.

DEPARTMENT STORES

Inno

Map 3, E3. Rue Neuve 111. Ⓜ de Brouckère or Rogier.
Mon–Thurs & Sat 9.30am–7pm, Fri 9.30am–8pm.
Brussels' largest department store has been recently refurbished and has four floors peddling goods ranging from perfume and lingerie to home furnishings, clothing, and shoes. Prices vary from the high-rise to the bargain basement.

Marks & Spencer

Map 3, E4. Rue Neuve 17–21. Ⓜ de Brouckère or Rogier.
Mon–Thurs 9.30am–6pm, Fri 9.30am–8pm, Sat 9.30am–6.30pm.
British expats find a home from home in the staples which this
chain is famous for. It sells good-quality clothing and underwear, along with the ubiquitous M&S flower-scented soaps and
bath products. There is a small food hall in the basement.

GALLERIES

City 2

Map 3, F3. Rue Neuve. Ⓜ Place Rogier.
A huge temple to shopping with an abundance of boutiques,
restaurants and cinemas, as well as a department store and the
massive Fnac store. Hell or heaven depending on your taste or
credit limit.

Galerie Agora

Map 4, D4. Off rue des Éperonniers. Ⓜ Centrale.
Although near the grandeur of the Grand-Place, this galerie is
an exotic bazaar of ethnic clothes, incense, tattooists, piercers
and all the tacky accoutrements that make shopping a rush.

Galerie Louise and Galerie de la Toison d'Or

Map 6, H1. Ⓜ Porte de Namur or Louise.
Galleries housing a series of boutiques selling top–of–the–range
designer clothing – Armani, Gautier, Helmut Lang – at
heart–attack city prices: take a peek at the clothes in Ottimo
(Mon–Sat 10am–6.30pm). A variety of shoe shops along the
same expensive lines such as Nouchka, in both the Espace
Louise section, of the galleries and the Toison d'Or section, are
open Mon–Sat 10.30am–6.30pm. The whole sprawl is nevertheless hugely tacky, with red carpet and a glorious golden
mock fountain in the centre.

Galeries St Hubert
Map 4, E3–F2. Ⓜ de Brouckère.

An impressive 1846 glass-roofed gallery divided up into the Galerie de la Reine and the Galerie du Roi. It contains a selection of well-established conservative shops. Those worth looking out for are Longchamps, Galerie du Roi 21, for quality women's accessories, Van Schelle at Galerie du Roi 36 and Nicholson at Galerie de la Reine 36; all sell the leading brands in fashion. Neuhaus (see p.232) has one of their poshest shops here and there are various art and philosophy bookshops dotted along the galleries to browse in. For a more highbrow interlude during your shopping day, the excellent art house Arenberg cinema in the Galerie de la Reine has an eclectic film programme, or you could simply relax in one of the cafés.

Galerie d'Ixelles
Map 6, H–I1. Ⓜ Porte de Namur.

Small gallery in Matonge, the African quarter just off the chaussée d'Ixelles, with a fantastic atmosphere. It contains a series of small stores selling ethnic jewellery as well as various record stores and hairdressers specializing in Afro hair.

FASHION

Emporio Armani
Map 3, E8. Pl du Grand Sablon 37. Tram #92, #93, #94.
Mon, Wed–Sat 10.30am–7pm, Sun 11am–6pm.
Sleek and smart casual suits, jeans, underwear and accessories for both men and women in the mainstream Armani vein. The store is spacious and the staff are welcoming

Coco's
Map 3, E7. Rue St Jean 45. ℂ512 53 77 Ⓜ Gare Centrale.
Ring for times.

FASHION

Eccentric second-hand clothes and bric-à-brac store owned by an amiable woman who seems to have steadily collected everything over a period of decades. It covers two floors and is in a beautiful old Brussels house covered in Belgian royal family memorabilia and 1970s kitsch.

Elvis Pompilio

Map 4, A6. Rue du Midi 60. Ⓜ Bourse.
Mon–Sat 10.30am–6.30pm.
From eccentric hats which look like wedding-cakes to simple berets and his trademark cowboy hats, Belgian hatter Elvis Pompilio deserves his high-fashion reputation. The women's shop and the adjacent men's shop at rue des Lombards 24 are unmissable from any window-shopping trip: prices average at F5000. He also does made-to-measure and sells accessories such as parasols and specs which are more decorative than useful.

Francis Ferent

Map 6, G1. Av de la Toison d'Or 19a. Ⓜ Porte de Namur.
Mon–Sat 9.30am–6.30pm.
If you're on the market for some designer womenswear this is the place to head. It's expensive, but there's a wide selection – Donna Karan, Joseph, Vivienne Westwood, Alexander McQueen and Moschino to name but a few.

Gianni Versace

Map 6, F2. Bd de Waterloo 64. Ⓜ Louise.
Mon 1–6.30pm, Tues–Sat 10am–6.30pm.
Everything you expect from a Versace outlet – swish marble decor, stylish clothing, and enormous prices. Caters for both men and women.

Hennes & Mauritz (H&M)

Map 3, E3. Rue Neuve 80. Ⓜ de Brouckère or Rogier.
Mon–Thurs & Sat 9.30am–6.30pm, Fri 9.30am–7pm.

The Swedish store which has all the high-street fashion trends. Expect to find a mixture of cheap suits, club gear and youthful and casual clothing. There are male, female and kids' sections, as well as underwear and accessories. Items can be exchanged in all the H&Ms in Europe and they accept major European currencies. There are other branches on rue Neuve 36 and chaussée d'Ixelles 41–43.

L'Homme Chrétien
Map 3, D6. Rue des Pierres 27. Ⓜ de Brouckère or Bourse.
Mon–Sat 11am–7pm.

These are new spacious premises for this kitsch extravaganza of a store. There's a mixture of men and women's vintage and second-hand clothing and shoes, as well as the owner's own designs. These are a combination of quirky fashion-student type ideas – such as customised skirts made out of religious pictures – and stylised versions of high-street fashion. A tad overpriced but there are occasionally jumble-sale type bins worth rummaging through.

Privé Joke
Map 2, C5. Rue des Riches Claires 8 & 12. Ⓜ Bourse.
Mon–Sat 10.30am–7pm.

This shop stocks standard club and streetwear labels such as Carhartt, Ben Sherman and Lady Soul and they've recently expanded into boyswear and girlswear. It's host to occasional DJs who want to practise in the booth and there are always flyers for clubnights and raves to be picked up.

Stijl
Map 3, C5. Rue Antoine Dansaert 74. Ⓜ Bourse.
Mon–Sat 10.30am–6.30pm.

Huge men and womenswear emporium focusing on cutting-edge Belgian designers such as Ann Demeulemeester, Martin Margiela, Dries Van Noten, Dirk Bikkembergs and Raf

FASHION

Simons. They also sell Helmut Lang, John Smedley and Romeo Gigli. Their children's clothing shop, Kat en Muis at no. 32, means the whole family can look like it's straight out of a fashion shoot.

Virgin Shoes

Map 4, D6. Rue des Éperonniers 13. Ⓜ Gare Centrale. Mon–Sat 10.30am–12.30pm & 1.30–6.30pm.

Trendy men and women's shoes and boots in all shapes and sizes and all the colours of the rainbow. Their branch at rue Antoine Dansaert 10 does more mainstream-style footwear.

Zara

Map 3, E4. Rue Neuve 48–50. Ⓜ de Brouckère or Rogier. Mon 10am–7pm, Tues–Thurs 9.30am–7pm, Fri–Sat 9.30am–7.30pm.

This Spanish chain caters for the young professional with lots of smart, conservative suits for both men and women. They also do a wide range of dresses, accessories, jeans and shirts. There are several branches, with another one at avenue Louise 8–10. The same company owns the more upmarket menswear store Massimo Dutti on avenue de la Toison d'Or 22.

Euroline, rue du Marché-aux-Herbes 52 (Jan–March Mon–Sat 10am–8pm and Sun 10am–7pm; April–Dec Mon–Sat 9am–11pm and Sun 10am–7pm), is the ultimate in EU kitsch, with flags, car stickers and *objets d'art*, all with the golden stars of the EU insignia.

FASHION

FOOD AND DRINK

Au Suisse

Map 2, C5. Boulevard Anspach 73–75. Ⓜ Bourse.
Mon–Fri 10am–8pm, Sat & Sun 9pm.

Despite the name, a Belgian-style deli which serves up traditional nosh such as *maatjes* (Belgian herrings), *filet américain* (raw minced meat) or *tête pressée* (brawn), along with a lot more edible options. Two long counters line the deli, and you can eat in, also sampling some of their pastries, ice-cream milkshakes or coffee. The clientele is eclectic, from moustached locals to fashion victims. Their shop next door sells a wide variety of cheeses.

Bière Artisanale

Map 6, J2. Ch de Wavre 174. Ⓜ Porte de Namur.
Mon–Sat 11am–7pm.

A drinker's paradise – few can resist the temptation of Bière Artisanale's shelves, which, suprisingly for such modest premises, carry more than 400 different types of beer. It's quite cheap, too, and if drinking really is your hobby, you can buy the correct glass in which to serve your favourite tipple. To learn more about Belgian beer or to place an order for home delivery, look at their Web site *www.users.skynet.be/beermania/* or go along to one of the many classes (some given in English) and tasting-sessions organized here to spread the word.

Dandoy

Map 4, C3. Rue au Beurre 31. Ⓜ Bourse.
Mon–Sat 8.30am–6.30pm, Sun 10.30am–6.30pm.

This famous shop has been making biscuits since 1829, so it's no surprise they now have it down to a fine art. Their main speciality is known locally as "speculoos", a kind of hard gingerbread biscuit. This shop even has some larger-than-life biccies which are the size of small children and can cost as much as F2000. Moreover they come in a weird variety of shapes – the most unappetising one being the life-size biscuit Manneken Pis. They have two branches on the Grand-Place and a tearoom at their rue Charles Buls 14 branch.

De Muynck Regnier
Map 3, D6. Rue du Marché-aux-Herbes 56. Ⓜ Gare Centrale.
Daily 10am–9pm.

This specialist beer shop, handily placed near the Grand-Place, sells over 150 different types of beers including a number of rare Belgian varieties. Its popularity with tourists explains the slightly inflated prices, but there's a wide selection and the owner will quite happily chat away all day about any Belgian booze you care to mention.

LACE

F. Rubbrecht
Map 4, C3. Grand-Place 23. Ⓜ Gare Centrale.
Mon–Sat 9am–7pm, Sun 10am–6pm.

Traditional lace shop specializing in handmade Brussels lace. They do wholesale and retail, and also valuing and buying.

Manufacture Belge de Dentelle
Map 4, D3. Galerie de la Reine 6–8. Ⓜ Gare Centrale.
Mon–Sat 10am–7pm.

The city's largest lace merchant, in business since 1810. Sells a wide a variety of modern and antique lace at fairly reasonable prices. The service is helpfully old-fashioned.

Roses Lace Boutique
Map 4, C5. Rue Charles Buls 30. Ⓜ Gare Centrale.
Mon–Sat 10am–7pm.

There's a large collection of spooky lace-clad porcelain dolls in the window of this small shop, but it's a good place to go for gifts – they sell everything from parasols to lace crucifixes. But it's not cheap: a tiny lace tea coaster costs F275, whereas the tablecloths cost as much as F4900.

Lace

Renowned for the fineness of the thread and beautiful motifs, **Belgian lace** is famous the world over. Flanders lace, as it was once known, was worn in the royal courts of Paris and London – Queen Elizabeth I of England alone is said to have had more than 3000 lace dresses, and the famous ruffs of her courtiers were made out of lace, with starch to keep them stiff also introduced from Flanders. Lace reached its zenith of popularity in the mid-nineteenth century when an estimated 10,000 women and girls worked as lacemakers in the capital. By the end of the nineteenth century, though, much of the lace was machine-made.

Masterpieces from that period can still be viewed today – the Musée du Costume et de la Dentelle (see p.27) exhibits an interesting collection, including one of Empress Eugénie's skirts (the Empress owned a lace gown which 600 women had toiled over for ten months) and some of Empress Sissi of Austria's scarves and handkerchiefs.

If you're on the market for some Brussels lace, be warned – much of the lace on sale in the capital is actually made in China, and the authentic handmade stuff can be very pricey, particularly in the much-hyped lace shops in and around the Grand-Place. Your best bet is to head for the flea market at Jeu de Balle where you can usually pick up far nicer pieces for much less money. The shops listed on p.240, although not cheap, offer the pick of the lace in the city.

LACE

MARKETS

The Grand-Place daily **flower market** wins the prize for
the most picturesque of Brussels' markets (Mon-Sat 8am-
6pm); the Grand-Place also hosts a bird market on
Sundays 9am-1pm. Although the swankiest antiques and
collectibles market is held at **place du Grand Sablon**
(Map 3, E8; Sat 9am–6pm, Sun 9am–2pm), the real bar-
gains can be found at the flea market on **place du Jeu
de Balle** (Map 3, C10) in the Marolles quarter. It's held
every morning from 7am to 2pm, but it's at its biggest –
and most expensive – at weekends, where the eccentric
muddle of colonial spoils, quirky odds and ends and
domestic and ecclesiastical bric-à-brac give an impression
of a century's bourgeois fads and fashions. The largest and
most colourful food market is held every Sunday
(6am–1pm) at **Gare du Midi** (Map 2, A7), a bazaar-like
affair, with traders crammed under the railway bridge and
spilling out into the surrounding streets. Stands sell pitta,
olives, North African raï tapes, spices, herbs and pulses,
among the vegetables and cheap clothes. There's also a
picturesque market at **place du Châtelain** (Map 6, G7)
every Wednesday, cram-packed with tiny stalls selling
fresh vegetables, cheeses, cakes and pastries, as well as fine
laces, plants and flowers, and home-made wines.
Collector's markets are fairly random, although the
Woluwe St Pierre antiquarian book fair (Map 1, F3),
held in the Musée du Transport Urbain Bruxellois (see
p.107) on the first Saturday of every month, is a notable
exception.

MUSIC

BCM

Map 3, C6. Plattesteen 6. Ⓜ Bourse.

Mon–Sat 11am–6.30pm.

If you've come to Belgium to explore the techno scene, this is where to find your vinyl. They also stock lots of drum 'n' bass, speed-garage, and house.

DiscoSold

Map 2, E3. Bd Adolphe Max 97. Ⓜ Rogier.

Mon–Sat 10.30am–6.30pm.

This small second-hand record shop is well-known for its obscure but cool collection of soul, funk, pop and jazz as well as a large section devoted to classical music. The prices won't break the bank either; most CDs costing under F400.

Fnac

Map 3, E4. Rue Neuve City 2. Ⓜ Rogier or de Brouckère.

Mon–Thurs & Sat 10am–7pm, Fri 10am–8pm.

A store with a fairly wide selection of French and English tapes and CDs, along with books, newspapers and CD players. It's also the place to come to buy tickets for mainstream gigs and concerts in the capital.

Free Record Shop

Map 2, D4. Rue Fossé aux Loups 18. Ⓜ de Brouckère.

Mon–Sat 10am–7pm, Sun 12–6pm.

Huge generic store with an impressive range of CDs, vinyl and tapes. You name it, they have it: techno, house, easy listening, punk, rock, pop, folk, jazz, rap and classical. They also sell videos and computer games and there's a ticket booth for gigs and official raves.

MUSIC

Music Mania

Map 3, D5. Rue de la Fourche 4. Ⓜ de Brouckère.

Mon–Fri noon–6.30pm, Sat 11am–6pm.

The place to come for the latest release or that elusive vinyl or CD. This independent music store is frequented by rappers, straight-edge skaters and house or drum 'n' bass DJs alike and sells tickets before general sale to large and smaller gigs and parties. It's also a good source for flyers.

Virgin Megastore

Map 3, D4. Bd Anspach. Ⓜ de Brouckère.

Mon–Thurs, Sat 10am–7pm, Fri 10am–8pm, Sun noon–7pm.

Near the junction of rue Grétry. The full range of CDs, listening stands and games as well as the odd piece of vinyl.

Sports

Cycling and **football** are the nation's top sports. Belgium has a great cycling terrain and Brussels plays host to the many national cycling meets, having also been a stop-off point for the Tour de France. Eddy Merckx, fives times winner of the Tour, is still revered throughout the country even though he retired some twenty years ago. Less professional cyclists can join the joggers to stretch their legs in the Bois de la Cambre and the Forêt de Soignes.

Fans of football can follow the mixed fortunes of RSC Anderlecht, the only Belgian club to enjoy postwar success in Europe. Belgium, and Brussels in particular, awaits the year 2000 excitedly when they will host (jointly with Holland) the European Championship. Not only has a footballing event of this scale never been held in Brussels before but it's also a good opportunity to restore the city's place as an international football host after the Heysel tragedy.

However, it has to be said that perhaps the most common sports in Brussels are the extremely strenuous **"baby-foot"** (table football), as well as the many versions of bar billiards. There's also the traditional sport of *tir à l'arc en hauteur* which can be found in big parks like the Parc Josaphat and the Parc de la Woluwe and consists shooting down feathers from the top of a very tall pole with a bow and arrow.

ATHLETICS

Two major events dominate the **athletics** calendar of Brussels. The Ivo van Damme Memorial IAHF Grand Prix is one of the international Athletic Federation meetings that is held yearly (last fortnight in August) in the Stade Roi Baudouin (Map 5, B2) and attracts many of the stars of the sport. It's named after the Belgian 800m silver-medallist of the 1976 Olympics in Montréal. Ring ✆474 72 30 for tickets and details.

On a less professional note there is also the Brussels 20km Race held annually in May or June. This popular competition usually attracts a field of 20,000 runners, and more than 50,000 spectators. Although it consists of mostly serious runners, there are lots of festivities along the way and some people semi-walk it. The course takes participants halfway round the city near the EU Quarter, the Palais Royale, the avenue Louise, the Bois de la Cambre and through the tunnels of the Brussels inner ring road. It starts and finishes at the Esplanade du Cinquantenaire, and participants are charged F350 for the privilege of running their socks off for four hours. Ring ✆511 90 00 for details and to sign up.

FOOTBALL

Brussels' position in European **football** went down several notches following the Heysel disaster. Not only was the city's reputation in tatters, but Heysel was banned from staging European matches. Even the home club who played in the stadium complex, Racing Jet Brussels, moved out to Wavre, 30km away.

However, after being rebuilt and renamed the Stade Roi Baudouin, the new ground will be host to the Euro 2000 matches.

Recent proofs of good conduct have included the 1996 Cup-Winners' Cup Final between Paris St Germain and Rapid Vienna, with its potentially explosive mix of fans, which passed off without a hitch, as did the crucial 1998 Belgium v Ireland World Cup qualifier.

Heysel

The **Heysel** disaster is synonymous with football violence. The stadium, built in 1930 in the Parc des Expositions in northwest Brussels, was the site for the 1985 European Cup Final between Liverpool FC and Juventus.

Liverpool fans had started drinking early in the day, and were joined by neo-Nazi elements in the stands, as was manifest from the pamphlets later found near the seats. Local policing was disorganised and parts of the stadium were in need of renovation. Shortly before kick-off, a group of Liverpool fans charged through the supposedly neutral block Z and 39 supporters (mainly Italian) were crushed to death when the sector wall collapsed. The match was played out to avoid further pandemonium, resulting in a win for Juventus. English clubs were banned from Europe for five years.

The stadium obviously had to be refurbished, and after various arguments, the Belgian FA agreed to foot the bill. The Stade du Roi Baudouin was built in its place, although some of the original Heysel infrastructure remains. The stadium, already largely finished, with a projected capacity of 50,000, all-seated, is due to host the opening match of Euro 2000. It boasts its own new métro station at the end of the 1A line, and can also be accessed from the Heysel métro station. The stadium ticket office, marked Kartenverkoop/Vente Tickets, is along avenue du Marathon by Tribune no.1 and sells tickets in four different colour-coded price brackets. Ring ©477 12 11 for details on tickets.

In terms of league football Brussels has been dominated by one club – Anderlecht. Most of the city's other clubs have either folded, migrated or merged to help form the city's poor relation, Racing White Daring Molenbeek (RWDM). Anderlecht's facilities and resources put other Belgian clubs in the shade, but this difference is all the more marked in Brussels as RWDM attract only a few thousand fans. A third city club, Union Saint-Gilloise, were *the* Brussels club until their relegation in 1973. They have an identifiable neighbourhood feel and their sardonic Bruxellois humour can still be heard in the club bar. The few fans who still shuffle up the rue du Stade do so now out of duty rather than pleasure.

ROYAL SPORTING CLUB ANDERLECHT

Map 1, B3. Stade Constant Vanden Stock, av Théo Verbeeck 2 ©522 15 39 for information and tickets. Ⓜ St Guidon.

Founded in 1908, Anderlecht won their first title only in 1947. Two years after that, an England ex-goalie by the name of Bill Gormlie was appointed first team coach, ushering in a decade of seven titles that established Anderlecht as the country's biggest club.

In the early 1960s Real Madrid, CDNA Sofia and Bologna were all beaten, while at home Anderlecht won five titles in a row. In 1964, the Belgian team that beat Holland 1-0 was composed entirely of Anderlecht players. All of Anderlecht's three European successes came during the late 1970s and early 1980s, the club's golden period. Their greatest triumph was their Cup Winners' Cup victory in 1976, with a 4-2 victory over West Ham in the final. Other successes included victory over Liverpool in the European Super Cup in 1978 and an impressive win over Benfica in the UEFA Cup Final in 1983.

After that, the money needed to convert the stadium meant that there was less to spend on players. The Mauves (because of their strip) have thus under-achieved in Europe for most of the Nineties – the only highlight being an appearance in the 1990 Cup Winners' Cup Final, which they went on to lose to Sampdoria. Various corruption sagas have also haunted the club. Recently the club president Vanden Stock admitted that he had paid a Spanish referee a million francs after a UEFA semi-final with Nottingham Forest.

The only comfort remaining to fans is that they now have a quite classy stadium, and it's where the Belgian team practised and played during the Heysel refurbishment.

RWD MOLENBEEK

Map 1, B2. Stade Edmond Machtens, rue Charles Malis 61 ©411 99 00. Ⓜ Beekkant.

RWDM was formed by merging two Brussels clubs, Daring and Racing White, in 1973. Only two years later, a goal from international Jacques Teugels against Anderlecht won the club their first and only title. Key player Johan Boskamp became a local hero – until his move to Anderlecht. Though they were unable to keep their title, the team remained in the top six, and in 1977 they were only one away goal away from a UEFA Cup Final against Juventus. The club have done little since, though coach René Vandereycken did take them back into Europe for 1996–97.

To get there, go to Métro Beekkant, then take bus #85 or a ten-minute walk down rue Jules Vieujant, followed by a left down rue Osseghem.

UNION SAINT-GILLOISE

Map 1, A3. Stade Joseph Marien, ch de Bruxelles 223 ©344 16 56. Ⓜ Horta.

A more romantic ground would be difficult to imagine. The Stade Joseph Marien, named after a former club president, is bordered by the forest of Parc Duden on one side and by a wonderful old club bar on the other.

FOOTBALL

People crowded up the hillside in their thousands to see Union in their golden prewar days, when they were the biggest club in Belgium. The last decent Union side, that of the late 1950s and early 1960s, made occasional forays into the Fairs' Cup, beating Roma and Olympique Marseille.

Union were too proud to agree to any of the mergers that swallowed up the lesser Brussels clubs in the 1970s. The result was that the club celebrated their centenary in 1997 by being relegated to the third division. With amateur football and possibly worse looming, the forest is ghostly silent.

To get there, take the tram to Horta and then tram #18, getting off at Van Haelen. From there the stadium is a five-minute walk up rue des Glands.

....

Young multinational bar lads flock to O'Reilly's (see p.197), which has established itself as the raucous venue for satellite international and particularly English Premiership matches. For big Irish matches, the Irish Club (©231 12 16/231 12 08) usually organizes big screen social evenings.

....

CYCLING

Cycling is immensely popular in Belgium, both as a sport and a hobby. Those interested in cycling as a spectator sport will know that the Tour de France has come through Belgium, and stopped off in Brussels. In honour of the great Belgian cyclist, the Eddy Merckx Grand Prix on the last Sunday of August is a timed event attracting top professionals. However, as of last year, Provélo (©502 73 55) organizes an amateur version which is an excellent opportunity to take advantage of the car-free 22km circuit within Brussels, starting and ending at the Gare du Nord, via the Botanique, Montgomery tunnel, the canal and Heysel. Families are welcome.

Eddy Merckx

Four cyclists have achieved the extraordinary distinction of winning the Tour de France five times: Jacques Anquetil, Bernard Hinault, Miguel Indurain and – the best of them all – Belgium's **Eddy Merckx**. In his very first Tour, in 1969, Eddy finished eighteen minutes in front of the runner-up (this is a race in which five minutes is a big gap), destroying the field in a style that was to earn him the nickname "The Cannibal". As strong on mountain climbs as in races against the clock (he set a world record for the greatest distance covered in an hour), and as strong in one-day events as in the huge multi-stage tours, Merckx amassed a tally of titles that no rider is ever likely to equal: five victories in the Giro d'Italia (Tour of Italy); three times winner of the Paris–Nice race; three times World Road Champion; five times winner of the Liège–Bastogne–Liège race; three times winner of the Paris–Roubaix (the so-called "Hell of the North"); seven times winner of the Milan–San Remo . . . the list goes on. In the 1974 season he managed to win the tours of Italy and France, then the World Championship, a Grand Slam that only Stephen Roche has matched. Indeed, so complete was his dominance that a disconsolate rival once observed: "If Merckx has decided he wants to win today, then he will." He retired in 1978, having totalled 525 victories, and has since divided his time between punditry, running his own bike factory, and nurturing the talent of his son Axel, who is now following hot in his father's wheel-tracks, achieving a very commendable 10th place in the 1998 Tour de France. So, should you be in Brussels for the August Grand Prix. keep your eyes peeled and you just might just see the Greatest Living Belgian giving his expert analysis to the TV crews.

If you're **hiring** a bike go to Provélo (Sept–June Mon–Fri 9am–6pm, rue E. Solvay 32; July–Aug Tues–Sun 1–7pm rue de l'infante Isabelle; ☎502 73 55) who also organize other bike tours of Brussels and/or the outskirts. Alternatively, make sure you check out the Train-plus-Vélo schemes offered at most railway stations – a bike is thrown in with the price of a train ticket (☎555 25 25) to 19 destinations in Belgium. For free spirits who already have their own bike, you can take it on the train for F150 per single journey, F300 for a return journey.

GOLF

Most **golf courses** are outside Brussels and the Federation Royal Belge de Golf (☎0672 23 89) can provide information on full-size golf courses in Belgium. The best 18-hole course in Brussels itself is the **Royal Amicale Anderlecht Golf Club**, rue Scholle 1 (☎521 16 87) which has training and driving ranges and is well laid-out in wooded surroundings with lakes. The **Brabantse Golf** at Steenwagenstraat 11, Melsbroek (☎751 82 05) is near the airport and is a pleasant and not too challenging full practice course of 5km long. The **Golf de l'Empereur** near Waterloo is both challenging and beautiful, with the clubhouse in an old farmhouse. It has both 18- and 9-hole courses. You can play **crazy golf** at Parc de Wolvendael on avenue de Wolvendael 44 (daily 10am–6pm; tram #92, #41; ☎375 34 62).

SKATING

Ice-skaters will be delighted at the whimsical faerie-atmosphere surrounding the rink on the Grand-Place in December and January. Other public rinks include the Patinoire de Forest, avenue du Globe 36 (☎345 16 11), which is open all year round, and Poséidon, avenue des

Vaillants 4 (Sept–April; ☎762 16 33). **Rollerbladers** and **skateboarders** should go to Mont des Arts near Gare Centrale or the Roller Park, quai de Beistbroeck (☎522 59 19), which closes at midnight on Friday and Saturday.

SPORTS CENTRES AND GYMS

Winner's at rue Bonneel 13 (☎280 02 70) has an inside **climbing**-wall, as well as **squash** courts and a **gym**. The **Physical Golden Club** at place du Châtelain 33 (Mon–Fri 12–10pm, Sat–Sun 10am–4pm; ☎539 30 36) has become highly prestigious in beefcake circles since the rise in popularity of that great Belgian export Jean-Claude van Damme. Indeed, van Damme started off here and his ex-coach is still the manager. It has two thousand square metres of muscle-building machines, runs aerobics, step and fitness classes, has saunas and sunbeds and, of course, the popular **martial arts** classes for all those Hollywood wannabes. The **American Gym** at boulevard Général Jacques 144 (Mon–Fri 10am–10pm, Sat 10am–3pm, Sun 10am–2pm; ☎640 59 92) has similar facilities.

The Centre Sportif de Woluwe St Pierre at avenue Salomé 2 (☎773 18 20) has a full range of sporting facilities including a multi-sports hall and squash and **tennis** courts (the latter are open till 11pm). The Complexe Sportif du Palais du Midi at rue van der Weyden 3–9 (Map 2, C6; ☎279 59 56) is more centrally located and has a sports hall which it rents out to teams including the first division Brussels **basketball** team.

SWIMMING POOLS

The city has a number of pools in local sports centres including an Olympic-sized one at the **Centre Sportif de Woluwe St Pierre** (Mon–Thurs 8am–7pm, Fri 8am–8pm,

Sat 8am–7pm). Alternatively, the **Océade** water park in Heysel (see "Kids' Brussels") is a great place to go for water slides, wave-making machines and other aquatic mischief.

TENPIN BOWLING

The less active will be pleased to learn the city has a number of bowling alleys, the biggest, and most centrally located, being the **Crosly Super Bowling** at boulevard de l'Empereur 36 (Map 2, D6; daily 2pm–2am; ℂ512 08 74). It has twenty lanes and a late bar.

Kids' Brussels

Although many of the main sights and museums in Brussels (the Manneken Pis, the Grand-Place, the Musée d'Art Moderne) are about as interesting to kids as pig iron production in Micronesia, worry not – Brussels can be child-friendly.

In the town centre, the **Centre Belge de la Bande Dessinée** museum, **Scientastic**, and the **Théâtre de Toone**, are the main attractions for younger and older children alike. Out of town, Heysel gives the impression it was specifically designed for the under-12s, and is home to both **Mini-Europe** and **Océade**, as well as the excellent **Planétarium** which holds regular exhibitions. Elsewhere, the **Musée des Sciences Naturelles** is host to an impressive display of dinosaur skeletons and is ideal for pre-teens, whereas the **Musée du Jouet**, with its huge collection of toys throughout the ages, seems to be a hit with everybody regardless of age.

Most of the city's parks have playgrounds – the most popular one is at the lovely Bois de la Cambre (see p.259), a large, undulating place, ideal for running around and letting off some steam. The city also has a summer fun fair – **Foire du Midi** – which is held near the Gare du Midi from mid-July to mid-August. Here you'll find the usual riot of candy floss, amusement arcades and rides, including a large Ferris wheel. Full listings of children's exhibitions, shows and fairs can be found in the "Jeunes Publics" section of Wednesday's *Le Soir* supplement.

ACTIVITIES

City Kart
Map 1, C3. Sq des Grées du Lou 59 ℂ332 36 96. Tram #52.
Sat & Sun 9.30am–2pm, Wed 12.30–5pm; children (4–16) F100
Wed, F350 Sat, F500 Sun.
Ideal for budding Schumachers, these karts can go up to
60kph. Saturday and Sunday mornings are reserved for junior
racing, with different age ranges competing in heats. On
Wednesday afternoons the kids can race as much as they want
and have lunch thrown in. Reservations necessary.

Océade
Map 5, C2. Bd du Centenaire 20 ℂ474 13 11. Ⓜ Heysel.
Ring for times. Adults F460, children F360.
Water fun park with a number of attractions including high-
speed slides, wavepools, whirlpools and solariums.

CINEMA

UGC De Brouckère
Map 3, D4. Pl de Brouckère 38 ℂ0900 29 930. Ⓜ de Brouckère.
Sat 9.30am–11.30am. Children F60.
Screens children's films – mainly animation – every Saturday
morning. Moreover, you can leave your kids in the hands of
the supervisors, whilst you go off to watch a film for the
grown-ups. A free ice cream is included in the price of the
children's ticket.

MUSEUMS AND SIGHTS

Centre Belge de la Bande Dessinée

Map 3, F4. Rue des Sables 20 ©219 19 80. Ⓜ Botanique or Rogier.
Tues–Sun 10am–6pm. Adults F180, under-12 F60.

As popular with adults as it is with children, the comic museum documents the illustrious history of the Belgian comic book with numerous displays ranging from Tintin and the Smurfs to comic-book production. If your kids like comics, this place is guaranteed to shut them up for an hour.

Mini-Europe

Map 5, C3. Bd du Centenaire 20 ©478 05 50. Ⓜ Heysel.
Daily 9.30am–6.30pm (check for seasonal variations). Adults F395, children F295.

Mini-Europe is pure tack, but children love it. All the historic European sights are reproduced in miniature, and you can even re-enact the eruption of Vesuvius and the fall of the Berlin wall.

Musée des Enfants

Map 6, L8. Rue de Bourgmestre 15 ©640 01 07. Bus #71.
Wed, Sat 2.30–5pm. Closed August. Adult and child tickets F200.

Like Scientastic, this museum's strong point is that it's interactive – there are lots of buttons to press and knobs to turn. It's aimed more at younger children (under 10) than pre-teens. As well as looking at the many exhibits, children can paint, cook, or just generally run around and cause mayhem.

Musée du Jouet

Map 2, F4. Rue de l'Association 24 ©219 61 68. Ⓜ Botanique or Madou.
Daily 10am–6pm. Adults F120, children F80.

A large toy museum with more than 25,000 toys – dolls, trains, steam engines, pedal cars – with at least 5000 on show at any one time. Some of them date back to 1860, but you can play only with the more modern ones. The museum is pretty interactive and there's a big play area. Most suitable for 5- to 12-year-olds.

Musée des Sciences Naturelles

Map 6, L2. Rue Vautier 29 ©627 42 38. Ⓜ Porte de Namur.
Tues–Sat 9.30am–4.45pm, Sun 9.30am–6pm. Adults F150, children (6–17) F100, (0–5) free.

The centrepieces of this collection are the 65-million-year-old, five-metre-high dinosaur skeletons, which were found in southern Belgium in 1878, when prospectors were digging for gold. If Jurassic monsters aren't your thing, there are four more floors covering mammals (stuffed lions, tigers and bears), sea creatures (including a gigantic whale skeleton) fauna, and sections on how people live in the Arctic.

National Planetarium

Map 5, B3. Av de Bouchout 10 ©478 95 26. Ⓜ Heysel.
Sun–Fri 9am–4.30pm. Ring for programme list. F120.

A great place for children to take time out and look skyward. Apart from the regular shows such as a "voyage through the cosmos" and "the movement of the stars", there are a number of permanent exhibits on the ground floor including displays on rockets, satellites and astronomical instruments. Temporary exhibitions are held in the entrance hall.

....

There is a special price combination ticket (adult F640, child F580) for Mini-Europe, the Atomium and Océade – available from each venue.

....

Scientastic

Map 3, C6. Level -1 of the Métro Bourse station ©715 91 30.
Ⓜ Bourse.
Easter, July–Aug, Christmas 2–5.30pm, rest of year Sat–Sun

2–5.30pm. Adults F150, under-26 F130.

Both younger and older children seem to love the hands-on nature of this small science museum, which has over seventy interactive exhibits including visual illusions such as an impossible box, and sensory games like "smell your way out of the maze".

PARKS

Bois de la Cambre
Map 1, D3. At the intersection of av Louise and bd de la Cambe. Tram #93, #94.

The capital's largest and most popular inner city park. There's plenty of room for the kids to go crazy, and when they get bored of that, you can take them to Halle du Bois – a giant playground in the middle of the park equipped with a bouncy castle and toboggan run. It's open on school holidays and weekends 2–6pm and only costs F100 per child.

Parc du Cinquantenaire
Map 2, J6. Entrance av de Cortenberg. Ⓜ Mérode or Schuman.

The main attraction of this spacious park are the child-friendly museums it hosts. See p.91.

THEATRE

Théâtre de Toone
Map 4, D3. Petite rue des Bouchers, impasse Schuddeveldgang 6 ©217 27 53. Ⓜ Bourse or de Brouckère.
Tues–Sat 8.30pm. Adults F400, children F250.

World-famous puppet theatre housed in a seventeenth-century building a few steps from the Grand-Place. Performances are in several languages (ring in advance) and range from *The Three Musketeers* and the *Hunchback of Notre Dame*, to *Faust* and

Hamlet. There's also a puppet museum which can be visited free of charge during the intermission. Suitable for children, who love the puppets, and adults, who appreciate the sly references to recent news.

....

Also of interest . . .
The Atomium p.104, Autoworld p.93,
Musée Royal de l'Armée et d'Histoire militaire p.94,
La Boutique de Tintin p.230.

....

THEATRE

Gay and lesbian Brussels

Brussels often seems to be lagging a good decade behind the times on gay politics – the city's first gay and lesbian pride event wasn't held until 1996. But at least one senior politician is now openly gay and the age of consent for gay men is 16. The actual **gay scene** is fairly well-developed. There's a good selection of gay bars, clubs and restaurants, and although Brussels can hardly be described as a gay capital in the same rank as Amsterdam, the city compares favourably with many of its European counterparts.

The area just south of the Bourse remains the centre of the action, particularly in the triangle between rue des Pierres, rue du Marché au Charbon, and rue St Géry, which is the closest the capital has to a designated gay quarter. Although many bars in this area aren't specifically gay, no one will bat an eyelid if a gay couple walks in. Gay venues are beginning to spring up in other areas, too, most notably in the up-and-coming Ste Catherine district, but also around rue des Bouchers, close to place de la Monnaie. The same cannot be said of the **lesbian scene**, which remains quite cloistered. Although a few venues welcome both gays and lesbians equally, there are only a handful of out-and-out lesbian bars spread randomly around the city.

Listings of gay and lesbian events, and a number of useful addresses, can be obtained from Tels Quels (see "Information Services") who also organize events such as the Gay and Lesbian Film Festival held every January at the Botanique (see p.213). An informative English-language Web site for listings is *www.geocities.com/~eggbrussels*.

The city's many **gay associations** include Égalité (✆295 98 87) which, as its name suggests, has a political slant and lobbies the powers that be for equal rights for gays and lesbians, whereas Infor Homo (✆733 10 24), and the student equivalent Cercle Homosexuel Étudiant (✆650 25 40), both organize regular nights out and gay activity programmes. There are actually more **lesbian associations** in Brussels than there are lesbian venues – the most popular ones being Amazing Grace (✆218 36 51) and Attirement d'Elles (✆512 45 87).

Many **gay associations** in Brussels direct their energies towards educating people about **Aids** and providing support for victims of the disease. The most high-profile ones are Aide Info Sida (✆514 29 65) and Act Up (✆512 02 02), which also aims to change government policies towards Aids. Act Together at rue d'Artois 5 (✆512 05 05) provides support for families of victims, and has an English-speaking helpline.

INFORMATION SERVICES

Tels Quels

Map 3, C6. Rue Marché au Charbon 81 ✆512 45 87. Ⓜ Bourse. Sun–Thurs 5pm–2am, Fri–Sat 5pm–4am.

Gay and lesbian meeting place on the same street as *Au Soleil*, and just round the corner from *Chez Maman*. Although there's a small café, it's best known for its documentation centre which has information on gay and lesbian rights and forthcoming events. It also hosts occasional art exhibitions and group discussions. *Tels Quels*, their monthly French-language publication, includes political reports and a full gay and lesbian listings section for bars, clubs and restaurants, as well as hairdressers, saunas and sex shops.

GAY RESTAURANTS

Le Comptoir
Map 3, D7. Pl de la Vieille Halle aux Blés 24 Ⓒ514 05 50.
Ⓜ Gare Centrale.
Daily 7pm–3am.
A well-known gay restaurant and bar, just off rue Chêne, popular with a chic and stylish crowd, who are attracted by the excellent food and decadent ambience. After you've gorged yourself on the tasty *nouvelle cuisine* in the restaurant upstairs, head to the floor below where you can burn it off to the latest dance, house and techno tracks.

L'Entre Deux
Map 3, D7. Pl de la Vieille Halle aux Blés 42 Ⓒ511 68 73. Ⓜ Bourse.
Daily 7pm–midnight.
A laid-back and gay-friendly restaurant, just up the road from *Le Comptoir*, well-known for serving tasty, but pricey, French and Belgian food. It's busiest on Tuesday, when transvestite king pin Maman – of *Chez Maman* fame – struts his/her stuff to the amusement of all.

H2O
Map 3, C6. Rue du Marché au Charbon 27 Ⓒ512 38 43. Ⓜ Bourse.
Daily 7pm–2am.
A fashionable gay restaurant close to the Bourse, popular with late-twenty something couples, who come to sample the simple

GAY RESTAURANTS

but tasty world cuisine. Some may find the fantasy theme decor – Tolkien-style sculptures and pictures, and aquamarine-coloured walls – slightly off-putting, but there's always an upbeat atmosphere, and the service is both friendly and attentive. It's very cheap, and reservations are not always necessary. Hetero-friendly.

GAY BARS AND CLUBS

Le Belgica

Map 3, D6. Rue Marché au Charbon 32. Ⓜ Bourse.
Thurs–Sat 10pm–3am.
Arguably the capital's most popular gay bar and pick-up joint. Admittedly the walls of this small corridor-like abode could do with a lick of paint or two, and the Formica tables and dilapidated chairs have seen better days, but if you're out for a lively, friendly atmosphere, you could do a lot worse. Come on Friday and Saturday night and the place is thronged with young gay men, as well as a few old ones, living it up until the early hours. Moreover, being the elder statesman of the Brussels gay scene, nobody seems to care whether you're male, female, gay or straight.

Cercle 52

Map 3, C5. Rue des Chartreux 52 ℂ514 30 78. Ⓜ Bourse.
Tues–Sat 10pm–late.
Long-established gay club a couple of minutes' walk from place St Géry. Most people come here to cruise and use (there are a number of back rooms), but if you're just here for the music you could do a lot worse – it plays a good selection of house and techno throughout the week, and disco at the weekends. Membership F300 and free thereafter.

Chez Maman

Map 3, C6. Rue des Grands Carmes 7. Ⓜ Bourse.
Thurs–Tues 9pm–3am.

This tiny bar has achieved an almost cult-like status in Brussels – mainly because of the supremely flamboyant proprietor Maman and his hugely popular half-hour transvestite shows. People flock from all corners of the city to see him strut up and down the bar singing his heart out Marlene Dietrich-style.

La Démence

Map 3, C9. Rue Blaes 208 ℂ 511 97 89. Ⓜ Porte de Hal.
Every third Sunday 11pm–7am.
The city's most popular gay club, held on two floors every three weeks in *The Fuse* (see p.207). Although the music's pretty down-to-earth – mainstream rave, house and garage anthems pump out on both floors – the crowd is a bit difficult to pigeonhole. Expect to find a hybrid mix of muscle men, transsexuals, trendy fashion victims, and out-and-out ravers. Back rooms available.

L'Incognito

Map 4, B3. Rue des Pierres 36. Ⓜ Bourse.
Daily 11pm–late.
A popular gay bar, with a lively atmosphere and camp music – Madonna, Celine Dion, disco, and French pop. It's well situated, not far from the Grand-Place, but can be a bit cliquey. Not particularly lesbian-friendly.

The Slave

Map 3, C6. Plattesteen 7. Ⓜ Bourse.
Mon–Fri 9pm–4am, Sat & Sun 9pm–6am.
An off-the-beaten-track leather bar, with plenty of back rooms, S&M gear, and video pornography. Scares the pants off most gay people, but something of a Brussels underground institution.

GAY BARS AND CLUBS

The Soum

Map 3, C6. Rue du Marché au Charbon 44. Ⓜ Bourse.
Daily 4pm–late.

A small, dark bar popular with a flamboyant crowd, and decked out with kitsch plastic plants, fairy lights, and a tiny dance floor. Young and old alike come here to chew the cud over cocktails, and take advantage of the generous booze promotions. It can be busy midweek.

LESBIAN BARS AND CLUBS

Pussy Galore

Map 3, C9. Rue Blaes 208 ℄511 97 89. Ⓜ Porte de Hal.
Second Friday of the month.

The lesbian spin-off of *La Démence*, held upstairs in *The Fuse* (see p.207). The music – ambient dance – is a little tamer than most house clubs, and the mixed-age crowd a little more laid-back.

Le Sapho

Map 3, C5. Rue St Géry 1 ℄512 45 52. Ⓜ Bourse.
Fri–Sat 10pm–late.

One of only two solely lesbian bars in the capital, so it usually attracts a good crowd. The atmosphere is friendly and, unlike in many of the capital's gay bars, members of the opposite sex are not made to feel unwelcome.

Festivals and special events

usic and film feature most prominently in the Brussels calendar of annual festivals, although flower lovers, and those who appreciate dance and fine art, will not be disappointed. The more traditional festivals – the medieval-style **Ommegang** and the **Planting of the Meiboom** – centre on the Grand-Place, while most of the modern ones like the jazz or film festivals take place in various venues around the city and bring the whole of the capital to life. The main annual events are listed below; for information on the dozens of mini-festivals held in Brussels during the year, check *The Bulletin* or ask at the tourist office. Alternatively, it's well worth catching a train to one of the many festivals held in the towns outside the capital. In particular, the Procession of the Holy Blood, held in Bruges, is famous throughout Belgium for its medieval pageant.

JANUARY

Brussels Film Festival
Last two weeks (℗0900 10 440)
Although not as well known as many European film festivals, this annual event is on the up – cult icon Dennis Hopper recently put in a personal appearance after winning the festival's top award for "Most Outstanding Career". The films on show vary hugely, but there's usually a theme – in 1998 it was a celebration of 25 years of Irish cinema and included all things Neil Jordan, as well as contributions from John Huston, Jim Sheridan and Stephen Frears. Films are screened at various locations around the city.

FEBRUARY

Animation and Cartoon Festival
Middle two weeks (℗218 27 35)
Little-known animation fest, which screens as many as 120 new and old cartoons from around the world over the course of the event. Held at Auditorium du Passage 44, boulevard du Jardin Botanique.

MARCH

Ars Musica
Mid-March to early April (℗219 26 60)
This contemporary classical music festival has in the past featured internationally renowned composers. Performances are usually held in the Palais des Beaux Arts or La Monnaie (see p.222). Tickets cost around F500.

Festival of Fantasy Film, Science Fiction and Thrillers
Last two weeks (℡201 14 95)

This well-established festival has achieved an almost cult-like status with cult-film lovers, and is the place to see all those entertainingly dreadful B-movies, as well as more modern sci-fi classics, thrillers and fantasy epics. It's held at Auditorium du Passage 44, boulevard du Jardin Botanique.

APRIL

Ghent – Gentse Floralien
End of April (℡09/222 73 36)

Held every five years in the Flanders Expo building, Maaltekouter 1, Sint Denijs Westrem, this is one of the world's biggest flower festivals. The one-and-a-half kilometre "inside garden", which is home to a wide range of flowers from around the globe, is also the setting of the main event – the international flower competition. Here, you witness first hand the cut and thrust of flower competition, perennial pitted against perennial, and hot house plants (not in bloom) against hot house plants (not in bloom), to name but a couple of the categories. The next festival is scheduled for the year 2000, and the centrepiece will be the innovative "Garden of the 21st Century".

MAY

Jazz Marathon
May–June (℡456 04 85)

Sometimes regarded as the poor relation of the Jazz Festival (see below), the Jazz Marathon is a blast nonetheless. Hep jazz cats can listen to non-stop groove around the city for three cool days, and although most of the sixty-plus bands are little known, the quality of the vibe is usually very high. Entrance fees vary depending on the venue, but you can buy a three-day pass from Fnac or the tourist office for a bargain F400. Alternatively head for one of the free jazz concerts on the Grand-Place.

Concours Musical International Reine Elisabeth de Belgique

May to mid-June (℗507 82 00)

A world-famous classical music competition founded more than forty years ago by Belgium's violin-playing Queen Elisabeth. The categories change annually, rotating piano, voice and violin – 1999 is the voice, 2000 is the violin – and the winners perform live in the Grand-Place in July. Tickets for the competition can be difficult to get hold of and can cost as much as F2000, but the venues do include the splendid Palais des Beaux Arts and the Conservatoire Royal de Musique.

Couleur Café Festival

End of June (℗227 59 60)

A trendy two-day live music festival held in a big tent on the site of the *Tour & Taxi* nightclub (see p.209). Expect a fair share of African rhythms, acid-jazz and world music, as well as ragga and hip-hop.

Bruges – The Procession of the Holy Blood

Ascension Day (℗05/044 86 86)

This historic Roman Catholic procession was first mentioned in a statute dating back to 1291, and has been held in Bruges on Ascension Day every year since 1970. Colourfully dressed in biblical and medieval-inspired costumes, the marchers bring to life scenes from both the New and Old Testament, including the legend of how knight and crusader Diederik van den Elzas helped bring back the "relic of the holy blood" (a piece of cloth, said to be stained with the blood of Christ) to Bruges from Jerusalem. The relic itself is displayed in the Chapel of the

Holy Blood on place Burg, and can be viewed every Friday. Ascension Day will be May 13 in 1999, June 1 in 2000, May 24 in 2001 and May 9 in 2002.

JULY

Sundays in Bois de la Cambre
July, August and October

A free open-air classical music or jazz concert is held every Sunday in Bois de la Cambre, 11am–1pm. Popular with Belgian families. See p.259.

Ommegang
First Tuesday and Thursday

One of the capital's best-known annual events, the Ommegang is a procession from Grand Sablon to the Grand-Place that began in the fourteenth century as a religious event, celebrating the arrival of a statue of the Virgin from Antwerp. Nowadays the Ommegang has people in period costumes and the descendants of nobles playing the roles of their ancestors. It all finishes up with a traditional dance on the Grand-Place and is so popular it is now held twice in the same week. If you want a ticket for a seat on the Grand-Place for the finale, you'll need to reserve at the tourist office there at least six months ahead.

Brosella Folk and Jazz Festival
Second weekend (©269 69 56)

A small, long-established jazz and folk festival held at Théâtre de Verdure, Parc d'Osseghem near Métro Heysel. The surrounding chaos (things rarely start on time) somehow adds to the attraction and the bands, mostly Belgian, but occasionally international, offer good entertainment.

Bruges – The Cactus Festival
Second week (℗05/033 20 14)

This open-air live music festival is held in the beautiful Minnewater Park in central Bruges. The Cactus Festival is a cosy, low-key affair, and you get to hear up-and-upcoming pop, rock and indie acts from Belgium and abroad, as well as blues, reggae and Irish folk. One-day tickets cost F550 (F450 in advance), whereas a two-day ticket will set you back F1000 (F800 in advance) – they can be purchased from the Fnac store in Brussels at the City 2 complex (Ⓜ Rogier).

Ghent – Gentse Feesten
Mid- to late July (℗09/239 42 67)

For ten days every July, Ghent loses its conservative feel and embraces the youth-oriented street festival known as the Gentse Feesten. Local bands perform free outdoor gigs throughout the town, and the place seems to become a haven for every type of street performer in the country, buskers, comedians, actors or puppeteers. There's also an outdoor market, selling everything from jenever, a gin-like traditional Ghent liquor, to handmade crafts.

Torhout and Werchter – Torhout-Werchter Festival
First weekend (℗01/660 04 06)

Belgium's premier rock and pop festival and one of the largest open-air music festivals in Europe. In recent years the all-star line-up has included Massive Attack, Nick Cave and the Bad Seeds, Pulp, Björk, as well as the Beastie Boys, Garbage and Sonic Youth. Bands first play at Torhout in West Flanders (Fri–Sat), before moving on to Werchter in Brabant (Sat–Sun). A combined weekend ticket costs F2000, with single days costing as much as F900 to F1400. To get to Torhout, take the train from Gare du Midi or Gare Centrale to Bruges (40min), and then the train from Bruges to Torhout (10min). Special buses will take you from

Torhout train station to the festival site for free. To reach
Werchter, take the train to Leuven (25min), after which a special
festival bus will take you to the site for a cost of F150.

AUGUST

Planting of the Meiboom
August 9

This annual event involves the planting of the meiboom (maypole) at the corner of rue des Sables and rue du Marais – a procession involving much boozing, food and general partying.
The story goes that in 1213 a wedding party was celebrating
outside the city's gates when it was attacked by a street gang
from Leuven. They were beaten off (with the help of a group
of archers who happened to be passing by) and, in thanks, the
duke gave them permission to plant a maypole on the eve of
their patron saint's feastday.

Tapis des Fleur
Mid-August weekend

If you like flowers, and floral designs, head down to the Grand-
Place in mid-August. Every two years (2000 and 2002 are the
next) its historic cobblestones are covered with a lovely floral
carpet made up of over 700,000 begonias from Ghent.

Ghent – Festival van Vlaanderen
Second weekend in September and the last week of October
(✆09/243 94 94 or 02/548 95 95)

One of the high points of the Flemish cultural calendar, the
internationally renowned Festival of Flanders comprises more
than 120 classical music concerts and operas held throughout
sixty Flemish towns. Most of the festival's international symphony orchestras can be seen in Brussels – in 1998 the city was host
to the London Symphony Orchestra, the Los Angeles

Philharmonic, the Chicago Symphony Orchestra and the Vienna Philharmonic to name but a few. However, it's also worth heading out of the capital, particularly to the Flanders Festival-Ghent, which presents a different theme every year. In 1998 the month-long programme, entitled "Ladies First", emphasised the important role played by women in the classical music field. For full concert listings, contact the tourist office – ℂ02/504 03 90.

OCTOBER

Audi Jazz Festival
Mid-October to November
A month-long jazz extravaganza, featuring a wide range of local and international acts which in the past have included Courtney Pine, Andy Shepherd and Ray Charles. Like the Jazz Marathon, concerts are held in many live music venues (see p.269) around the city. Contact the tourist office for further information.

Europalia
Mid-October to mid-January (ℂ507 85 50)
The Europalia festival focuses on a different person or country each year and comprises paintings and exhibitions, as well as theatre, dance and live music. Like Dublin and Glasgow in the recent past, Brussels will be a City of Culture in the year 2000. Although the Palais des Beaux Arts is at the centre of the festival, a number of venues are used throughout the city.

DECEMBER

Le Marché de Noël
Mid-December (ℂ513 89 40)
The capital's traditional Christmas market and fair, held on the Grand-Place for three days every December and featuring food,

booze and various wares from EU countries. Admittedly, the piped Christmas tunes are a bit tacky, but it gets even the most cynical humbugs in the Christmas spirit. After the market is over the Christmas tree is put up and a large skating rink is installed.

Directory

AIRLINES British Airways (☎548 03 36), Aer Lingus (☎548 98 48) and American Airlines (☎508 77 11) all have their main offices at rue du Trône 98. Air UK (☎717 20 70), Cathay Pacific (☎712 64 48), KLM (☎717 20 70), Sabena (☎723 23 23) and Tap Air (☎720 02 23) have their main offices at Zaventem airport. The main Iberia office is on avenue Louise 54 (☎548 94 90), as is United Airlines at 350 (☎646 55 88); British Midland is at avenue des Pléiades 1200 (☎771 77 66).

AIRPORT INFORMATION For general information at Zaventem (☎753 21 11; 24 hours). For specific enquiries ring ☎753 39 13 or 723 31 11 (7am–10pm).

BANKS AND EXCHANGE Banks are generally open Mon–Fri 9am–4pm, with a one-hour lunch break between noon and 2pm. A few banks are open Saturday mornings. Most banks have a bureau de change, and cash travellers' cheques and Eurocheques. ATMs dispense a minimum of F1000 – although both General Bank and BBL are notorious for running out of money on Saturday night or Sunday morning. Even more incredible is the fact that the city's main domestic and international train station – Gare du Midi – does not have a cash dispenser. Bureau de change offices are widespread, the most central one being the

24-hour Crédit Général Automatic Exchange at Grand-Place 7. However, expect to be charged a flat fee, or lose money on a low exchange rate.

CAR RENTAL Major operators have branches at both Zaventem airport and Gare du Midi train station. Europcar (Gare du Midi ✆522 95 73, Zaventem ✆721 05 92); Avis (Gare du Midi ✆513 69 69, Zaventem ✆720 09 44); Hertz (Gare du Midi ✆524 31 00, Zaventem ✆720 60 44). Both Europcar (✆640 94 00) and Avis (✆524 31 00) have branches in Ixelles, as does Budget (✆646 51 30).

CREDIT CARD COMPANIES American Express is based on boulevard du Souverain 100 (✆676 21 11 or 24-hour ✆676 23 23). If you lose your card (Bankcontact, Eurocard, Visa, Mastercard, or Mr Cash) ring ✆070 34 43 44. For Diners Club ✆206 79 00.

DISABILITY Brussels is not easy for the disabled traveller, although the new trams with a low-level platform have improved disabled access, and Braille information panels have been introduced in some métro stations. If you live in Brussels the STIB runs a special low-cost (F50), door-to-door mini-bus service within the greater Brussels area ✆515 23 65. Accommodation-wise, many of the larger hotels have full disabled access, although smaller and cheaper ones often don't.

ELECTRICITY 220 volts AC. Most European appliances should work, providing you have a standard two-pin plug adapter. North Americans will need this plus a transformer.

EMBASSIES Australia, rue Guimard 6 (✆286 05 00); Canada, avenue de Tervueren 2 (✆741 06 11); Germany, avenue de Tervueren 190 (✆774 19 11); Great Britain, rue d'Arlon 85 (✆287 62 11); India, chaussée de Vleurgat 217 (✆640 91 40); Ireland, rue Froissart 89–93 (✆230 53 37); Japan, avenue des Arts 58 (✆511 23 07); New Zealand, boulevard du Régent 47–48 (✆512 10 40); South Africa, rue de la Loi 26 (✆285 44 00); USA, boulevard du Régent 25–27 (✆508 21 11).

EMERGENCIES Dial 101 for the police, and 100 for the ambulance or fire service. Doctors can be reached 24 hours a day at ℗479 18 18.

HEALTH Residents of European Union countries are entitled to free medical treatment and prescribed medicines under the EU Reciprocal Medical Treatment arrangement provided you have a completed E111 form (available from post offices in Britain and Social Security offices elsewhere).

HOSPITALS The main ones are: Brugmann Hospital, Campus Brugmann, place van Gehuchten (℗477 21 11); Érasme Hospital, route de Lennik 808 (℗526 34 02); Saint-Luc Hospital, avenue Hippocrate 10 (℗764 11 11 or 764 16 12) and St Pierre Hospital, rue Haute 322 (℗535 31 11).

INTERNET ACCESS The CyberTheatre, avenue de la Toison d'Or 4, Ixelles (next to Ⓜ Porte de Namur) has more than twenty terminals with Internet access, although you have to pay F300 to join (membership entitles you to a free 1hr session), and it costs F150 per hour after that. Emailing is free, as long as you buy a drink.

LEFT LUGGAGE Major train stations have luggage offices (daily 6am–midnight). Most train stations also have coin-operated lockers taking F20 and F50 pieces.

LOST PROPERTY For property lost on aircraft ring ℗723 60 11; if lost at the airport contact ℗753 68 20. The lost property office for the métro, trams and buses is at avenue de la Toison d'Or 15 (℗515 23 94).

NEWSPAPERS AND MAGAZINES The three main French-language dailies are *Le Soir*, *La Libre Belgique*, and *La Dernière Heure*; the main Flemish ones are *De Standard* and *De Morgen*. The only English-language publication is *The Bulletin*. Most English papers are on sale here on the day of publication, though at about double the normal cover price.

PHARMACIES Most pharmacies are open from 8.30am to 6.30pm. There is a rota-system for pharmacies on call at night, Sundays and bank holidays. A list is displayed in the window of all chemists.

POLICE There are two basic types of police: the Gendarmerie Nationale, and the police. The former, who wear blue uniforms with red stripes on their trousers, patrol the motorways and deal with major crime; the latter, in their dark blue uniforms, cover everything else. The central police station is at rue Marché au Charbon 30 (C517 96 11).

POST OFFICES Most post offices are open Mon–Fri 9am–5pm, although the post office at avenue Fosny 48a next door to Gare du Midi is open 24 hours a day, and the central post office on the first floor of Centre Monnaie (place de la Monnaie) is also open on Saturdays.

PUBLIC HOLIDAYS The main holidays when shops and banks will be closed are: Jan 1 (New Year's Day); Easter Monday; May 1 (Labour Day); May 21 (Ascension Day); June 1 (Whitsuntide); July 11 (Flemish Community Day); July 21; Aug 15 (Assumption); Sept 27 (French Community Day); Nov 1 (All Saints' Day); Nov 11 (Armistice 1918); Dec 25 (Christmas Day).

TELEPHONES Local calls cost a minimum of F10, but to make an international call you'll need to put in a minimum of F50. Many phones accept prepaid cards which can be bought from newsagents, post offices and railway stations for F200 and F400. To make an international call dial 00, wait for the continous tone, and then dial the country code followed by the area code – omitting the initial zero – and then the number. For directory enquiries in English dial 1405. To ring Brussels from abroad dial 00 322, and then the telephone number.

TRAVEL AGENCIES Acotra World Travel Agency (Mon–Fri 8.30am–6pm) at rue du Marché-aux-Herbes 110 (C512 86 07) is one of the bigger travel agencies, and specializes in discount train, ferry and plane tickets. Nouvelles Frontières (℡513 68 15), on chaussée d'Ixelles, just opposite place Fernand Cocq, is also good for cheap flights.

CONTEXTS

A history of Brussels

Early settlement and the Middle Ages

Brussels takes its name from Broekzele, or "village of the marsh", the community which grew up beside the wide and shallow River Senne in the sixth century reputedly around a chapel built here by St Géry. A tiny and insignificant part of Charlemagne's empire at the end of the eighth century, it was subsequently inherited by the dukes of **Lower Lorraine** (or Lotharingia – roughly Wallonia and northeast France), who constructed a fortress here in 979; the first city walls were added a few decades later. The village benefited from its position on the trade route between Cologne and the burgeoning towns of Bruges and Ghent to become a significant trading centre in its own right. The surrounding marshes were drained to allow for further expansion, and by the end of the twelfth century Brussels had a population of around 30,000.

In 1229 the city was granted its first charter by the dukes of Brabant, the new feudal overlords who controlled things here, on and off, for around two hundred years, governing through seven *échevins*, or **aldermen**, each of whom represented one of the patrician families who monopolised the administration. This self-regarding oligarchy was deeply unpopular with the skilled workers who made up the **guilds**, the only real counterweight to the aristocrats. The guildsmen rose in rebellion in 1302 and again in 1356, when the Count of Flanders, Louis de Maele, occupied Brussels during his dispute with Jeanne, the Duchess of Brabant. The guildsmen rallied to the Brabantine cause under the leadership of **Everard 't Serclaes** and, after ejecting the count's garrison, exacted terms from the returning duchess. Jeanne was obliged to swear an oath – the *Joyeuse Entrée* – which stipulated the rights and responsibilities of the ruler and the ruled, effectively a charter of liberties which also recognised the guilds and gave them more political power. This deal between the duchess and her craftsmen led to a period of rapid expansion and it was at this time that a second town wall was constructed, an eight-kilometre pentagon whose lines are followed by the boulevards of today's **petit ring**.

The early decades of the fifteeenth century proved difficult: the cloth industry began its long decline and there was more trouble between the guildsmen and the patricians. Temporary solutions were, however, found to both these problems. The craftsmen started making luxury goods for the royal courts of Europe, while the city's governing council was modified to contain seven aristocrats, six guildsmen and two aldermen – a municipal compromise that was to last until the late eighteenth century. There was a change of overlord too, when, in 1430, marriage merged the territories of the duchy of Brabant with those of **Burgundy**. Initially, this worked against the interests of the city as the first Burgundian rulers – Philip the Good and his son Charles the Bold – paid little regard to Brussels, and indeed Charles' ceaseless warmongering resulted in a steep increase in taxation. But when Charles' daughter, **Mary of Burgundy**, established her court in Brussels, the city gained political stature and its guildsmen found a ready market for the luxury goods they were already making – everything from gold jewellery and silverware through to tapestries and illuminated books. Painters were drawn to Mary's court, too, and Rogier van der Weyden was appointed the city's first official artist.

Mary married **Maximilian**, a **Habsburg** prince and future Holy Roman Emperor in 1477. She died in a riding accident five years later and her territories passed to her husband, who ruled until 1519. Thus Brussels – as well as the whole of present-day Belgium and Holland – was incorporated into the Habsburg empire. A sharp operator, Maximilian whittled away at the power of the Brabantine and Flemish cities and despite the odd miscalculation – he was imprisoned by the burghers of Bruges in 1488 – had to all intents and purposes brought them to heel by the end of the century. Maximilian was succeeded by his grandson **Charles V**, whose vast kingdom included Spain, the Low Countries and large parts of Germany and Italy. By necessity, Charles was something of a peripatetic monarch, but he favoured Brussels, his home town, more than any other residence, running his empire from here for a little over twelve years, which made the city wealthy and politically important in equal measure. Just like his grandfather, Charles kept the city's guilds firmly under control.

The Reformation and the Revolt against Spain

The **Reformation** was a religious revolt that stood sixteenth-century Europe on its head. The first stirrings were seen in the welter of debate that spread across much of western Europe under the auspices of theologians such as Erasmus (see p.99), who wished to cleanse the Catholic church of its corruptions and extravagant ceremony; only later did some of these same thinkers – principally Martin Luther – decide to support a breakaway church. The seeds of this **Protestantism** fell on fertile ground among the merchants of Brussels, whose wealth and independence had never been easy to accommodate within a rigid caste society. Similarly, their employees, the guildsmen and their apprentices, who had a long history of opposing arbitrary authority, were easily convinced of the need for reform. In 1555, **Charles V abdicated**, transferring his German lands to his brother Ferdinand, and his Italian, Spanish and Low Countries territories to his son, the fanatically Catholic **Philip II**. In the short term, the scene was set for a massive confrontation between Catholics and Protestants, while the dynastic ramifications of the division of the Habsburg empire were to complicate European affairs for centuries.

On his father's abdication, Philip II decided to teach his heretical subjects a lesson. He garrisoned Brussels and the other towns of the Low Countries with Spanish mercenaries, imported the Inquisition and passed a series of anti-Protestant edicts. However, other pressures on the Habsburg empire forced him into a tactical withdrawal and he transferred control to his sister **Margaret of Parma** in 1559. Based in Brussels, the equally resolute Margaret implemented the policies of her brother with gusto. Initially, the repression worked, but in 1565 the Protestant workers struck back. In Brussels and most of the other big cities hereabouts they ran amok, sacking the churches and destroying their rich decoration in the **Iconoclastic Fury**.

Protestantism had infiltrated the nobility, but the ferocity of the rioting shocked the upper classes into renewed support for Spain. Philip was keen to capitalize on the increase in support and, in 1567, he dispatched the **Duke of Albe**, with an army of 10,000 men, to the Low Countries to suppress his religious opponents absolutely. Margaret was not at all pleased by Philip's decision and, when Albe arrived in Brussels, she resigned in a huff, initiating a long period of what was, in effect, military rule. One of Albe's first acts in the capital was to set up the Commission of Civil Unrest, which was soon nicknamed the "**Council of Blood**" after its habit of executing those it examined. No fewer than 12,000 citizens went to the block, most famously the counts of **Egmont** and **Hoorn**, who were beheaded on the Grand-Place in June 1568.

Once again, the repression soon backfired. The region's greatest landowner, Prince William of Orange-Nassau, known as **William the Silent** (1533–84), raised the Low Countries against the Habsburgs and swept all before him, making a triumphant entrance into Brussels, where he installed a Calvinist administration. Momentarily, it seemed possible for the whole of the Low Countries to unite behind William and all signed the **Union of Brussels**, which demanded the departure of foreign troops as a condition for accepting a diluted Habsburg sovereignty. But Philip was not inclined to compromise. In 1578, he gathered together another army which he dispatched to the Low Countries under the command of **Alessandro Farnese**, the Duke of Parma. Parma was successful, recapturing most of modern Belgium including Brussels and finally Antwerp in 1585. He was, however, unable to advance any further north and the Low Countries were divided into two – the **Spanish Netherlands** and the **United Provinces** – beginning a separation that would lead, after many changes, to the creation of Belgium and the Netherlands.

The Spanish Netherlands

Parma was surprisingly generous in victory, but the city's weavers, apprentices and skilled workers – the bedrock of Calvinism – still fled north to escape the new Catholic regime, fuelling an economic boom in the province of Holland. The migration badly dented the economy of the **Spanish Netherlands** as a whole, but Brussels – the capital – was relatively immune, its economy buoyed up by the Habsburg elite, whose conspicuous consumption fostered luxury industries like silk weaving, diamond processing and lace making. The city's industries also benefited from the digging of the Willebroek canal, which linked Brussels to the sea for the first time. This commercial restructuring underpinned a brief flourishing of artistic life both here and, in comparable circumstances, in Antwerp, where it was centred on **Rubens** and his circle, including Anthony van Dyck and Jacob Jordaens.

Meanwhile, months before his death in 1598, Philip II had granted control of the Spanish Netherlands to his daughter and her husband, appointing them the **Archdukes Isabella** and **Albert**. Failing to learn from experience, the ducal couple continued to prosecute the war against the Protestant north, but with so little success that they were obliged to make peace – the **Twelve Year Truce** – in 1609. When the truce ended, the new Spanish king Philip IV stubbornly resumed the campaign against the Protestants, this time as part of a general and even more devastating conflict, the **Thirty Years' War** (1618–48), a largely religious-based conflict between Catholic and Protestant countries that involved most of western Europe. Finally, the Habsburgs were compelled to accept the humiliating terms of the **Peace of Westphalia**, a general treaty whose terms formally recognized the independence of the United Provinces and closed the Scheldt estuary, thereby crippling Antwerp. By these means, the commercial pre-eminence of Amsterdam was assured and its Golden Age began.

The Thirty Years' War had devastated the Spanish Netherlands, but the peace was perhaps as bad. Politically dependent on a decaying Spain, economically ruined and deprived of most of its more independent-minded citizens, the country turned in on itself, sustained by the fanatical Catholicism of the **Counter-Reformation**. Literature disappeared, the sciences vegetated and religious orders multiplied to an extraordinary degree. In **painting**, artists – such as Rubens – were used to confirm the ecclesiastical orthodoxies, their canvases full of muscular saints and angels, reflecting a religious faith of mystery and hierarchy; others, such as David Teniers, retreated into minutely observed realism.

The Peace of Westphalia had also freed the king of France from fear of Germany, and the political and military history of the Spanish Netherlands after 1648 was dominated by the efforts of **Louis XIV** to add the country to his territories. Fearful of an over-powerful France, the United Provinces and England, among others, determinedly resisted French designs and, to preserve the balance of power, fought a long series of campaigns beginning in the 1660s. It was during one of these wars, the **War of the Grand Alliance**, that Louis XIV's artillery destroyed much of medieval Brussels, a disaster that led to the construction of the lavish **Grand-Place** that survives today (see Chapter Two).

The **War of the Spanish Succession** – the final conflict of the series – was sparked by the death in 1700 of Charles II, the last of the Spanish Habsburgs, who had willed his territories to the grandson of Louis XIV. An anti-French coalition refused to accept the settlement and there ensued a haphazard series of campaigns that dragged on for eleven years. Eventually, with the **Treaty of Utrecht** of 1713, the French abandoned their attempt to conquer the Spanish Netherlands, which now passed under the control of the Austrian Habsburgs in the figure of the Emperor Charles VI.

The Austrian Netherlands

The transfer of the country from Spanish to Austrian control made little appreciable difference: a remote imperial authority continued to operate through an appointed governor in Brussels and the country as a whole remained poor and backward. This sorry state of affairs began to change in the middle of the eighteenth century when the Austrian oligarchy came under the influence of the **Enlightenment**, that belief in reason and progress – as against authority and tradition – that had first been proselytized by French philosophers. In 1753, the arrival of a progressive governor, the

The Belgian language divide

The Belgians are divided between two main groups, the **Walloons**, French-speakers who account for around forty percent of the population, and the **Flemish**, or Dutch speakers, who form about sixty percent, out of a total population of some ten million.

The Flemish-French **language divide** has troubled the country for decades, its historical significance rooted in deep class and economic divisions. Prosperity has shifted back and forth between the two communities over the centuries: in medieval times Flanders grew rich on its textile trade; later Wallonia developed mining and steel industries. However, Francophones have always dominated the aristocracy, and, since the Middle Ages, the middle classes as well. The setting-up of the Belgian state in 1830 crystallized this antagonism, with the final arrangements favouring the French-speakers. French became the official language, Flemish was banned in schools (the Belgian Civil Code was only translated into Flemish in 1961), and the industries of Wallonia were regarded as pre-eminent. Nowadays, however, Flanders is the industrial powerhouse of Belgium, and the heavy industies of Wallonia are in decline, an economic change of fortunes which has made the Flemish-speakers more assertive in their demands for linguistic and cultural parity. However, Flemish "parity" is often perceived as "domination" by Walloons.

The line between the two cultures – effectively cutting the country in half, west to east – was drawn in 1962, but, in response to increasing acrimony between the two communities, the constitution was redrawn in 1980 on a federal basis, with three separate **communities** – the Flemish North, the Walloon South and the German-speaking east around the towns of Eupen and Malmédy – responsible for their own cultural and social affairs and education. At the same time, Belgium was simultaneously divided into three **regions** – the Flemish North, the Walloon South and Brussels (which is officially bilingual, although a majority of its population is French-speaking), with each regional authority dealing with matters like economic development, the environment and employment.

Although the niceties of this partition have calmed troubled waters, in **bilingual Brussels** and at national government level the division between Flemish and French speakers still influences many aspects of working and social life. Schools, political parties, literature and culture are all segregated along linguistic lines leading to a set of complex regulations which can verge on the absurd. Governmental press conferences, for example, must have questions and answers repeated in both languages, one after the other. Across Belgium as a whole, bitterness about the economy, unemployment and the government smoulders within (or seeks an outlet through) the framework of this linguistic division, and individual neighbourhoods can be paralyzed by language disputes. The communities of Fourons/Voeren, for instance, a largely French-speaking collection of villages in Flemish Limburg, almost brought down the government in the mid-Eighties when the Francophone mayor, Jose Happart, refused to take the Flemish language exam required of all Limburg officials. Dismissed, he stood again and was re-elected, prompting the prime minister at the time, Wilfred Martens, to offer his own resignation. The Fourons affair was symptomatic of the obstinacy that besets the country to this day. Jose Happart could probably pass that Flemish exam easily – indeed rumour has it that he is fluent in the language – but he simply chose not to submit, fuelling the confict and giving succour to the political extremists on both sides – namely the Vlaams Blok on the Flemish side, and, for the French-speakers, the Front des Francophones (FDF).

The casual visitor to Belgium will rarely get a sniff of these bilingual tensions. Although it's probably better to speak English rather than Flemish or French in the "wrong" part of Belgium, if you make a mistake the worst you'll get is a look of glazed indifference.

THE BELGIAN LANGUAGE DIVIDE

Count of Cobenzl, signified a transformation of Habsburg policy. Cobenzl initiated an ambitious programme of public works and set about changing the face of Brussels – which had become an urbanised eyesore – by pushing through the grand Neoclassical boulevards and avenues which still characterise the Upper Town (see Chapter Three).

In 1780, the Emperor **Joseph II** came to the throne, determined to "root out silly old prejudices", as he put it – but his reforms were opposed by both left and right. The liberal-minded **Vonckists** demanded a radical, republican constitution, while their enemies, the conservative **Statists**, insisted on the Catholic status quo. There was pandemonium and, in 1789, the Habsburgs dispatched an army to restore order. Against all expectations, the two political groups combined and defeated the Austrians near Antwerp in what became known as the **Brabant Revolution**. In January 1790, the rebels announced the formation of the United States of Belgium, but the country remained in turmoil and when Emperor Joseph died in 1790, his successor, **Léopold**, quickly withdrew the reforming acts and sent in his troops to restore imperial authority.

French occupation and the Kingdom of the Netherlands

The new and repressive Habsburg regime was short-lived. French Republican armies brushed the imperial forces aside in 1794, and the Austrian Netherlands were annexed the following year, an annexation that was to last until 1814. The **French** imposed radical reforms: the Catholic church was stripped of much of its worldly wealth, feudal privileges were abolished, and, most unpopular of all, conscription was introduced. The invaders were deeply resented and French authority had largely evaporated long before Napoleon's final defeat just outside Brussels at the battle of **Waterloo** in 1815.

At the **Congress of Vienna**, called to settle Europe at the end of the Napoleonic Wars, the main concern of the great powers was to create a buffer state against any possible future plans the French might have to expand to the north. With scant regard to the feelings of those affected, they therefore decided to establish the **Kingdom of the Netherlands**, which incorporated both the old United Provinces and the Austrian Netherlands, and on the throne they placed Frederick William of Orange, appointed **King William I**. From the very beginning, the union proved problematic – there were even two capital cities, Brussels and The Hague. Nonetheless, the union struggled on until August 25, 1830, when the singing of a duet, *Amour sacré de la Patrie* in the Brussels opera house hit a nationalist nerve. The audience poured out onto the streets to raise the flag of Brabant in defiance of King William, thereby initiating a countrywide **revolution**. William sent in his troops, but Great Britain and France quickly intervened to stop hostilities and in January of the following year, at the **Conference of London,** the great powers recognized Belgium's independence, with the caveat that the country be classified a "neutral" state, that is one outside any other's sphere of influence. To bolster this new nation, they dug out the uncle of Queen Victoria, Prince Léopold of Saxe-Coburg, to present with the crown.

Independent Belgium

Léopold I (1830–65) was careful to maintain his country's neutrality and encouraged an industrial boom that saw coal mines developed, iron-making factories established and the rapid expansion of the railway system. His successor, **Léopold II** (1865–1909), further boosted industry and supervised the emergence of Belgium as a major industrial power. The king and the reforming

INDEPENDENT BELGIUM

Brussels burgomaster Anspach also set about modernizing the capital. New boulevards were built; the free university was founded; the Senne – which by then had become an open sewer – was covered over in the city centre; many slum areas were cleared; and a series of grandiose buildings was erected, the most unpopular of which was the Palais de Justice (see p.67), whose construction involved the forced eviction of hundreds of workers. To round the whole thing off – and turn Brussels into a city deserving of its king – Léopold held the golden jubilee exhibition celebrating the founding of the Belgian state in the newly inaugurated Le Cinquantenaire (see p.91), a mammoth edifice he had built just to the east of the old city centre.

The first fly in the royal ointment came in the 1860s and 1870s with the first significant stirrings of a type of **Flemish nationalism** which felt little enthusiasm for the unitary status of Belgium, divided as it was between a French-speaking majority in the south of the country – the Walloons – and the minority Dutch-speakers of the north. The Catholic party ensured that, under the Equality Law of 1898, Dutch was ratified as an official language, equal in status to French – the forerunner of many long and difficult debates.

The twentieth century

At the beginning of the twentieth century, Brussels was a thriving metropolis which took a progressive lead in a country that was determined to keep on good terms with all the great powers. Nonetheless, Belgium could not prevent getting caught up in **World War I**. Indifferent to Belgium's proclaimed neutrality, the Germans had decided as early as 1908 that the best way to attack France was via Belgium, and this is precisely what they did in 1914. They captured almost all of the country, the exception being a narrow strip of territory around De Panne. Undaunted, the new king **Albert I** (1909–34) and the Belgian army bravely manned the northern part of the Allied line. It made Albert a national hero.

The **Germans** returned in May 1940, launching a *blitzkrieg* that overwhelmed both Belgium and the Netherlands. This time there was no heroic resistance by the Belgian king, now **Léopold III** (1934–51), who ignored the advice of his government and surrendered unconditionally and in great haste. It is true that the Belgian army had been badly mauled and that a German victory seemed inevitable, but the manner of the surrender infuriated many Belgians, as did the king's refusal to form a government in exile. It took time for the Belgians to adjust to the new situation, but by 1941 a Resistance movement was organizing acts of sabotage against the occupying forces – and **liberation** by the Allies came three years later.

After the war, the Belgians set about the task of economic reconstruction, helped by aid from the United States, but hindered by a divisive controversy over the wartime activities of King Léopold. Many felt his surrender to the Germans was cowardly and his subsequent willingness to work with them treacherous; others pointed out his efforts to increase the country's food rations and his negotiations to secure the release of Belgian prisoners. Inevitably, the complex shadings of collaboration and forced co-operation were hard to disentangle, and the debate continued until 1950 when a referendum narrowly recommended his return from exile. Léopold's return was, however, marked by rioting in Brussels and across Wallonia, where the king's opponents were concentrated, and Léopold abdicated in favour of his son, **Baudouin** (1951–1993).

The development of the postwar Belgian economy follows the pattern of most of western Europe – reconstruction in the 1950s; boom in the 1960s; recession in the

1970s; and retrenchment in the 1980s and 1990s. During this period, Brussels has been transformed from one of the lesser European capitals into the home of the EU and NATO, but, above all, the postwar period has been dominated by the increasing **tension between the Walloon and Flemish communities**. Every national institution is now dogged by the prerequisites of bilingualism – speeches in parliament have to be delivered in both languages – and in Brussels, the country's one and only **bilingual region**, every instance of the written word, from road signs to the yellow pages, has to be bilingual as well. Brussels has also been subtly affected by the **Linguistic Divide** (or Language Frontier), which was formally delineated in 1962. Bilingual Brussels is now encircled by Flemish-speaking regions and, partly as a result, many Francophones living in the city have developed something of a siege mentality; the Flemish, on the other hand, can't help but notice the prevalence of French in what is supposed to be their capital city.

Belgium's top twenty-five beers

Belgium's **beer-making** history goes back centuries and from whatever bar of the world you come from you'll know that this is serious beer country. Official estimates suggest there are more than 400 to choose from with the rarest and most precious of them given all the reverence of a fine wine. (In fact, as any Trappist will tell you, you should always remove the cork from a bottle of beer a good half hour before serving.) The professional beer lover will already know the few brews listed below but for the tippling amateur we have produced what we consider to be the best of Belgium from over 800 beers available. Cheers!

Bush Beer (9.6%)

A Wallonian speciality; it is claimed the original Bush beer is the strongest beer in Belgium. It's actually more like a barley wine, and has a lovely golden colour, and an earthy aroma.

Chimay (red 5.5%, blue 7.1%)

Made by the five remaining Trappist breweries in Belgium, Trappist beers are widely regarded as being amongst the best beers in the world. The most famous range is Chimay, produced at the Abbey of Notre Dame, and they are characteristically fruity and strong, deep in body, and sometimes spicy with a hint of nutmeg or thyme. The two bestsellers, Chimay Red and the stronger Chimay Blue, have been described as the beer world's answer to a port.

La Chouffe (6.4%)

Produced just north of Bastogne in the Ardennes, this peculiar beer is instantly recognisable by the red hooded gnome (or *chouffe*) which adorns its label. It is a refreshing drink, which leaves a peachy aftertaste.

Don't drink the water!

In the eleventh century a Benedictine monk dipped his crucifix into a brewer's kettle to encourage the populace to drink beer instead of plague-contaminated water: the plague stopped. The monk later became known as St Arnold and was made the patron saint of brewers. In Brussels brewers pay homage to Arnold at an annual church service in July, and in recent years this has been extended to a sacred "day of beer" when beer tasting goes on throughout the whole city, and colourfully robed brewers march in procession to the Grand-Place. When visiting Brussels raise your glass at least once to St Arnold.

Corsendonk (Pater Noster 5.6%)

The creation of Jef Keersmaekers, the most famous Corsendonk, the Pater Noster, is known for its Burgundy-brown colour and its smoky bouquet.

Forbidden Fruit (9%)

Forbidden Fruit is worth buying just for the label which was once given a half-page in *Playboy*; it depicts a fig-leaf clad Adam offering a strategically covered Eve a glass of beer in the garden of Eden. The actual drink is dark, strong and has a spicy aroma, and has something of a cult following in Belgium.

Framboise (5–7%)

Known as "the pink champagne" of the beer world, Framboise seems very popular with tourists visiting the capital. It starts off life as a Lambic beer, but in time-honoured tradition it is then further fermented with the addition of raspberries. Despite its strength, it tastes like a luscious fruit drink.

Kriek (5–7%)

Kriek beer has the bouquet and delicate flavour of cherries, and the sherryish background of the base beers. Traditionally only cherries grown in the Brussels suburb of Schaarbeek were used, and even today some producers claim they maintain this tradition by using cherries grown in domestic gardens in the area.

....

See our Chapter 11 for our favourite places to drink. If you fancy bringing a couple of bottles home with you, have a peek at Bière Artisanale on p.239.

....

Grimbergen (Dubbel 5.2%, Tripel 7.2%)

These sweet beers have a hint of liquorice and are something of an acquired taste. The Dubbel is raisiny with a brandy-like finish whereas the Tripel is golden, intensely aromatic, and has a winey fruitiness.

Hoegaarden White (3.8%)

The role model of all Belgian white beers, Hoegarden – named after a small town east of Leuven – is light, and extremely refreshing, despite its cloudy appearance. Also known as "Blanche", it is brewed from equal parts of raw wheat and malted barley and is the ideal drink for a hot summer's day. Fairly recently white beers faced extinction on the grounds that they were too old-fashioned. However, in the last few years they have experienced a miraculous revival and have become the drink of the terrace café for many young people.

Leffe (Leffe Brune 5.2%, Leffe Blond 5.5%, Triple 6.7%)

Leffe is made by a secular brewery on behalf of an abbey – in this case the abbey Nostre Dame de Leffe in the Ardennes. The beers are characteristically strong and malty and come in three main varieties; Leffe Blond is bright, fragrant, and has a slight orangey flavour, whereas Leffe Brune is dark, aromatic, and full of body. Perhaps the most popular of all is Leffe Triple, which is strong, has a beautiful golden colour, and makes an ideal aperitif.

Orval (6.2%)

One of the world's most distinctive malt beers, Orval is made at Notre Dame d'Orval which was founded in 1070 by Benedictine monks from Calabria. It's a lovely golden colour, is very refreshing, and makes a great aperitif.

Rochefort (Rochefort 6–6%, Rochefort 8–7.3%, Rochefort 10–9%)

Renowned for its fine cheeses, Rochefort also produces a lesser-known, though equally impressive, range of traditional beers. Produced at Notre Dame de Saint-Rémy, which dates back to 1230 (although they didn't start brewing there until 1595) the beers are typically dark and sweet and come in three versions – Rochefort 6, Rochefort 8, and the extremely popular Rochefort 10, which has a deep reddish-brown colour and a delicious fruity palate.

Timmermans Lambic Blanche (7%)

The first ever Lambic-based white beer. The orange peels and coriander give it a gingery flavour; however, people tend to either love it or hate it.

Westmalle (Westmalle Dubbel 5.2%, Golden Triple 7.2%)

According to the producers of Westmalle – the monks at the Sacred Heart monastery just north of Antwerp – their beer not only cures loss of appetite, and insomnia, but reduces stress by half. This prescription also tastes good. Their most famous beer, the Westmalle Golden Triple, is deliciously creamy and aromatic, and the highly popular Westmalle Dubbel is dark and supremely malty.

Westvleteren (green top 3.6%, red 5%, blue 6.4%, yellow 8.8%)

Made at the abbey of St Sixtus in West Flanders, Westvleteren beers come in four varieties: the Green Top is gold and light, the Red Top is a ruby colour and has an almost chocolate-like taste, the Blue Top is sweet and fruity, and the Yellow Top is both rich and creamy.

Books

History

Pieter Geyl *The Revolt of The Netherlands 1555–1609* (Cassell/Barnes and Noble). Geyl presents a concise account of the Netherlands during its formative years, chronicling the uprising against the Spanish and the formation of the United Provinces. Without doubt the definitive book on the period.

E. H. Kossmann *The Low Countries 1780–1940* (OUP, UK). Gritty, technically detailed but ultimately rather turgid narrative of the Low Countries from the Austrian era to World War II. Concentrates on the narrow arena of party politics.

A. de Meeüs *History of the Belgians* (Praeger o/p). Entertaining if rather confused attempt at an exhaustive history of the Belgians, from "prehistoric dawns" to modern times. Good on incidental detail.

Geoffrey Parker *The Dutch Revolt* (Penguin in the UK and US o/p). Compelling account of the struggle between the Netherlands and Spain. Probably the best work of its kind. Also *The Army of Flanders and the Spanish Road 1567–1659* (Cambridge UP). The title may sound academic, but this book gives a fascinating insight into the Habsburg army which occupied "Belgium" for well over a hundred years – how it functioned, was fed and moved from Spain to the Low Countries along the so-called Spanish Road.

Art and architecture

Max J. Friedlander *From Van Eyck to Bruegel* (Phaidon/Cornell UP o/p). Scholarly and thoughtful account of the early Flemish masters, though stylistically and factually (in the light of modern research) beginning to show its age.

Eugene Fromentin *The Masters of Past Time: Dutch and Flemish Painting from Van Eyck to Rembrandt* (Phaidon). Entertaining essays on the major Dutch and Flemish painters.

R. H. Fuchs *Dutch Painting* (Thames & Hudson). If the excellent sample of Dutch paintings at Brussels' Musée des Beaux Arts whets your appetite, then the first book you should turn to is this thoughtful and well-researched title which tracks through the history of its subject from the fifteenth century onwards.

R. H. Fuchs et al *Flemish and Dutch Painting (from Van Gogh, Ensor, Magritte and Mondrian to Contemporary)* (Rizzoli). Excellent, lucid account giving an overview of the development of Flemish and Dutch painting.

Walter S. Gibson *Bosch* (Thames & Hudson). Everything you wanted to know about Bosch, his paintings and his late fifteenth-century milieu. Superbly illustrated. Also, try the beautifully illustrated, *Bruegel* (Thames & Hudson), which takes a detailed look at the artist with nine well-argued chapters investigating the components of Pieter Bruegel's art.

Paul Haesaerts *James Ensor* (Thames & Hudson o/p). It may weigh a ton, but this excellent volume is an outstanding exploration of the work of this often neglected, Ostend-born painter. The illustations and photos are well-chosen.

Melissa McQuillan *Van Gogh* (Thames & Hudson). Extensive, in-depth look at van Gogh's paintings as well as his life and times.

Benoit Peeters *Tintin and the World of Hergé: an Illustrated History* (Methuen/Joy St Books). Examines the life and career of Hergé, particularly the development of Tintin, and the influences on his work.

Christopher White *Peter Paul Rubens: Man and Artist* (Yale UP o/p). A beautifully illustrated introduction to both Rubens' work and social milieu.

Travel and specific guides

Charlotte and Emily Brontë; ed. Sue Lonoff *The Belgian Essays* (Yale UP). The Brontë sisters left their native Yorkshire for the first time in 1842 to make a trip to Brussels. Charlotte returned to Brussels the following year. This handsome volume reproduces the twenty-eight essays they penned (in French) during their journey and provides the English translation opposite. It makes a delightful read with particular highlights being "The Butterfly", "The Caterpillar" and "The Death of Napoleon".

S. A. Delta ed. *Guide Delta Bruxelles 1998*. Over five hundred pages of detailed and perceptive hotel and restaurant reviews – ideal if you're moving to Brussels. Only in French.

Michael Jackson *The Great Beers of Belgium* (Prion). Belgium produces the best beer in the world. Michael Jackson is the best beer writer in the world. The result is cheeky, palatable and sinewy with just a hint of fruitiness.

Ernest Gilliat-Smith *The Story of Brussels* (J.M. Dent o/p). Quirky, good-humoured account of Brussels written in 1906. Pick it up at the library or a second-hand bookshop.

Tim Webb *Good Beer Guide to Belgium and Holland* (CAMRA Books). Detailed and enthusiastic guide to the best bars and breweries. A good read, and very well informed to boot.

Literature

Charlotte Brontë *Villette*, *The Professor* (Penguin in the UK and US). Although less well-known than *Jane Eyre*, these two novels set in Brussels and Belgium are touching stories of the complications of love in a foreign country.

Hugo Claus *The Sorrow of Belgium* (Penguin/Pantheon). Born in Bruges in 1929, Claus is generally regarded as Belgium's foremost Flemish-language novelist, and this is generally regarded as his best novel. It charts the growing maturity of a young boy living in Flanders under the Nazi occupation. Claus' style is somewhat dense to say the least, but the book gets to grips well with the guilt, bigotry and mistrust of the period, and caused a minor uproar when it was first published in the early 1980s. His *Swordfish* (Dufour) is a story of an isolated village rife with ethnic and religious tensions. The effects of this prove too much for a boy in his spiral down to madness.

Alan Hollinghurst *The Folding Star* (Vintage). Not a Belgian novel, but the British writer Hollinghurst's evocation of a thinly disguised Bruges, in this novel of sex, mystery and obsession, is completely compelling. The enthusiastic descriptions of gay male sexual encounters make this a climactic book in more ways than one.

Jean Ray *Malpertuis* (Atlas). This spine-chilling Gothic novel was
written by a Belgian in 1943. It's set in Belgium, too, where the
suffocating Catholicism of the Inquisition provides a perfect
backcloth.

Georges Rodenbach *Bruges la Morte.* (Atlas). First published in
1892, this slim and subtly evocative novel is all about love and
obsession – or rather a highly stylised, decadent view of it. It's
credited with starting the craze for visiting Bruges, the "dead city"
where the action unfolds.

Glossaries

FRENCH TERMS

ABBAYE Abbey or group of monastic buildings.
AÉROPORT Airport.
AUBERGE DE LA JEUNESSE Youth hostel.
BEAUX ARTS Fine arts.
BEFFROI Belfry.
BÉGUINAGE Convent occupied by béguines, ie members of a
sisterhood living as nuns but without vows and with the right of
return to the secular world.
BICYCLETTE Bicycle
BOURSE Stock exchange.
CHAPELLE Chapel.
CHÂTEAU Mansion, country house, or castle.
COUR Court(yard).
COUVENT Convent, monastery.
DÉGUSTATION Tasting (wine or food).
DONJON Castle keep.
ÉGLISE Church.
ENTRÉE Entrance.
ÉTAGE Floor (of a museum etc).

FERMETURE Closing period.

FOUILLES Archeological excavations.

GARE Railway station.

GÎTE D'ÉTAPE Dormitory-style lodgings situated in relatively remote parts of the country which can house anywhere between ten and one hundred people per establishment.

GRAND-PLACE Central town square and the heart of most Belgian communities.

HALLES Covered, central food market.

HÔPITAL Hospital.

HÔTEL Either hotel, or – in its earlier sense – (private) town house

HÔTEL DE VILLE Town hall.

JARDIN Garden.

JOURS FERIÉS Public holidays.

MAISON House.

MARCHÉ Market.

MOULIN Windmill.

MUNICIPAL Civic, municipal.

MUSÉE Museum.

NOTRE DAME Our Lady.

PALAIS Palace.

PLACE Square, market place.

PONT Bridge.

PORTE Gateway.

QUAI Quai, or station platform.

QUARTIER District of a town.

SORTIE Exit.

SYNDICAT D'INITIATIVE Tourist office.

TOUR Tower.

TRÉSOR Treasury

FLEMISH TERMS

ABDIJ Abbey or group of monastic buildings.

BEIAARD Carillon (ie a set of tuned church bells, either operated by an automatic mechanism or played by a keyboard).

BEGIJNHOF Convent occupied by béguines (begijns), ie members of a sisterhood living as nuns but without vows and with the right of return to the secular world.

BELFORT Belfry.

BEURS Stock exchange.

BOTERMARKT Butter market.

BRUG Bridge.

BURGHER Member of the upper or mercantile classes of a town, usually with certain civic powers.

FIETSPAD Bicycle path, and **fiets** — bicycle.

GASTHUIS Hospital.

GEMEENTE Municipal: eg Gemeentehuis – town hall.

GILDE Guild.

GERECHTSHOF Law Courts.

GROENTENMARKT Vegetable market.

GROTE MARKT Central town square and the heart of most Belgian communities.

HAL Hall.

HOF Court(yard).

HUIS House.

INGANG Entrance.

JEUGDHERBERG Youth hostel.

KAAI Quai.

KAPEL Chapel.

KASTEEL Castle.

KERK Church; eg Grote Kerk – the principal church of the town; Onze Lieve Vrouwekerk – church dedicated to the Virgin Mary.

KONINKLIJK Royal.

KORENMARKT Corn market.

KUNST Art.

KURSAAL Casino.

LAKENHALLE Cloth hall. The building in medieval weaving towns where cloth would be weighed, graded and sold.

LUCHTHAVEN Airport.

MARKT Marketplace.

MOLEN Windmill.

OMMEGANG Procession.

PALEIS Palace.

POORT Gate.

POSTBUS Post office box.

PLEIN A square or open space.

RIJK State.

SCHEPENZAAL Alderman's Hall.

SCHOUWBURG Theatre.

SIERKUNST Decorative arts.

SCHONE KUNSTEN Fine arts.

SPOOR Track (as in railway) – trains arrive and depart on track (as distinct from platform) numbers.

STADHUIS Town hall.

STATION (Railway or bus) station.

STITCHING Institute or foundation.

STEDELIJK Civic, municipal.

STEEN Fortress.

TOREN Tower.

TUIN Garden.

UITGANG Exit.

VOLKSKUNDE Folklore.

ART AND ARCHITECTURAL TERMS

AMBULATORY Covered passage around the outer edge of the choir of a church.

APSE Semicircular protrusion at (usually) the east end of a church.

ART DECO Geometrical style of art and architecture popular in the 1930s.

ART NOUVEAU Style of art, architecture and design based on highly stylized vegetal forms. Popular in the early part of the twentieth century.

BASILICA Roman Catholic church with honorific privileges.

BAROQUE The art and architecture of the Counter-Reformation, dating from around 1600 onwards, and distinguished by extreme ornateness, exuberance and complex spatial arrangement of interiors.

CARILLON A set of tuned church bells, either operated by an automatic mechanism or played by a keyboard.

CARYATID A sculptured female figure used as a column.

CLASSICAL Architectural style incorporating Greek and Roman elements – pillars, domes, colonnades, etc – at its height in the seventeenth century and revived, as **Neoclassical**, in the nineteenth century.

CLERESTORY Upper storey of a church, incorporating the windows.

FLAMBOYANT Florid form of Gothic (see below).

FRESCO Wall painting – durable through application to wet plaster.

GABLE The triangular upper portion of a wall – decorative or supporting a roof.

GOBELINS A rich French tapestry, named after the most famous of all tapestry manufacturers, based in Paris, whose most renowned period was in the reign of Louis XIV. Also loosely applied to tapestries of similar style.

GOTHIC Architectural style of the thirteenth to sixteenth century, characterized by pointed arches, rib vaulting, flying buttresses and a general emphasis on verticality.

MISERICORD Ledge on choir stall on which occupant can be supported while standing; often carved with secular subjects (bottoms were not thought worthy of religious ones).

NAVE Main body of a church.

NEOCLASSICAL Architectural style derived from Greek and Roman elements – pillars, domes, colonnades, etc – popular in the Low Countries during French rule in the early nineteenth century.

ROCOCO Highly florid, light and graceful eighteenth-century style of architecture, painting and interior design, forming the last phase of Baroque.

RENAISSANCE Movement in art and architecture developed in fifteenth-century Italy.

RETABLE Altarpiece.

ART AND ARCHITECTURAL TERMS

ROMANESQUE Early medieval architecture distinguished by squat forms, rounded arches and naive sculpture.

STUCCO Marble-based plaster used to embellish ceilings, etc.

TRANSEPT Arms of a cross-shaped church, placed at ninety degrees to nave and chancel.

TRIPTYCH Carved or painted work on three panels. Often used as an altarpiece.

TYMPANUM Sculpted, usually recessed, panel above a door.

VAULT An arched ceiling or roof.

ART AND ARCHITECTURAL TERMS

INDEX

Stay in touch with us!

ROUGHNEWS is Rough Guides' free newsletter.
In three issues a year we give you news, travel issues, music reviews, readers' letters and the latest dispatches from authors on the road.

I would like to receive ROUGH*NEWS*: please put me on your free mailing list.

NAME . . . .

ADDRESS . . . .

Please clip or photocopy and send to: Rough Guides, 62-70 Shorts Gardens, London WC2H 9AB, England

or Rough Guides, 375 Hudson Street, New York, NY 10014, USA.

ROUGH GUIDES: Travel

ROUGH GUIDES: Mini Guides, Travel Specials and Phrasebooks

MINI GUIDES

Antigua
Bangkok
Barbados
Big Island of Hawaii
Boston
Brussels
Budapest
Dublin
Edinburgh
Florence
Honolulu
Lisbon
London Restaurants
Madrid
Maui
Melbourne
New Orleans
St Lucia

Seattle
Sydney
Tokyo
Toronto

TRAVEL SPECIALS

First-Time Asia
First-Time Europe
More Women Travel

PHRASEBOOKS

Czech
Dutch
Egyptian Arabic
European
French

German
Greek
Hindi & Urdu
Hungarian
Indonesian
Italian
Japanese
Mandarin Chinese
Mexican Spanish
Polish
Portuguese
Russian
Spanish
Swahili
Thai
Turkish
Vietnamese

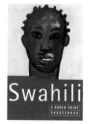

ROUGH GUIDES:
Reference and Music CDs

REFERENCE
Classical Music
Classical:
 100 Essential CDs
Drum'n'bass
House Music

World Music:
 100 Essential CDs
English Football
European Football
Internet
Millennium

**ROUGH GUIDE
MUSIC CDs**
Music of the Andes
Australian
 Aboriginal
Brazilian Music
Cajun & Zydeco
Classic Jazz
Music of Colombia
Cuban Music
Eastern Europe
Music of Egypt
English Roots
 Music
Flamenco
India & Pakistan
Irish Music
Music of Japan
Kenya & Tanzania
Native American
North African
Music of Portugal

Jazz
Music USA
Opera
Opera:
 100 Essential CDs
Reggae
Rock
Rock:
 100 Essential CDs
Techno
World Music

Reggae
Salsa
Scottish Music
South African
 Music
Music of Spain
Tango
Tex-Mex
West African Music
World Music
World Music Vol 2
Music of Zimbabwe

AVAILABLE AT ALL GOOD BOOKSHOPS

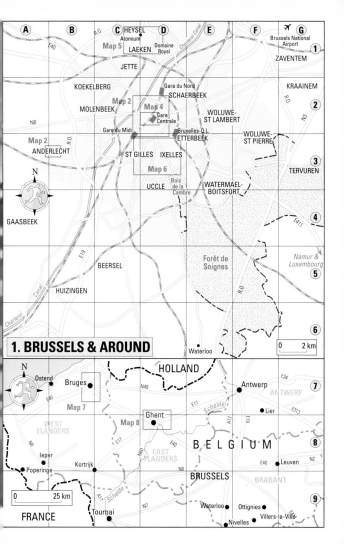

1. BRUSSELS & AROUND

0   2 km

0   25 km

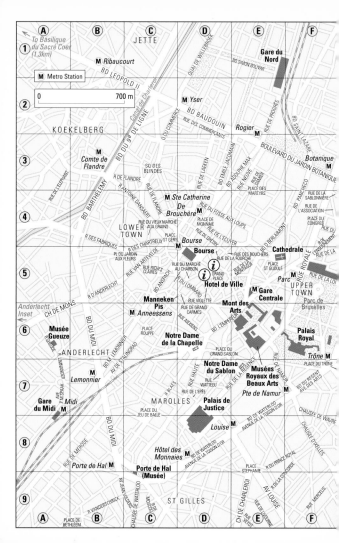

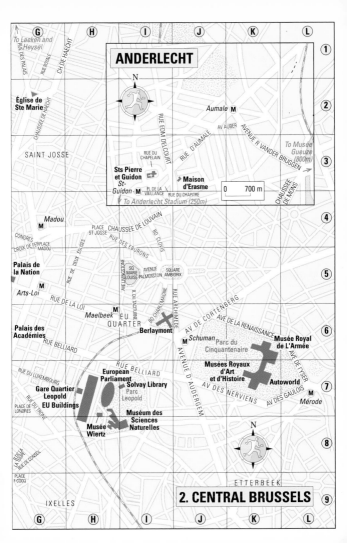

ANDERLECHT

To Laeken and
Rue DES PALAIS

RUE ROYALE

CH DE HAECHT

Église de
Ste Marie

CHAUSSÉE DE HAECHT

SAINT JOSSE

RUE EDM DELCOURT

RUE DU
CHAPELAIN

Aumale **M**

AV AUBER

RUE D'AUMALE

AVENUE R VANDER BRUGGEN

To Musée
Gueuze
(800m)

CHAUSSÉE DE MONS

Sts Pierre
et Guidon
St-Guidon **M**

PL DE LA
VAILLANCE

Maison
d'Erasme

RUE DU CHAPITRE

0   700 m

To Anderlecht Stadium (250m)

Madou **M**

PLACE
ST JOSSE

CHAUSSÉE DE LOUVAIN

BD CLOVIS

CONGRES

CROIX DE FERPLACE
MADOU

RUE DES EBURONS

RUE DE L'ÉGLISE

Palais de
la Nation

RUE DE DEUX EGLISES

SQ
MARIE
LOUISE

AVENUE
LOUISE-PALMERSTON

SQUARE
AMBIORIX

RUE ARCHIMEDE

Arts-Loi **M**

RUE DE LA LOI

R DU TACITURNE

BD CHARLEMAGNE

AVE DE CORTENBERG

AVE DE LA RENAISSANCE

Palais des
Académies

RUE BELLIARD

Maelbeek **M**

EU
QUARTER

Berlaymont

Schuman **M**

Parc du
Cinquantenaire

Musée Royal
de L'Armée

AVE DE L'YSER

RUE BELLIARD

RUE DU LUXEMBOURG

European
Parliament

Solvay Library

AVENUE D'AUDERGEM

Musées Royaux
d'Art
et d'Histoire

Autoworld

Mérode **M**

Gare Quartier
Leopold
EU Buildings

Parc
Leopold

AVE DES NERVIENS

AVE DES GAULOIS

PLACE DE
LONDRES

Muséum des
Sciences
Naturelles

PLACE DU TRONE

Musée
Wiertz

RUE DE CONSEIL

LA RELLA

IXELLES

PLACE
F COCQ

ETTERBEEK

2. CENTRAL BRUSSELS

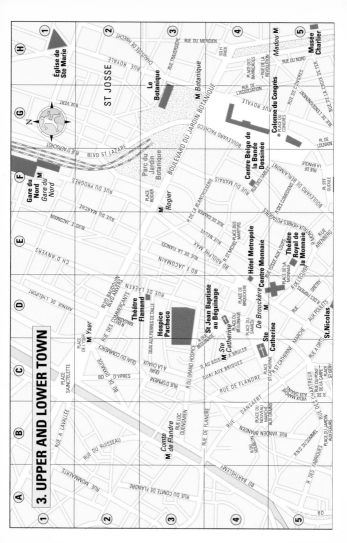

3. UPPER AND LOWER TOWN

Église de Ste Marie

ST JOSSE

Le Botanique

M Botanique

RUE DU MERIDIEN

RUE TRAVERSIÈRE

SQ H FRICK

PLACE DES BARRICADES

RUE DE LA RÉVOLUTION

Centre Belge de la Bande Dessinée

RUE DE L'ASSOCIATION

RUE ROYALE

Colonne du Congrès M

PLACE DU CONGRÈS

RUE DU CONGRÈS

RUE DE LA CROIX DE FER

Musée Charlier M

Madou M

RUE DU NORD

RUE DE L'ENSEIGNEMENT

PL DE LOUVAIN

BOULEVARD DU JARDIN BOTANIQUE

BOULEVARD PACHECO

Parc du Jardin Botanique

BLVD ST LAZARE

RUE D'AERSCHOT

N

RUE VERT

Gare du Nord M Gare du Nord

RUE DU PROGRÈS

PLACE ROGIER

Rogier

RUE DU MARCHÉ

BLVD E. JACQMAIN

CH D'ANVERS

AVENUE DE L'HÉLIPORT

RUE DE BERLAIMONT

RUE DU MARAIS

RUE DES SABLES

RUE DE LA BLANCHISSERIE

RUE DE DAMME

RUE DAMIER

RUE NEUVE

PLACE DES MARTYRS

RUE ST MICHEL

RUE ADOLPHE MAX

RUE DE LA FIANCÉE

BD E. JACQMAIN

Hôtel Metropole

Théâtre Royal de la Monnaie

Théâtre Flamand

Centre Monnaie

De Brouckère M

RUE DE LAEKEN

RUE DES COMÉDIENS

BOULEVARD DE BERLAIMONT

R DES COMÉDIENS

RUE FOSSÉ AUX LOUPS

PLACE DE LA MONNAIE

RUE DE L'ÉVÊQUE

RUE NEUVE-AUX-HERBES-POTAGÈRES

R AU BEURRE

RUE D'ARENBERG

Hospice Pacheco

St Jean Baptiste au Béguinage

PLACE DU BÉGUINAGE

RUE DU BÉGUINAGE

Ste Catherine M

RUE DE BRUXELLES

PLACE STE CATHERINE

Ste Catherine

St.Nicolas

Comte M de Flandre

Théâtre Flamand

PLACE DES COMMERCANTS

RUE DU COMMERCE

RUE MAGASINS

RUE YSER M

PLACE DE L'YSER

BD BAUDOUIN BOULEVARD

QUAI DU COMMERCE

QUAI AUX PIERRES DE TAILLE

R DU GRAND HOSPICE

QUAI AU BOIS À BRÛLER

QUAI AUX BRIQUES

RUE DU MARCHÉ

ST CATHERINE

RUE DE FLANDRE

AUX POULETS

RUE A ORTS

RUE DES HALLES

GRÉTRY

RUE D'OMMEGANG

RUE DE LAEKEN

RUE SAINCTELETTE

PLACE SAINCTELETTE

RUE A. LAVALLÉE

RUE J. LAVALLÉE

RUE DU RUISSEAU

BD DE DIXMUDE

BD DE DIXMUDE

BD D'YPRES

RUE DE FLANDRE

RUE DANSAERT

RUE VANDEN BRANDEN

RUE DU NOUVEAU MARCHÉ AUX GRAINS

PLACE DU NOUVEAU MARCHÉ AUX GRAINS

VIEUX MARCHÉ AUX GRAINS

RUE DES CHARTREUX

RUE DE FLANDRE

RUE AUX FLEURS

RUE DU CANAL

RUE DES FABRIQUES

R DES FABRIQUES

BD DU JARDIN AUX FLEURS

PLACE DU JARDIN AUX FLEURS

RUE DE LA LAITERIE

RUE ST GÉRY

RUE DU VIEUX MARCHÉ

BD BARTHÉLEMY

RUE DU COMTE DE FLANDRE

RUE LOC GUENGNEM

RUE MOMMAERTS

RUE DE FLANDRE

RUE DU COMTE DE FLANDRE

BD

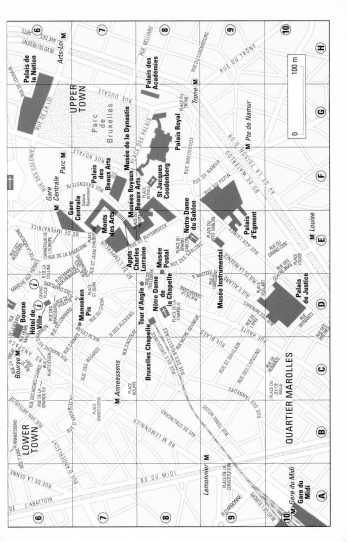

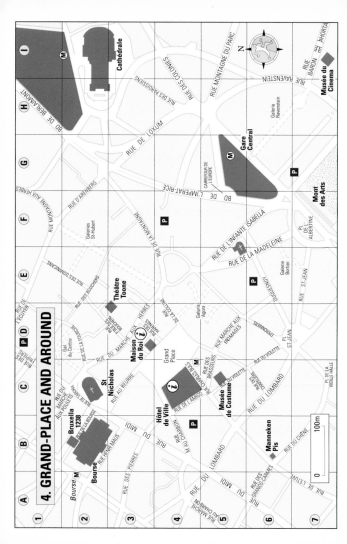

4. GRAND-PLACE AND AROUND

Cathédrale

Musée du Cinema

Gare Central

Mont des Arts

Galerie Ravenstein

Galerie Bortier

Galeries St-Hubert

Galeria Agora

Théâtre Toone

Maison du Roi

St Nicholas

Bruxella 1238

Bourse

Grand Place

Hôtel de Ville

Musée de Costume

Mannekin Pis

RUE DE BERLAIMONT
BD DE BERLAIMONT
RUE DES PARISSIENS
RUE DES COLONIES
RUE MONTAGNE DU PARC
RUE BARON HORTA
RUE RAVENSTEIN
RUE DE LOXUM
RUE D'ARENBERG
RUE MONTAGNE AUX HERBES
BD DE L'IMPERATRICE
CARREFOUR DE L'EUROPE
RUE DE L'INFANTE ISABELLA
RUE DE LA MADELEINE
RUE DES DOMINICANS
RUE DE LA MONTAGNE
RUE DES BOUCHERS
RUE DE LA COLLINE
RUE DES HARENGS
RUE MARCHE AUX HERBES
RUE DE LA FOURCHE
RUE DES BOUCHERS
GAL DU CENTRE
RUE DE L'ECUYER
RUE DES FRIPIERS
RUE DU MARCHE AUX POULETS
RUE AU BEURRE
PL. DE LA BOURSE
RUE HENRI MAUS
RUE DU MIDI
RUE DES PIERRES
RUE DE LA TETE D'OR
RUE CHAIR ET PAIN
RUE DE LA VIOLETTE
RUE CHARLES BULS
RUE DE L'AMIGO
RUE DES BRASSEURS
RUE DU MARCHE AUX FROMAGES
PL. ST-JEAN
RUE ST-JEAN
DUQUESNOY
RUE VIOLETTE
RUE DES EPERONNIERS
PL. DE L'ALBERTINE
RUE DU LOMBARD
RUE DU CHENE
RUE DU LOMBARD
M AU CHARBON
RUE AU CHARBON
RUE DU MIDI
RUE MARCHE AU CHARBON
RUE DES GRANDS-CARMES
PL. DE LA VIEILLE HALLE
RUE DE L'ETUVE

Bourse M

0   100m

5. LAEKEN & HEYSEL

Pavillon Chinois

Tour Japonaise

Serres Royales

N

Château Royal

Belvédère

AV DU PARC ROYAL

AUTOROUTE A12

HEYSEL

Parc d'Osseghem

LAEKEN

Parc de Laeken

Monument de Léopold Ier

AV DU PARC ROYAL

Laeken Cemetery

Parc des Expositions

AV DE L'ATOMIUM

Atomium

AV DU GROS TILLEUL

Jardin Colonial

Château du Stuyvenberg

Parc Reine Elisabeth

BD DU CENTENAIRE

Stade du Roi Baudouin (Heysel Stadium)

Océade

Bruparck

Mini-Europe

Planétarium

AV DU GROS TILLEUL

AV HOUBA DE STROOPER

AV DE L'IMPÉRATRICE CHARLOTTE

M

AV DU BOUQOIN

AV BOUQOIN

AV HOUBA DE STROOPER

AV ROMMELAERE LN

AV STIENON

0   200m

A B C D E F G H I

1 2 3 4 5 6 7

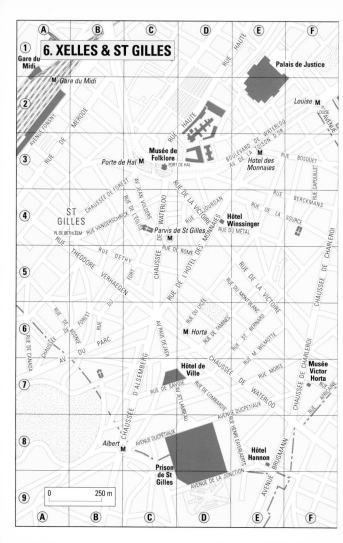

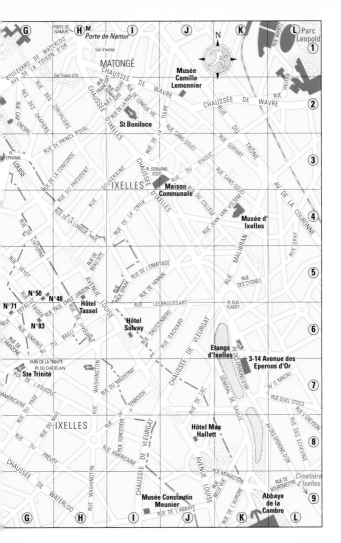

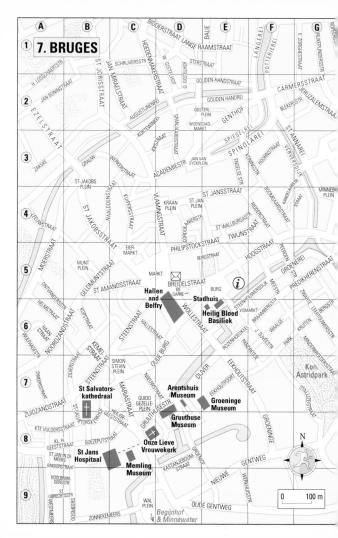

7. BRUGES

| | A | B | C | D | E | F | G |

1

2

3

4

5

6

7

8

9

BIDDERSTRAAT LANGE RAAMSTRAAT
BALIE
LANGEREI
POTTERIEREI
E ZORGHESTRAAT
RIJKUEGHUNDFHESTR

H. LOSSCHAERTSTR
ST JORISSTRAAT
SCHRIJVERSSTR
JAN MIRAELSTRAAT
HOEDENMAKERSSTRAAT
W GISTELHOF
STERSTRAAT
LICHTELD
GOUDEN-HANDSTRAAT
CARMERSSTRAAT
JERUZALEMSTRAAT

JAN BONINSTRAAT
AUGUSTIJNENREI
KORTEWINKEL
GOUDEN HANDREI
OOSTERL PLEIN
WOENSDAG-MARKT
GENTHOF
BLEKERSSTR
ST ANNAREI

EZELSTRAAT
GRAUW
WEVERSSTRAAT
SPINOLAREI
SPINOLAREI
HOORNSTRAAT
VERVERSDIJK
ST ANNAREI

ZAKSKE
ST-JAKOBS PLEIN
NAALDENSTRAAT
KUIPERSSTRAAT
ACADEMIESTR
VLAMINGSTRAAT
JAN VAN EYCKPLEIN
ENGELSE STR
KONINGSTR
MINNEB PLEIN

EELYKSTRAAT
ST JAKOBSSTRAAT
EIER-MARKT
KRAAN PLEIN
ST JAN PLEIN
ST JANSSTRAAT
RIDDERSTRAAT
BOOMGAARDSTRAAT
KANDELAARSTR
MINNEB PLEIN

MOERSTRAAT
MUNT PLEIN
GELDMUNTSTRAAT
A-NIERSTR
ST WALLBURGSTR
ST WALLBURGSTRAAT
TWIJNSTRAAT

ONTVANGERSSTR
HELMSTRAAT
ST AMANDSSTRAAT
PHILIPSTOCKSTRAAT
BURGSTRAAT
HOOGSTRAAT
PEERDEN
GROENEREI
PREDIKHERENSTRAAT

HAAN-STRAAT
WOLFHAGESTR
NOORDZANDSTRAAT
STEENSTRAAT
HALLESTRAAT
MARKT
BREIDELSTRAAT
DE GARRE
BURG
ⓘ
STEENHOUWERSDIJK
VISMARKT
BRAAMBERGSTR
MEESTR
PARK
ZWARTE-LEERTOUWERSSTR
KRUITEN

DWEERSSTRAAT
ZILVERSTRAAT
KEMEL STRAAT
SIMON STEVIN PLEIN
OUDE BURG
Hallen and Belfry
Stadhuis
Heilig Bloed Basiliek
WOLLESTRAAT
ROZENHOEDKAAI
PANDREITJE
J SUVESTR
WAALSE
MINDERBROEDERSSTRAAT

ZUIDZANDSTRAAT
St Salvators-kathedraal
MARIASTRAAT
NIEUWSTRAAT
GUIDO GEZELLE-PLEIN
GRUUTHUSESTR
DIJVER
Arentshuis Museum
Groeninge Museum
EEKHOUTPOORT
EEKHOUTSTRAAT
Kon. Astridpark
ST JUUZESTRAAT

KTE VULDERSSTRAAT
ST SSALVATORSKERKHOF
HEILIGE GEESTSTRAAT
Gruuthuse Museum
GROENINGE

KL. H GEESTSTRAAT
GOEZEPUTSTRAAT
Onze Lieve Vrouwekerk
KASTANJEBOOM-STRAAT
GENTWEG

ST JAN IN DE MEERS
BAKKERSSTRAAT
St Jans Hospitaal
Memling Museum
NIEUWE
WERFHUISSTR

KOOLBRAN-DERSSTR
ST OBRECHTSSTR
WAL PLEIN
OUDE GENTWEG

WESTMEERS
OOSMEERS
ZONNEKEMEERS
Begijnhof & Minnewater

N

0   100 m

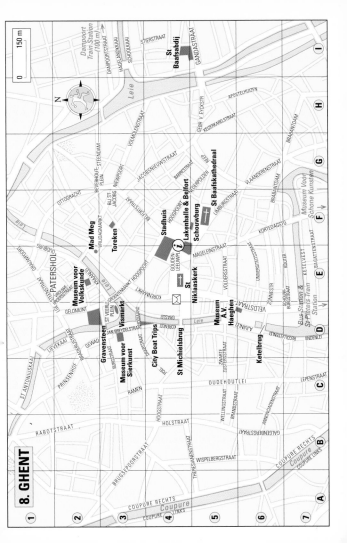

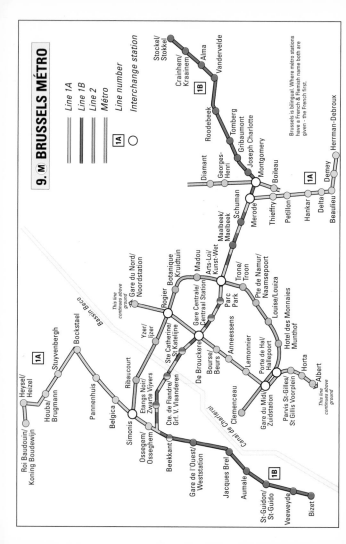

9. M BRUSSELS MÉTRO

Line 1A
Line 1B
Line 2
Métro
Line number
Interchange station

1A
○

Brussels is bilingual. Where métro stations have a French & Flemish name both are given – the French first.